PRIERIAS: THE LIFE AND WORKS OF SILVESTRO MAZZOLINI DA PRIERIO, 1456–1527

PRIERIAS

THE LIFE AND WORKS OF
SILVESTRO MAZZOLINI DA PRIERIO, 1456–1527

MICHAEL TAVUZZI

Duke University Press   Durham and London 1997

© 1997 Duke University Press
All rights reserved
Printed in the United States of America on acid-free paper ∞
Designed by Katy Giebenhain
Typeset in Garamond by Keystone Typesetting, Inc.
Library of Congress Cataloging-in-Publication Data appear
on the last printed page of this book.

Contents

PREFACE

Every undergraduate who takes a course in Reformation history comes to know Silvestro Mazzolini da Prierio's name (in at least the toponymic form, Prierias) because he was Luther's first literary opponent. Yet, very few teaching such a course are themselves likely to know much more about him than that. I hope that this work will fill this lacuna.

I did not come upon Silvestro principally through Luther, but while researching a topic in the history of philosophical logic. Silvestro played a significant part in the Renaissance Thomist debate on the nature of first and second intentions and allied issues—a debate that I shall consider in detail elsewhere. While attempting to put together a brief bio-bibliographical footnote, I soon discovered that there was no satisfactory account of Silvestro's life and works. The only attempt turned out to be Franz Michalski's very brief *De Sylvestri Prieratis . . . vita et scriptis . . .* (Münster, 1892). I also became aware, to my dismay, that Michalski's work, though by no means unsympathetic to Silvestro, is almost entirely unreliable. Yet, since its publication there has been an interminable, uncritical repetition of its contents.

The result was the decision to embark on this biography, which, even though it represents a distraction from my continuing, primary research interests, I do not regret, for Silvestro is certainly worthy of attention in his own right and, moreover, he provides an invaluable point of entry into the peculiar world of the friars' intelligentsia during the period immediately preceding the Reformation—a matter which, all in all, still awaits serious scholarly attention.

I do not claim to have written an in-depth biography of Silvestro. The complete lack of any kind of personal, intimate documentation, such as letters and diaries, has prevented the composition of an exhaustive, psychological account of the man, so that he remains very much an enigma. Nevertheless, I believe that this chronicle of his public life shows that, even if he was not a first-rank figure, he did play an extremely important role in some of the most significant events of the early sixteenth century (such as the cases of Reuchlin, Pomponazzi, and Luther). An acquaintance with the entire course of his life casts some new light on all of these.

I have organized this account into four chapters following a chronological division which corresponds to the four principal phases of Silvestro's official life. Within these chapters I have inserted brief descriptions of all his numerous literary works. These discussions do not do justice to the contents of these works, for the works range in their thematic diversity from logic and astronomy to dogmatic and moral theology, canon law, liturgics, homiletics, spirituality, hagiography, demonology, and witchcraft. To be able to deal with all this satisfactorily would require a book many times lengthier, as well as a wide-ranging expertise that I do not possess. Perhaps my brief bibliographical remarks will induce specialists in these disciplines to pay more attention to Silvestro's works than has been the case so far.

I wish to express my gratitude to those who contributed to the completion of this work, especially the Rev. Dr. Simon Tugwell O.P., President of the Dominican Historical Institute, Rome, who read the entire manuscript at various stages of its composition and made very many suggestions for its improvement. I wish to thank him, moreover, for his truly fraternal forbearance with my interminable chatter about Silvestro on innumerable occasions. I have also to express my gratitude to Professor Edward P. Mahoney for his unfailing support and to the editorial staff of the Duke University Press for their help in preparing this work for publication. Finally, I wish to thank the anonymous readers of the Press whose acute observations enabled me to make much better sense of some important aspects of Silvestro's life.

Prierias: The Life and Works of Silvestro Mazzolini da Prierio, 1456–1527

Silvestro da Prierio, *Conflatum ex S. Thoma,* Perugia 1519, detail of frontispiece. (Biblioteca Casanatense, Rome. Courtesy of the Ministero per i Beni Culturali ed Ambientali). Central medallion of Thomas Aquinas set in a burst of rays listing his most important works. Below, Silvestro da Prierio—M[AGISTER] SILVESTER—in pious and scholarly poses.

I   FRIAR PREACHER, 1456–1487

Beginnings

Silvestro Mazzolini da Prierio, commonly known as Prierias and whom I shall henceforth call Silvestro, was born either in 1456 or 1457. This is evident from two autobiographical remarks in his *Conflatum ex. S. Thoma.* This work, although it was published in 1519, must have been completed during the first half of 1516 since its prefatory letter by Pope Leo X is dated 28 June of that year. In the first remark Silvestro tells us that he is in his sixtieth year and in his forty-fifth year as a Dominican friar.[1] In the second, along with a conventional avowal of humility, he repeats the information about his age.[2]

Silvestro hailed from the small village of Priero near Mondoví in the province of Cuneo in Piedmont. Priero today is a small rural center with a population of a few hundred. It lies in a hilly region, the northern aspect of the Ligurian Alps, and is situated some six kilometers from Ceva on the railway line between Turin and Savona. During the second half of the fifteenth century Priero formed part of the Duchy of Savoy, which was ruled at the time of Silvestro's birth by the Duke Ludovico (1413–1465). That it was not in any way a significant place is indicated by the fact that Leandro Alberti da Bologna's remarkably detailed *Descrittione di tutta Italia* (1550) makes no mention of it.

Leandro Alberti (1479–1552), who was himself a Dominican and had been one of Silvestro's students in Bologna at the beginning of the sixteenth century, confirms Silvestro's provenance from Priero in his *De viris illustribus Ordinis Praedicatorum* (1517). This work is structured in the form of a dialogue between Alberti himself and a variety of interlocutors, and its description of Silvestro is placed in the mouth of another Dominican, the famous novelist Matteo Bandello di Castelnuovo (1485–1561). Writing in 1516, when Silvestro was already a person of great moment and reputation, Alberti indulges in no mean comparison: he likens Silvestro's learning and virtues to those of Aristotle and claims that Silvestro honored the hamlet of Priero as Stagira had been honored by Aristotle.[3]

Since it was customary at the time for members of religious orders, especially the friars, to be designated by their place of origin, Silvestro was usually called "de Prierio" in Latin and "da Prierio" in Italian. Several versions of the Latin appellation, in the first place "Prierias," are found in the titles, prefaces, and colophons of Silvestro's numerous Latin works. But of course in his publications Silvestro was often at the mercy of the whim of his printers and allowance has to be made for the exigencies of diverse grammatical constructions. In his Italian works, Silvestro is invariably referred to as "da Prierio." Whenever it is a matter of Silvestro's self-designation in the various letters, entries in conventual registers, and other documents that we shall encounter in the course of this biography, he always styles himself, in Latin, "Silvester de Prierio" and, in Italian, "Silvestro da Prierio."

That Silvestro's family name was Mazzolini is certain since it appears in the title of the dedication to Leo X in the *Conflatum*[4] and in that of the first book of the *Errata et argumenta* (1520).[5] Some authors have suggested, quite erroneously, that his family name was Di Prierio.[6] But it is likely that they simply wished to bolster a little what must have been rather humble social origins by attempting to connect him with the Di Prierio, a noble family of Liguria. But of Silvestro's family, the Mazzolini of the undistinguished hamlet of Priero, nothing is known other than what concerns his two nephews, Aurelio and Silvestro, who followed their uncle into the Dominican Order. Since neither of Silvestro's nephews will reappear in this biography it will be most convenient to deal briefly with them at this point.

Aurelio Mazzolini da Prierio (d. 1561), while not achieving his uncle's prominence and fame, made, nonetheless, a respectable, although rather slow, academic career. He was adopted at a very young age and raised in Bologna by the "beata" Elena Duglioli Dall'Olio (1472–1520), who is reputed to have had Silvestro as her spiritual director during the opening years of the sixteenth century.[7] He was received in the Dominican Order in the convent of San Domenico in Bologna in 1506 and made his religious profession on 29 December 1507. His first academic appointment, as master of studies in San Domenico's studium generale, took place only as late as 1530, when he is believed to have had frà Michele Ghislieri, the future Pope Pius V, as one of his students. At the time the regent master was Bartolomeo Spina da Pisa, who had been one of Silvestro's favorite disciples and had benefited greatly from his patronage and protection during his own academic ascent. Perhaps his promotion of Aurelio was principally an acknowledgment of his debt to his old mentor. Be that as it may, Aurelio later served as bachelor of the *Sentences* in Bologna during 1540–42, graduated as master of theology in the University of Bologna in 1542, and served as regent master in the studium during 1546–47. He subsequently attended as an official theologian the Bolognese sessions of the Council of Trent, but, as he has not left any literary remains, it is impossible to estimate his theological worth. His last important position was that of prior of the convent of Santa Maria di Castello in Genoa during 1555–57.[8]

Silvestro's other nephew, the homonymous Silvestro Mazzolini da Prierio, entered the order in Bologna when his uncle was vicar general of the Congregation of Lombardy (1508–1510) and made his religious profession on 12 October 1509. He certainly did not have the senior Silvestro's intellectual gifts, and one of the few records that we have of him presents him as the bursar in Santa Maria di Castello in 1557.[9] The only extant document that shows him in an intellectually demanding situation is not flattering.[10]

Let us now return to our Silvestro. Leandro Alberti tells us that he entered the Friars Preachers at a tender age.[11] This took place in 1471, when he was either fifteen or sixteen years old, the normal age of reception into religious orders at the time. This is clear from two autobiographical asides in the *Conflatum*[12] and, as well, a remark in the *Replica contra Lutherum* (1518).[13]

When he entered the order Silvestro was received into its reformed Observant Congregation of Lombardy. This congregation had been erected as a distinct juridical entity by Pope Pius II in 1459 and united the reformed convents situated principally in the territories of the two northern Italian, unreformed ("conventual") provinces of St. Peter Martyr (*Lombardiae Superioris*) and St. Dominic (*Lombardiae Inferioris*). Some of its houses, though, such as the renowned convent of San Marco in Florence and that of Santa Sabina in Rome, were located in central Italy and were situated within the territory of the unreformed Roman province.

The Congregation had its distant origins in the observant vicariate first founded in 1393 under the vicarship of Bl. John Dominici (1356–1419) in accordance with the directives for reform issued by Master General Bl. Raymond of Capua (1330–1399). A few years after Silvestro's death, the Observant Congregation of Lombardy would be reconstituted by Pope Clement VII in 1531 as the *Provincia Utriusque Lombardiae Regularis Vitae* and the two unreformed provinces of St. Peter Martyr and St. Dominic demoted to the status of vicariates.[14]

The difference between the observant, "regular life" friars and the conventual, "common life" friars was not at all a matter of different degrees of apostolic fervor and efficacy or of intellectual dedication and prowess. Popular preachers and learned academics, especially in the Thomistic tradition but not exclusively so, were to be found among both groups. Certainly both parties numbered among their members a large majority that performed their tasks conscientiously and led decent lives, as well as their fair share of poltroons, ignoramuses, and buffoons, and a very small number of thieves, lechers, syphilitics, and such like. It is significant that at least two of the annual chapters of the Congregation of Lombardy itself, those held in Florence in 1485 and in Venice in 1492, found it necessary to prescribe that each convent had to have a jail with a securely locked door and equipped with stock, chains, and fetters so that recalcitrant friars could be suitably disciplined.[15]

That this state of affairs has been acknowledged only very rarely is perhaps the result of the ideological preoccupations of writers of Dominican history during the second half of the nineteenth and the first half of the twentieth century. Their primary concern seems to have been the historical justification of the particular character that had been assumed by the Dominican revival at the time of Henri-Dominique Lacordaire (1802–1861) and, especially, the term of office of Master General Vincent Jandel (1855–1872). Antonin Mortier, for example, managed to produce with his famous history of the Dominican masters general (pub. 1907–11) essentially an outline of the reform movements in which the conventual provinces, and their members, are mentioned solely in order to illustrate situations in dire need of correction.[16]

The difference between the observants and the conventuals was first expressed by Raymond of Capua rather generally in terms of the former's resolution to fulfill the letter of the Dominican constitutions.[17] The fundamental issue was, however, different interpretations of the practical import of the vow of poverty. The conventuals accepted a certain measure of individual ownership of such goods as books and clothing and, especially, the custom of friars being allowed to have a personal fund (*peculium*), of which the order retained radical ownership, for approved, necessary expenditures. This entailed a degree of economic independence of individual friars from their communities—the state of affairs commonly known as the "private life" (and, in the terminology of the fifteenth century, somewhat paradoxically referred to as the "vita communis").

This situation had developed in the order from its very beginning. Whether it deserves to be judged adversely remains a moot point, for it seems to have been the inevitable result of both the emphasis that Dominicans placed on studies, with its implication of expensive needs such as books, and the intolerable constrictions that a rigid adherence to mendicancy, as well as monastic regularity, would have placed on apostolic activities.[18] Indeed, fifteenth-century advocates of conventuality, such as Raffaele da Pornassio (d. 1467), did not hesitate to argue that their way of life was as authentically Dominican as that of the observants, since it had been customary in the order from its earliest days, was envisaged by the Dominican constitutions with their stress on the necessity of apposite dispensations, and had been practiced by such eminent confreres as Albert the Great and Thomas Aquinas.[19] Whatever the case, the situation had certainly been aggravated in the aftermath of the ravages of the Black Death and the consequent economic insecurity of communities, and once ensconced, the practice of conventuality perpetuated itself.

A perfect example of a conventual friar is provided by Silvestro's greatest Dominican contemporary, Thomas De Vio Cajetan (1469–1534). Mortier, following J. Quétif and J. Échard's unfounded claim that at the time of Cajetan's entry into the order his convent of Gaeta belonged to the Congregation of Lombardy,[20] numbered Cajetan as a member of that congregation and, indeed, acclaimed him as one of its greatest glories.[21] But, in fact, Cajetan was a member of the unreformed province of the Kingdom of Naples (*Regni Siciliae*) and, as a young man, is reputed to have laughed at talk of reform.[22] Be that as it may, there is ample evidence of his conventuality. There is, for example, a record of the young Cajetan being reprimanded by Master General Gioacchino Torriani da Venezia in late 1495 for failing to settle a debt that he had personally contracted with another friar in Gaeta.[23] Furthermore, one of Cajetan's first acts, after his election as master general in 1508, was to ensure that the chamber that he had built at his own expense in the convent of Gaeta was handed over to a relative, frà Giovanni De Vio.[24]

It is impossible to say why Silvestro chose the Friars Preachers rather than some other order, and, especially, why he chose the observants rather than the conventuals. There was no Dominican house in Priero itself; if there had been, this might have determined his choice as much as the presence of an unreformed convent in Gaeta probably determined Cajetan's choice of the conventuals. That the choice was open to him cannot be doubted: Priero's neighboring towns hosted quite an array of convents belonging to both the Congregation of Lombardy and the Province of St. Peter Martyr. But Silvestro's youth at the time of his reception into the order, as well as the lack of any documentation, precludes any explanation in terms of the kind of personal motives that compelled his older fellow student and colleague Girolamo Savonarola, for example, to opt for the Congregation of Lombardy four years after him in 1475.[25]

Son of San Domenico in Savona

In Silvestro's time, when a young man entered the order he did so in a particular convent. There he received the religious habit, passed his novitiate year, and at the end of it made his religious profession—that is, took his solemn, permanent vows of poverty, chastity, and obedience. By doing so, he became a permanent member or "son" (*filius*) of that convent. Even though Dominicans have always made their religious profession expressly to the order's master general, a friar's essential juridical link with the order was at that time through affiliation to a convent. A friar usually remained in his own convent for the completion of his initial studies: those considered necessary for ordination to the priesthood and the beginning of apostolic work. Afterwards, he was often assigned to some other convent for reasons of further study or apostolic work. Nevertheless, he usually remained a member of the convent where he had been received, professed, and initially formed, for the rest of his life, enjoying certain rights within it and owing it certain obligations.

It was indeed possible for a friar to transfiliate to another convent, that is, cease to be a *filius* of the convent where he had been received, professed, and educated and become the *filius* of another convent. A friar thereby acquired rights in, and owed obligations to, the convent to which he had transfiliated as if it were the convent of his reception and profession. But transfiliation was an uncommon event and could only take place with the explicit permission of the order's master general.

It is generally claimed that when Silvestro entered the Congregation of Lombardy in 1471 he did so in the convent of Santa Maria di Castello in Genoa, became one of its *filii,* and remained there until the completion of his initial studies. The beginning of this tale is found in Quétif and Échard (1721) on the basis of a statement by Andrea Rovetta da Brescia (1691) which they felt should be treated with caution.[26] In fact, Rovetta says solely that in 1523 Silvestro was an *alumnus* (by which he means *filius*) of Santa Maria di Castello.[27] This, as we shall see, is correct; but it permits no conclusion about the convent of Silvestro's reception and profession.

The entry on Silvestro in the *Syllabus* of Santa Maria di Castello compiled by Amedeo Vigna in 1888 on the basis of six fifteenth- and sixteenth-century codices does mention him as one of the *filii* of that convent.[28] But, like Rovetta, it does not tell us when he became one. Of this we are informed, however, by a copy of the patent letter issued by Master General Cajetan permitting Silvestro's transfiliation to Santa Maria di Castello which is preserved in its *Liber consiliorum.* It records that Silvestro became a *filius* of Santa Maria di Castello, along with his nephews Aurelio and Silvestro, only on 5 March 1516, several months after his appointment as Master of the Sacred Palace.[29]

The Genoese *Syllabus* also states that Silvestro was originally received in the convent of San Domenico in Bologna. But this cannot be accepted without further investigation because of four pieces of evidence which point to a long-standing association with the convent of San Domenico in Savona:

1. A remark in Silvestro's *Quadragesimale Aureum,* published in 1515 but composed in 1507, informs us that he had suffered an almost fatal illness some thirty years earlier, that is, around 1482, while he was stationed in Mantua. He tells us that he was feverish for some fifteen months and was eventually diagnosed as having tuberculosis. He adds that, because of this, he was sent by his superiors to convalesce in the convent of Savona, where the air was deemed to be healthier. Silvestro points out that this was the convent, close to his home region, where he had received the religious habit.[30]

2. A further remark in the same work also suggests that Silvestro had been a novice in the convent of Savona. He reports the case of a usurer in Albenga who was supposed to have sold his soul to the devil and relates that he had first heard of the matter from some friars who were in Savona while he was a novice.[31]

3. It is certain that before transfiliating to Santa Maria di Castello in Genoa in 1516 Silvestro had been a *filius* of San Domenico in Savona. This is mentioned in a letter of Master General Cajetan, dated 5 December 1510, allowing him to transfiliate to the convent of Sant'Eustorgio in Milan if he so wished—a concession that Silvestro probably did not avail of for reasons that will be considered later.[32]

4. There is a letter, dated 26 February 1521, of Jeronimo Peñafiel, procurator and vicar general of the order, providing for the distribution of Silvestro's assets and literary remains in the eventuality of his death.[33] The convent of Savona is attributed a quarter of the capital. Silvestro must have been a *filius* of the Savonese convent for a significant period indeed if it was considered to have still such substantial rights in the matter.

Other than the entries in two of the Genoese codices on which Vigna based his *Syllabus,* there is no evidence at all for Silvestro's reception in San Domenico in Bologna. Nor is there any mention of the Bolognese convent (or of Sant'Eustorgio) in Peñafiel's letter as having any rights in the matter of Silvestro's bequests. Furthermore, Silvestro is not listed in the very accurate roster of the *filii* of the convent of San Domenico compiled by one of its archivists, Ludovico da Prelormo, during the second half of the sixteenth century and which explicitly mentions his two nephews.[34] Vigna's *Syllabus,* then, surely errs on this point. Vigna failed to notice that the authors of the codices from which he derived the remark "receptus Bononiae," the *Codice Carbone* (1554)[35] and the *Codice Bottaro* (1567),[36] were familiar with Cajetan's patent letter of 1516 and, probably on its basis, took it for granted that Silvestro had been received in Bologna just like his nephews.

The convent of San Domenico in Savona in which the young Silvestro was received in 1471 had been founded by 1288. But, other than this, nothing is known about it, not even the date of its reform and aggregation to the Congregation of Lombardy.[37]

Student in Bologna

Although Silvestro was undoubtedly received in San Domenico in Savona and must have made his novitiate and profession there, thus becoming one of its *filii,* this does not mean that he remained there for the whole of his initial studies. Rather, he completed these in the studium generale situated in the convent of San Domenico in Bologna. The evidence for this is in the preface to Silvestro's *Rosa aurea* (1503). The work is dedicated to the Count and Knight Ludovico da Thiene of Vicenza and was written in response to a request by his wife Adriana, who wished to be instructed on the Gospels so that her leisure could be devoted to spiritual edification. The preface contains a brief history of the Thiene family, which is preceded by an account of the impression that Vicenza had made upon Silvestro when he first arrived there. He stresses the beauty and fertility of Vicenza's surrounding countryside as well as the wealth and the elegant, refined manners of its citizens. It is in this context that he informs us that, before arriving in Vicenza, he had been studying in Bologna.[38] This move by Silvestro from Bologna to Vicenza corresponds precisely to the time when he would have terminated his initial studies.

In the preface to the *Rosa aurea* Silvestro also tells us when the greater part of the work was composed; obviously, if the work was first undertaken at the request of Adriana da Thiene, Silvestro's transfer from Bologna to Vicenza must have taken place earlier than the beginning of the work's composition. The events mentioned as preceding the composition of the bulk of the *Rosa aurea* are a harrowing siege of Ferrara by the Venetians and Silvestro's almost fatal illness.[39] These events are mentioned, as well, in the *Quadragesimale aureum,* where they are described as having taken place roughly thirty years earlier.[40] This latter work was published in 1515 but its content comprises Lenten sermons preached by Silvestro in Genoa in 1507. The reference to thirty years earlier could, then, have been written any time between 1507 and 1515 and indicates a date somewhere between 1477 and 1485 for the events in question. This span of time can be narrowed down further because the only war between Ferrara and Venice that falls within it is a well-known historical event that occurred in 1482.

Silvestro's departure from Bologna and first arrival in Vicenza took place, then, sometime after 1477 and before 1482. Since Silvestro had entered the order in 1471 at the age of fifteen or sixteen, he would have been ordained to the priesthood in 1480 at the age of twenty-three or twenty-four and completed his initial studies a year or two after that. It is certain, therefore, that Silvestro completed his initial studies in Bologna.

That San Domenico in Bologna was the convent where Silvestro completed his initial studies is not surprising. The convent of Savona was in all likelihood a small one and would not have had the resources to provide an adequate program of studies for its *filii*. Silvestro undoubtedly completed his novitiate in Savona. But this was a year of exclusively religious formation: a year of introduction to the laws and customs of the Dominican Order and, as well, to the rudiments of pious practices especially formal, liturgical prayer.[41] Silvestro probably also completed in Savona the two obligatory years of literary studies: grammar and rhetoric. A few years after his entry into the order the Congregation of Lombardy legislated, at the chapter held in Vicenza in 1483, that candidates were not to be accepted without having completed such studies previously.[42]

Silvestro is likely, then, to have been sent to Bologna for his philosophical and theological studies around 1474. That he did not begin these studies until then is confirmed by a remark in the *Conflatum* in which he tells us that he only commenced studying the works of Aquinas during his fourth year in the order.[43]

By Silvestro's time, the structure of the Dominican curriculum of philosophical and theological studies had been progressively determined by the legislation emanating from the order's general chapters and recorded in their *Acta*. The salient points of these determinations on academic matters would be summarily outlined in the paragraphs of commentary which accompanied the rather meager treatment of studies in the order's constitutions (dist. 2, chap. 14) when they appeared in print for the first time in 1505 at the behest of Master General Vincenzo Bandello di Castelnuovo.[44]

Dominican legislation about students and studies was promulgated in piecemeal fashion throughout the thirteenth century and received a fairly definitive, but still rather vague, formulation at the general chapter held in Genoa in 1305.[45] One must be careful, though, not to mythologize this legislation as has been done at times. It did not amount at all to some kind of fully worked out *ratio studiorum,* nor was it the a priori creation of some kind of daring foresight and inventiveness. Rather, it was very much the cumulative product of many occasional and pragmatic prescriptions that seem to have been principally motivated by two preoccupations. These were the concern to maintain a basic uniformity of training throughout the order and the desire to ensure that it harmonized with the requirements and structures of the universities.

It envisaged, after the completion of the two years of preparatory, literary studies (grammar and rhetoric), three years of logic: one year devoted to the *logica vetus* and two years devoted to the *logica nova*. This was to be followed by at least two years of philosophy (natural philosophy and metaphysics) and four years of systematic theology focusing on the *Sentences* of Peter Lombard. After the completion of the initial biennium of literary studies in their convent of affiliation, the friars were to complete their logical and philosophical studies in convents which housed studia particularia that specialized in these disciplines. The theological course was to be completed in a studium generale. There, the students enjoyed the status of *studentes formales:* they were officially embarked on a course of speculative, systematic theology which was the first step toward the acquisition of university degrees in theology. This course concentrated on the Bible and the *Sentences* of Peter Lombard and entailed participation in various formal academic exercises such as circles and disputations.

But it must be kept in mind that this ideal curriculum, which has received a considerable amount of attention from scholars,[46] was not meant for the normal, "run-of-the-mill" friars, the so-called *fratres communes* who constituted the great bulk of the order's membership.[47] Rather, it envisaged the few, especially intellectually gifted friars who were selected to be prepared for such specifically academic tasks within the order as that of conventual lector.

Unfortunately there is no official record of what might have been expected academically of the average friar. But it seems that he was envisaged as being trained exclusively in his convent of affiliation and under the sole guidance of his local conventual lector. After grammatical studies and, perhaps, a little logic and philosophy, he followed a course of theological studies which was essentially practical in import: it concentrated on the Bible and cases of conscience and was geared to preaching and hearing confessions.

Our knowledge of the details of the actual practice in this matter during Silvestro's time is only vague. But it is rather doubtful that the ideal curriculum was fully implemented even in the cases of friars chosen for academic careers. The general chapters of Montpellier (1456)[48] and Nejmegen (1459)[49] insisted that these friars complete at least a triennium of logic and philosophy. Complaints from the moderators of studia generalia about students being sent to commence the academic course in theology with little or no logic, philosophy, or even grammar were very common during the second half of the fifteenth century.[50]

Furthermore, it seems that at the end of whatever smattering of grammar, logic, and philosophy the average friar managed to acquire, he was considered sufficiently prepared to simply join the other members of his conventual community in their, perhaps rather erratic, continuing or "ongoing" study. This focused on the Bible, with the help of the *glossa ordinaria* and Petrus Comestor's *Historia,* and cases of conscience, employing some common *summa de casibus,* and was carried out under the direction of the conventual lector. It would certainly be anachronistic to think of the average friar of the time as being required to complete a predetermined course of philosophy and theology devised precisely as preparation for ordination to the priesthood in the manner of a post-Tridentine seminary. Rather, it seems to have been very much a matter of "on the job" training with few academic pretensions.

There is ample indirect evidence of the meager formal academic preparation received by the average friar during the second half of the fifteenth and the first half of the sixteenth centuries. A striking example are the very numerous records in the registers of the Dominican masters general of dispensations granted to friars allowing them to be ordained in their twenty-third rather than twenty-fourth year. These records stress that the dispensations were granted only on the condition that the beneficiaries were suitable. As far as academic requirements are concerned, suitability is indicated as involving at least a basic competence in grammar.[51] In not one of the hundreds of these records is there any reference to systematic theological formation. Another example is the ordination of the general chapter of Ferrara (1498) that no friar was thereafter to be promoted to holy orders unless he could recite the divine office decently and was sufficiently instructed in grammar.[52] A further example is the letter sent by Master General Cajetan to all the provinces of the order in 1508–09. It stresses that no friar was to be admitted to holy orders who was not sufficiently instructed in grammar and that no friar was to hear confessions who had not received a basic training in cases of conscience.[53] Again, in neither case is there any mention of systematic theology.

As far as Silvestro is concerned, since he completed his early studies in the rigorous studium generale in Bologna, they are likely to have been far less haphazard than those completed by the average friar in some minor convent. Furthermore, the Congregation of Lombardy stressed that its students were to be trained in conformity with the prescriptions of the order's legislation.[54] Silvestro probably completed something very much like the ideal curriculum of studies or at least the closest approximation to it available in the order at the time.

A provision peculiar to the Congregation of Lombardy's adaptation of the ideal course of studies seems to have been that even the most gifted friars did not commence the course of systematic theology immediately after philosophy. Instead, all friars undertook a primarily practical course of theology during which they were ordained to the priesthood. It was invariably only after ordination and usually only after a number of years of apostolate, which often included a period as conventual lector in some minor convent, that the intellectually gifted friars returned to the Bolognese studium as *studentes formales* for the academic course in theology which could lead, eventually, to the acquisition of degrees.[55] As we shall see, this was certainly the pattern that would be followed by Silvestro.

Student of Pietro da Bergamo

Of the various professors who are likely to have influenced Silvestro during his period of studies in Bologna, the most important was undoubtedly Pietro Maldura da Bergamo (d. 1482) who was regent master during 1471–77.[56] It has been argued that Pietro, the author of the vast thematic index to the works of Aquinas known as the *Tabula aurea* (1473), was the real inaugurator of the great Thomistic revival of the fifteenth and sixteenth centuries and that the studium of Bologna was its primary and continuing foyer.[57] Whatever the case, it is certain that Silvestro was formed in a center of a renewed Thomism which, being preoccupied with a return to its sources, the editing of sound texts, and discriminating between authentic and spurious works, might well be considered a Renaissance phenomenon in a deeper sense than that of mere chronological coincidence.

There are several references to Pietro in the *Rosa aurea*.[58] This work, although it was first published in 1503, had been commenced some twenty years earlier, at a time when Silvestro would still have thought of Pietro as the greatest Thomist that he had known and when his memories of him would still have been fresh. His references to him give the impression that he not only esteemed him highly but indeed revered him.[59] Several of his references to Pietro invoke Pietro's *Etimologiae id est concordantiae conclusionum* published in Bologna in 1477 during Silvestro's stay there.[60] There are further references to Pietro in another of Silvestro's early works, the *Additiones in Capreolum* (1497), and they are all to the *Etimologiae*.[61] A further such reference is in the *Summa silvestrina*, which, although it was published in 1515, was completed by 1506.[62]

The persisting influence of Pietro is best indicated by the nature of Silvestro's most ambitious literary project. The *Conflatum ex S. Thoma* (1519) is a great digest and anthology of all Aquinas's works. It is accompanied by a commentary by Silvestro which, if it had been completed, would have rivaled in extent the classic commentaries by Cajetan on the *Summa Theologiae* and by Francesco Silvestri on the *Summa contra Gentiles.* The *Conflatum* follows the thematic order of the *Summa Theologiae* and its selection and assembly of numerous parallel texts is evidently guided by Pietro's *Tabula aurea.* Its handling of difficult, controversial passages in Aquinas's text is also often determined by distinctions proposed by Pietro in the *Etimologiae.* The *Conflatum* includes one explicit reference to Pietro; in it Silvestro appeals to his authority in a polemic against Cajetan.[63] But to the *Conflatum,* as well as to Silvestro's doctrinal conflicts with Cajetan, I shall return at a later point.

Pietro da Bergamo was succeeded as regent master of the Bolognese studium in 1477 by Domenico de Pirris da Gargnano, who would hold the office till 1481.[64] There is no mention of Domenico in any of Silvestro's works, but this need not mean that he was not influenced by him. Domenico had different interests from those of Pietro. Alberto da Castello mentions Domenico in the *Chronica brevissima* (1516) as a preacher of Lenten sermons.[65] Domenico's only extant work is a *consilium* which deals with the practical, moral question of whether the then approved pawn shops (*Montes pietatis*) were wholly immune to usury.

It is just possible, then, that it was Domenico who communicated to Silvestro during his initial years of practical theology what would become for him a lifelong involvement with pastoral, moral issues and eventually result in the publication in 1515 of his most famous and popular work, the *Summa silvestrina.* It is instructive that one of Silvestro's earliest works was a *Consilium de monte pietatis,* which is no longer extant.[66] It is also likely that Domenico influenced Silvestro by first interesting him in, and perhaps forming his opinion on, the issues of demonology and witchcraft. This resulted in another of Silvestro's persistent preoccupations and the eventual publication of the *Tractatulus de diabolo* (1502), the apposite entries in the *Summa silvestrina* (1515), and the *De strigimagarum daemonumque mirandis* (1521). Domenico, while later serving as inquisitor in Bologna during 1485–89 and in Mantua during 1490–1511, advocated hard-line positions on these issues which anticipate those defended by Silvestro in his own works and by Silvestro's disciple, Bartolomeo Spina da Pisa, in the *Quaestio de strigibus et lamiis* (1523).[67]

The Thomist of greatest speculative significance who is likely to have been one of Silvestro's teachers at this time is Dominic of Flanders (Beaudoin Lottin) (d. 1479).[68] Dominic entered the Congregation of Lombardy in San Domenico in Bologna in 1461 some ten years after graduating as master of arts in the University of Paris, where he had studied under John Versorius (d. 1485) and taught for a while. He then studied theology and taught philosophy in Bologna for a decade before graduating a master of theology in the University of Bologna around 1470. In 1470 he was called by Lorenzo de' Medici to teach philosophy in the University of Florence and did so during 1470–72. From 1472 to 1474 he taught philosophy in Pisa, to where the university had been transferred. He died in 1479 of the plague while serving as regent master of the studium generale in the convent of Santa Maria Novella in Florence. But Dominic also taught in the Bolognese studium during the academic year 1474–75, when he lectured on book 2 of Aristotle's *Metaphysics,* and again in 1476–77.

If Silvestro was indeed one of Dominic's students, he does not appear to have been impressed by the experience. There are no traces in any of Silvestro's works of adhesion to the characteristic theses defended by Dominic in his great commentary on Aristotle's *Metaphysics*[69] and his many other works. Instead, in the *Conflatum,* Silvestro explicitly criticizes Dominic's most controversial metaphysical thesis: that the adequate subject of metaphysics is not the *ens commune* that is divided by uncreated and created being but only that *ens commune* that is divided by the ten categories.[70] The only explicit references to Dominic that I have been able to find in Silvestro's works are critical in intent and deal with the same speculative issue: the nature of the distinction between a predicamental relation and its fundament. The first reference is in the *Additiones in Capreolum* (1497) and simply lists Dominic's opinion among those rejected by Silvestro;[71] the second is in the *Conflatum* and is a churlish repetition of the first.[72]

Two of Silvestro's fellow students in Bologna deserve to be mentioned. The first is Paolo Barbo da Soncino (d. 1495).[73] Soncinas, a close friend of Giovanfrancesco Pico della Mirandola, was a student in Bologna during 1474–79 and was slightly ahead of Silvestro. In 1481 Soncinas would return to Bologna, where he matriculated as a *studens formalis* on 20 July. He later served as master of studies during 1486–87 and as bachelor of the *Sentences* during 1493–95. He graduated as master of theology in the University of Bologna on 30 May 1495 and died soon after, while serving as prior of San Domenico in Cremona, on 5 August 1495. Like Dominic of Flanders, Soncinas composed a lengthy commentary on Aristotle's *Metaphysics,*[74] but I have not found any explicit mention of it in Silvestro's works. Nonetheless, in the *Conflatum,* Silvestro expresses his negative evaluation of Soncinas's most controversial metaphysical thesis: the demonstration of the existence of immaterial substances pertains solely to natural philosophy and in no way to metaphysics.[75]

The second is Girolamo Savonarola da Ferrara (1452–1498). Savonarola made his novitiate in Bologna in 1475–76. Afterwards, since he had already completed his philosophical studies at the University of Ferrara before entering the order, he proceeded immediately to the study of theology during 1476–78 and completed a year as a *studens formalis* during 1478–79.[76] Accordingly, Silvestro and Savonarola, as well as Soncinas, were contemporaries as students of theology in San Domenico. This, in fact, would not be their only time of contact; as we shall see, they would both return to Bologna in 1487 after a little less than a decade of apostolic work.

It is disappointing that, although Silvestro and Savonarola must have known each other well, there is no mention of the Florentine reformer in any of Silvestro's works. This in itself is not surprising: Savonarola was not destined to enjoy great popularity among the friars of the Observant Congregation of Lombardy, who generally resented his attempt to effect a reform within the Congregation itself by the establishment of his independent Congregation of San Marco. Yet, in Silvestro's particular case, the impossibility of discovering his attitude to Savonarola is especially unfortunate. Perhaps Silvestro's knowledge of the Savonarola affair, and his possible conclusion that obstreperous friars were best dealt with by prompt and stern disciplinary measures, influenced his later handling of what, at least at first, might have seemed to be just another case of an inflexible, insubordinate friar: that of Martin Luther.

Preacher

Very little can be discovered about Silvestro's whereabouts and activities during the period of approximately a decade following his ordination to the priesthood around 1479 and the conclusion of his initial studies around 1480–81. The preface to the *Rosa aurea* gives the impression that he was first assigned to the convent of Santa Corona in Vicenza.[77] This house had been founded in 1260 by Bl. Bartolomeo da Breganza, bishop of Vicenza during 1255–71 and himself a Dominican. It was united to the Congregation of Lombardy by Pius II in 1463. Its magnificent romanesque church, built during 1260–70, preserved a relic of the Crown of Thorns from which it derived its title and which had been presented to Bartolomeo by St. Louis IX, King of France.[78] In the *Rosa aurea* (1503) Silvestro later devoted a *casus* to the problem of the kind of reverence that was to be payed to this relic.[79] While in Vicenza, Silvestro is likely to have dedicated himself almost exclusively to apostolic work. Nonetheless, it was probably at this time that he composed his short *Consilium de monte pietatis* that has been already mentioned. Many years later, in 1519, Silvestro indicated that at that time it was still in the archive of Santa Corona.[80]

The account of Silvestro's almost fatal illness presented in the *Quadragesimale aureum* informs us that, when he fell sick around 1482, he was stationed in Mantua.[81] But at the time there were two Dominican convents in that city. The older and larger convent, the centrally situated San Domenico, had been founded in 1233. Its large church took many years to complete and was finally consecrated by Pius II in 1460; it was demolished in 1924. The smaller convent of Santa Maria degli Angeli was founded in 1438, on the city's outskirts, as a reformed house.[82] By the time that Silvestro arrived in Mantua, San Domenico itself had also been reformed and aggregated to the Congregation of Lombardy so that he could have been in either house. But it is more likely that Silvestro was in the larger San Domenico because, before becoming ill, he worked as a junior lecturer and seems to have taught astronomy.

The evidence for this is in his *Commentarium in spheram.* Although this work was only published in 1514 when Silvestro was prior of San Domenico in Cremona, he informs us that he had completed it some thirty-two years earlier, around 1482.[83] The work is also described as one of Silvestro's first works in the inventory of his writings which accompanies the *Conflatum* (1519).[84] This inventory takes the form of a concluding letter to the reader. It is an especially important document since it contains a complete list of all of Silvestro's literary works up to 1519 and is accompanied by many remarks which shed light on the circumstances of their composition as well as their editorial misfortunes. Silvestro claims that he decided to compose this inventory because he felt that his death was near and wished to ensure that his works would not be appropriated by others. Now, since the *Commentarium* is an exposition of the standard, elementary astronomical text book of the time, the *De sphera* of John of Hollywood (Ioannes de Sacrobosco—strangely called Ioannes de Sacrobusto by Silvestro), and as it is expressly meant as a work for beginners, it represents the earliest literary product of Silvestro's lifelong commitment to teaching.[85]

It might also be the case that during this time in Mantua Silvestro composed a minor work dedicated to the Marquis of Mantua, Francesco II Gonzaga, dealing with the theology of the Precious Blood. The tract is no longer extant and we only know of it because of a reference to it in Silvestro's *Vita de Sancta Maria Magdalena* (1500).[86] Its substance probably corresponded to the content of the *quaestio* dealing with the same issue published later as part of the *Rosa aurea.*[87]

Silvestro's stay in Mantua was brought to an end by his superiors' decision to send him back to his convent of affiliation in Savona to help him recover from his serious illness.[88] But Silvestro did not spend this time in idle convalescence. Rather, if we are to judge by his account in the *Quadragesimale aureum,* he devoted himself unsparingly to strenuous apostolic activities and especially itinerant preaching in the region surrounding

Savona. He relates how he was moved by pity for the convent's lack of preachers who could minister to the villages in Savona's countryside during Lent. He decided to make a vow to God and the Blessed Virgin that if he could preach throughout Lent, fast every day, and hear confessions, he would recite the Rosary for an entire year and propagate this devotion everywhere. He then set out, despite his continuing fever and the fact that he fed himself exclusively on vegetables, plodding through the mud and snow, to preach eight to ten times each day in the poorest hamlets. He concludes by claiming that, although he could hardly believe it himself, he gradually regained his health, returned to Savona rather plump at Easter, and never fell sick again.[89]

Nor did his illness, or his intense apostolic labors, put an end to Silvestro's literary output. We have seen that it was at this time that he commenced composing the *Rosa aurea*. This is confirmed by a remark in the dedication to Adriana da Thiene in the *Vita di Sancta Maria Magdalena* (1500) that he had composed the *Rosa aurea* at a much earlier time.[90] It is also indicated by a remark in the *Conflatum* that he had written some parts of the *Rosa aurea* over thirty years earlier, during the early 1480s.[91]

But Silvestro's literary production at this time was essentially pastoral in intent. It was primarily concerned with homiletics and moral theology. The *Rosa aurea* is, after all, a collection of sermons for the liturgical year and of difficult cases of conscience. It was meant as an aid to those who, like Silvestro himself, were heavily involved in popular preaching, hearing confessions, and the direction of souls. During this period Silvestro was first and foremost a preaching friar who, reflecting the most authentic tradition of the Friars Preachers, believed that the efficacy of his apostolic effort was, but for the help of his God, wholly determined by the amount of intelligent preparation that he put into it.

Graduate Student

Silvestro's ten years or so of intense, predominantly apostolic work came to an abrupt end at the beginning of the second half of 1487. At this time, at the age of thirty-one, he was reassigned to the studium generale in San Domenico in Bologna as a *studens formalis*. This appointment was probably made at the chapter of the Congregation of Lombardy held in Bologna in May of that year and at the behest of its vicar general, Ludovico di Calabria. The vicars general of the Congregation had been conceded the right to assign *studentes formales* to the Bolognese studium generale by Master General Corrado d'Asti on 1 October 1462.[1] Such appointments had hitherto been a prerogative of the masters general and this was still the case with every other studium generale in the order.

What this appointment entailed was that Silvestro was to matriculate as a student in the theological faculty of the University of Bologna within which the Dominican studium in San Domenico was integrated. He became what we might call a "graduate student" who was officially embarked on the course of higher theological studies that could eventually, but not necessarily, lead a friar to the acquisition of the degrees of bachelor and master of theology and even the coveted appointment as regent master in one of the order's studia generalia. That Silvestro was chosen to be a *studens formalis* in Bologna precisely at this time is an indication of his worth and of the esteem that his superiors must have had for him, for the Congregation's chapter in 1487 also decided to limit the number of such students in the Bolognese studium and to subject prospective candidates to rigorous conditions of admission.[2]

The sequence of steps (*tirocinium*) which led to the master's degree usually followed the pattern of a number of years as *studens formalis,* a year as master of studies, a biennium as biblical lector or bachelor, and a further biennium as bachelor of the *Sentences.* The last of these stages in particular had not merely to be carried out but also to be officially approved by the order's authorities as conducive to the master's degree: as being *pro gradu et forma magisterii.* At that point, the recognized bachelor (*baccalaureus formatus, baccalaureus theologiae*) had to secure permission (be *licentiatus*) from either the master general or a general chapter of the order to be examined and graduate as a master in the faculty of theology of a recognized university. Finally, the newly graduated master of theology had to have his graduation formally recognized by a general chapter of the order. Only after this final step was a friar allowed to style himself "magister," was able to be appointed to a position for which the degree was required, and was able to enjoy the privileges and rights conceded by the order to its masters of theology. This was usually followed by an appointment as regent master in a studium generale for a triennium.[3] At the end of this period the experienced master normally left the studium and was either elected or appointed to a position of great responsibility, quite often to that of inquisitor in a major urban center. Only very rarely was a master recalled to a studium generale to serve a further term as regent master.

In the Congregation of Lombardy, which was particularly strict in matters of academic promotion, the progression through the various stages leading to the degrees of bachelor and master and the appointment as regent master was extremely selective, with a constantly diminishing number of candidates proceeding through the various stages. Only a very small minority of the friars originally matriculated as *studentes formales* did eventually become regent masters. Furthermore, the progression through the various stages was only very rarely chronologically continuous and was normally interrupted after each stage for indeterminate periods of apostolic activity.

The Congregation of Lombardy always sought to avoid an excessive multiplication of masters within its ranks and had decided early to limit the number of graduates from the studium in Bologna to that required to fill that studium's need for regent masters.[4] A friar of the Congregation who was successful in progressing through all the stages of the *tirocinium,* and this was exceptional enough, normally did not achieve the final goal of appointment as regent master in Bologna earlier than in his late forties. It is instructive that such eminent scholars as Crisostomo Iavelli da Casale (1470–1543)[5] and Francesco Silvestri da Ferrara (1474–1528),[6] who were fellow members of the Congregation and Silvestro's younger contemporaries, only became regent masters in Bologna at the age of forty-eight and forty-seven respectively. Silvestro, who would first become regent master in Bologna at the age of forty-two and hold the position twice, has the right to be considered exceptional.

Promotion to the master's degree was, however, by no means as arduous in the studia generalia of the conventual provinces of St. Peter Martyr and St. Dominic. Unlike the Congregation of Lombardy, which had San Domenico in Bologna as its sole studium generale, each of these provinces had three. The Province of St. Peter Martyr had San Tommaso in Pavia,

Sant'Eustorgio in Milan, and San Domenico in Turin.[7] The Province of St. Dominic had Sant'Agostino in Padua, San Domenico in Ferrara, and at least for a short while, Santi Giovanni e Paolo in Venice.[8]

In these studia a friar normally became a *studens formalis* immediately after the completion of his philosophical studies. Furthermore, the conventual provinces did not require that the various stages of the *tirocinium* be separated by periods of apostolic work. Finally, in the conventual studia the terms as biblical bachelor and bachelor of the *Sentences* were usually of only one year; only one of these was deemed necessary and either one could be recognized as being *pro gradu et forma magisterii*. Not surprisingly, masters of theology were far more numerous in the conventual provinces than in the Congregation of Lombardy, and it was not rare for a conventual friar to graduate as master at the age of thirty or even earlier.

Examples of this state of affairs are so familiar as to be almost superfluous. The case of Cajetan, who was created a master of theology at the age of twenty-five by Master General Gioacchino Torriani during the general chapter of Ferrara in 1494, supposedly at the insistence of the Duke of Ferrara, Ercole I d'Este, and following the celebrated, but actually rather restrained, disputation with the moribund Giovanni Pico della Mirandola (d.17 November 1494), is famous.[9] The friars of the Congregation of Lombardy, though, probably considered Cajetan's promotion notorious, since it took place after the completion of only three years of "graduate studies" in Padua.[10] In fairness to Cajetan, it must be stressed that there was nothing technically, legally irregular about his promotion, since the Dominican masters general had been conceded the faculty of creating a master of theology at each general chapter by Pope Boniface IX in 1402.[11] It was, however, extremely unusual, for Boniface's concession had envisaged such cases as those of senior friars, who despite their intellectual merits, had never had the chance to frequent a university faculty of theology because of long-standing apostolic or administrative commitments. Perhaps Cajetan's precocious promotion is, ultimately, best accounted for in terms of the patronage of Cardinal Oliviero Carafa, the order's cardinal protector.[12] Another, and even more apposite, example is Giovanni Rafanelli da Ferrara (d. 1515), who would be Silvestro's immediate predecessor as Master of the Sacred Palace. Rafanelli, a *filius* of the convent of San Domenico in Ferrara which belonged to the Province of St. Dominic, graduated as master of theology in the University of Ferrara at the age of twenty-eight.[13]

But an even greater abuse was rife among the conventual friars than the acquisition of the master's degree by means of accelerated and undemanding courses of studies. This was the practice of being promoted to the degree without any academic effort whatsoever (*ex saltu*) by means of papal bulls procured with the help of influential friends or simply purchased. An interesting example of such *magistri bullati, magistri per bullam,* is the famous author Francesco Colonna (1433–1527) of the Province of St. Dominic and a *filius* of Santi Giovanni e Paolo in Venice. Although primarily endowed with great literary talent and humanistic erudition, Colonna was not entirely lacking in theological interests and expertise, since he served one year as bachelor of the *Sentences* in Sant'Agostino in Padua during 1473–74.[14] Nevertheless, it has been suggested that he simply bought a papal bull in 1482 creating him a master of theology along with several other friars of his convent.[15] Be that as it may, the phenomenon was so widespread as to provoke its unequivocal condemnation by several general chapters, for example that of Ferrara in 1494.[16]

The preoccupation of so many conventual friars with the attainment of magisterial status was not motivated entirely by a disinterested desire for scientific recognition. Rather, notwithstanding that the conventuals certainly counted among their number many dedicated scholars of great repute, more often than not they seem to have been concerned with the rights and privileges conceded to holders of the degree within the order as well as the positions of influence that were made accessible by it.[17] A master was ex officio a member of the conventual council and the provincial chapter. He was also dispensed from the greater part of a normal Dominican's choral and other liturgical obligations, could choose from among the better cells of his convent and the most financially rewarding preaching limits (*termini*), could take his meals in his cell—thereby avoiding the abstinence from meat imposed in the conventual refectory—and could possess a mule and stable it in one of his convent's courtyards. The master's degree was normally required for the position of regent master in one of the conventual studia generalia, which usually entailed a substantial emolument, for the powerful office of inquisitor, for elevation to the episcopate, or for appointment as preacher or spiritual director in a noble house or princely court.

Of course such nonscientific motivations are not likely to have been entirely foreign to some of the friars of the Congregation of Lombardy as well. But, given the very limited number of friars who became masters by means of the rigorous and selective process operative in the Congregation, its holders of the degree are all likely to have been of a respectable academic standard. The Congregation of Lombardy would, in fact, be praised for its academic preeminence by the highest authorities of the order.[18] Furthermore, it was common in Silvestro's time for members of the conventual provinces to be submitted to the humiliation of being examined by professors from the Congregation before they could take up the academic posts to which they had been appointed within their own conventual studia.[19]

According to his own account, Silvestro matriculated as a *studens formalis* in the Bolognese studium on 9 August 1487 and remained such for two academic years: 1487–88 and 1488–89.[20] During this biennium the regent master was Vincenzo Bandello, who would later serve as vicar general of the Congregation of Lombardy during 1489–91 and 1493–95 and as master general during 1501–06. The bachelor of the *Sentences* was Antonio da Cremona and the master of studies for the academic year 1487–88 was Girolamo Savonarola and for the academic year 1488–89 Silvestro da Mantova.

On 9 October 1487 Silvestro was present at a chapter of the convent of San Domenico attended, as well, by Savonarola.[21] Savonarola had returned to the studium in Bologna at the same time as Silvestro, the beginning of the academic year 1487–88. He had been immediately appointed master of studies since he had already completed a year as *studens formalis* during 1478–79 and had subsequently served for a number of years as *lector principalis* in the convent of San Marco in Florence.[22] The academic year 1487–88 was, then, the second period that Savonarola and Silvestro were together in Bologna, and this time Silvestro might even have had Savonarola as one of his teachers. Whatever the case, he certainly had him as his principal academic supervisor, since Silvestro formed part, during that year, of the group of *studentes formales* entrusted to Savonarola's care. But, once again, there is no record of the contact that there must have been between them. Savonarola left Bologna at the end of that academic year and would not proceed any further in the stages leading to the master's degree. They might have met once more, though, before Savonarola met his end in Florence in 1498, for Savonarola returned to Bologna to preach during Lent of 1493.[23]

Among the junior students in San Domenico during Silvestro's second year as a *studens formalis*, 1488–89, was the young Tommaso De Vio. Cajetan, as we have seen, was a member of the unreformed Province of the Kingdom of Naples. Master General Bartolomeo Comazzio had first assigned him as a student to Bologna on 8 April 1485 immediately after the completion of his novitiate in his convent of Gaeta.[24] But nothing came of this assignment, since Cajetan subsequently commenced his logic course in the studium generale of the convent of San Domenico Maggiore in Naples. Master General Gioacchino Torriani reassigned Cajetan to Bologna as a student of philosophy on 18 June 1488.[25] But Cajetan remained in Bologna for only a few months, for on 4 December 1488 the master general allowed him to return to Gaeta because of poor health.[26] When Cajetan recovered sufficiently to recommence his studies early in 1491 he did so in the studium generale of the unreformed convent of Sant'Agostino in Padua.[27]

There must have been some contact between Silvestro and Cajetan at this time, but it was probably minimal. Cajetan was only a young student of nineteen and still at the early stages of his initial studies, while Silvestro was already an established preacher and beginning a formal academic career. Silvestro would have been aware of Cajetan as a very junior student and, to those who have the slightest knowledge of the psychology of such relationships in religious communities, it is not surprising that in later years Silvestro would never be intimidated by Cajetan's eminent offices or hesitate to polemicize against him on speculative issues when he believed him to be in error. But to the matter of the relationship between Silvestro and Cajetan I shall return in a later chapter.

Lecturer

Silvestro's academic performance and religious demeanor during the biennium as *studens formalis* must have been excellent, for at the beginning of the following academic year, 1489–90, he was appointed master of studies.[28] This meant that he became, in effect, the administrative secretary, the academic *fac totum,* and especially, the supervisor of the *studentes formales* in the Bolognese studium generale.[29] During this academic year and probably also during the following, 1490–91, he also taught logic and possibly astronomy to the junior students of the studium.

That Silvestro taught logic is evident from the preface of the *Compendium dialecticae* (1496).[30] He tells us there that he had taught logic in Bologna while Angelo Faella da Verona was the regent master and it is known that Angelo held this post during 1489–92. It has often been asserted that at this time, or even as late as the end of the 1490s by authors who have failed to grasp the chronology of the matter, Silvestro taught logic in the University of Bologna's faculty of arts. But there is, in fact, no evidence for his having taught logic other than in the Dominican studium or at any other time than the biennium 1489–91.

The authors who have made such claims base themselves exclusively on Silvestro's dedication of the *Apologia in dialecticam suam* (1499) to his students "in Gymnasio Bononiensi." But, first, these authors misunderstand the terminology of the time. Whenever a Dominican of this period used expressions such as "in Gymnasio Bononiensi" and "in Gymnasio Patavino" he usually meant the Dominican studia generalia that were integrated within the faculties of theology of the universities of those cities. When he wanted to talk of the faculties of arts of those universities he used the expressions "in Gymnasio publico Bononiensi" and "in Gymnasio publico Patavino." Second, the preface clearly shows that when he referred to his teaching logic in Bologna, Silvestro, writing in 1499 when he was already a master of theology and was serving as regent master of the studium, had in mind an earlier period when, as he tells us, he had not been even a *baccalaureus formatus.*[31] It is clear, then, that the *Apologia in dialecticam suam* is not dedicated to students studying logic under Silvestro in the Faculty of Arts of the University of Bologna in the late 1490s. It is dedicated to students studying theology under him in the Dominican studium during 1498–99, at least some of whom had followed his logic course in the same studium at the beginning of the 1490s.

We have seen that during Silvestro's term as master of studies and lecturer in logic the regent master in Bologna was Angelo Faella. The bachelor of the *Sentences* was Giovanni Cagnazzo da Taggia. Cagnazzo later became regent master during 1494–99 and Silvestro's immediate predecessor in the office. Cagnazzo authored a famous *Summa de casibus* (1515), known as *Summa Tabiensis,* which almost rivaled in popularity Silvestro's *Summa silvestrina.* At the same time as he was appointed regent master, Cagnazzo was also appointed inquisitor in Bologna and held the post for almost twenty years, till 1513. He died in 1521.[32]

Silvestro continued his academic ascent during the two subsequent academic years, 1491–92 and 1492–93. The general chapter of Le Mans, held in May 1491, had appointed him for this period as biblical bachelor in Bologna.[33] This office involved cursory lecturing on the Bible: a fairly general exposition of the text which sought to communicate to students a basic, comprehensive acquaintance with it. Such lecturing avoided the subtler or more problematic theological issues which were the proper concern of the bachelor of the *Sentences* and, especially, the regent master.

Reformer in the Kingdom of Naples

At the end of the biennium as biblical bachelor, and after a total of six uninterrupted years of academic work, Silvestro left Bologna once again in the middle of 1493. He was now thirty-seven years old and perhaps keen for a spell of apostolic work, especially preaching. At first he returned to his convent in Savona and remained there until the middle of 1494. There is a bizarre reference to this period, more precisely to Lent 1494, in *De strigimagarum daemonumque mirandis* (1521).[34] Silvestro relates an incident which took place while he was traveling at this time in the vicinity of Genoa. A member of the party to which he had attached himself asked him to bless his mule, which had supposedly wounded itself and was bleeding from its hoofs. Silvestro blessed the animal in the name of the Holy Trinity, whereupon it was immediately healed. Later during the journey, another member of the party inquired whether someone had indeed blessed the mule. When this person discovered that Silvestro had done so, he expressed his disappointment and acknowledged his impotence once one of God's servants had entered the fray. Silvestro subsequently took this person to be really the devil himself and to have been the real cause of the mule's misfortunes.

Silvestro informs us, in the *Vita de Sancta Maria Magdalena* (1500), that he spent the period from the middle of 1494 till the middle of 1495 in the Kingdom of Naples.[35] Although Silvestro does not also tell us what he was doing there, there can be little doubt about the matter. As early as 1489 there had been pressures on the Congregation of Lombardy, probably emanating from the King of Naples, Ferdinando I d'Aragona, to take over and reform a number of convents of the Province of the Kingdom of Naples. But the chapter of the Congregation held in Pavia in 1489 decided not to do so. This refusal was repeated by the chapter held in Como in 1490. Nonetheless, Federico d'Aragona, the son of the Neapolitan king, used his influence in Rome with the result that Pope Alexander VI, in a bull of 21 January 1493, commanded the Congregation to take over eleven convents. These were three convents in Naples, San Domenico Maggiore, S. Pietro Martire, and Spirito Santo, and those of Capua, Gaeta, Arienzo, Sessa, Salerno, Fondi, Aversa, and Piedimonte. To these, a little later, Alexander VI added a twelfth convent, that of Aquila. The vicar general of the Congregation, Vincenzo Bandello, wrote to Alexander VI imploring him to suspend the effects of the bull until such time as he could come to Rome and explain his reasons against the request. Alexander VI accepted this but, after receiving Bandello, judged his reasons to be insufficient. At this point the Congregation had no choice and gradually took over the twelve convents, commencing with San Domenico Maggiore in Naples on 26 October 1493. All were placed under the supervision of Andrea Pezzotelli da Brescia as substitute vicar general.

Once settled in these houses, the friars of the Congregation of Lombardy found them impossible to reform, as they had feared to begin with, since their conventual inmates simply did not want to be reformed by them. Accordingly, they gradually abandoned these convents and returned to the convents of the Congregation in northern Italy. Nonetheless, on 16 February 1496, Alexander VI insisted on the matter. The new vicar general of the Congregation who had been elected in 1495, Sebastiano Maggi, went to Rome and managed to convince Alexander VI of the hopelessness of the situation. The Congregation was then allowed to retreat from the Neapolitan convents so that by October 1496 it still held only the convent of Arienzo, and even from that its friars were anxious to leave. At this point King Federico d'Aragona of Naples turned directly to the vicar general and pleaded that the Congregation remain at least in Arienzo. He must also have approached Alexander VI at the same time, for the pope issued a brief on 6 April 1496 ordering the friars of the Congregation to remain in Arienzo under threat of excommunication. They accordingly did so and would in fact remain there until 1601, when the convent of Arienzo was aggregated to the reformed Congregation of Abruzzo.

There is no need to enter into the matter any further. It has been adequately dealt with by A. D'Amato, who has published all extant archival sources.[36] What is of interest is that it accounts for Silvestro's presence in the Kingdom of Naples during 1494–95. In the middle of 1494 he must have been conscripted as a member of the party of friars of the Congregation who, against their wishes and expecting the worst, were despatched, at the pope's behest, to attempt the ill-conceived task of reforming the Neapolitan conventuals. This is confirmed by Silvestro's incidental remark, in the *Vita,* that, during his sojourn in the Kingdom of Naples, he had learned of a particular devotion to St. Mary Magdalen that was customary in precisely the twelve convents with which he had become acquainted.[37]

It is less certain where and how Silvestro was actually employed during this period. But he is more precise about the location in a brief remark in the *Errata et argumenta* (1520), where he informs us that as a young man he had worked for a while in the city of Naples itself.[38] If we combine this information with our knowledge of Silvestro's previous academic career, it is plausible that Silvestro was assigned to the convent of San Domenico Maggiore and engaged in some academic work in its studium generale. This is corroborated by the fact that the attempted reform of San Domenico Maggiore had involved the restructuring of its studium on the pattern of that of Bologna.[39] Silvestro would have been an obvious choice for such a task.

Bachelor of the Sentences

After the Neapolitan interlude, Silvestro spent two academic years, 1495–96 and 1496–97, exercising the office of bachelor of the *Sentences.* During this biennium, he lectured formally on Peter Lombard's *IV Sententiarum* in order to qualify as a bachelor of theology or *baccalaureus formatus,* and did this with the eventual promotion as master of theology in mind: *pro gradu et forma magisterii.* Thus he must have done so under a regent master and within a recognized studium generale of such standing as to enable him to proceed eventually to the higher degree in Bologna without any difficulty.

That Silvestro undoubtedly did this at this particular time is indicated by his *Compendium Capreoli* published in April 1497. The *Compendium* is a lengthy digest of John Capreolus's *In IV Sententiarum* (or *Defensiones Theologiae Divi Thomae Aquinatis*), which had appeared in print in 1483–84. A digest of Capreolus's work, which follows the order of Aquinas's *Commentary on the Sentences,* is precisely the kind of task that would have been engaged in by a Dominican and a Thomist while lecturing on the *Sentences.* Significantly, both the title[40] and the colophon[41] of the *Compendium* style Silvestro "Baccalaureus Theologiae." This designation does not appear in Silvestro's single preceding publication, the *Compendium dialectice* published in June 1496. This clearly shows that Silvestro must have ended the required biennium as a bachelor of the *Sentences* at the end of the academic year 1496–97 and had not done so, as could be thought, while he was stationed, perhaps, in the studium generale of San Domenico Maggiore in Naples during 1494–95.

Where precisely Silvestro formally read the *Sentences* and qualified as a *baccalaureus theologiae* is a problem that I have not been able to solve. In Silvestro's case, a specimen of the standard formula "Frater . . . assignatur baccalaureus ordinarius in conventu . . . ad legendum sententias pro gradu et forma magisterii," which we have for so many of his contemporaries, is not to be found in the registers of the then master general, Gioacchino Torriani (1487–1500).[42] Furthermore, the extant text of the *Acta* of the general chapter of Ferrara 1494, which is likely to have made provisions for the assignment of bachelors in the various studia generalia during the period in question, is defective and lacks the customary section of academic assignments.[43] One would automatically think of the studium generale in Bologna as the most likely place. But this was probably not the case since the records of the Bolognese studium show no trace of Silvestro's presence in it at this time and, moreover, clearly indicate Giorgio Cacatossici da Casale as the bachelor of the *Sentences* in Bologna during 1495–97.[44] There remains the remote possibility that Silvestro did function as bachelor of the *Sentences* in the studium in Bologna at this time as *extraordinarius* while Giorgio da Casale did so as *ordinarius.* But this is unlikely: although the practice of instituting extraordinary bachelors of the *Sentences* was customary in the conventual studia such as those in Pavia, Padua, and Ferrara, thereby enabling a greater number of friars than otherwise to proceed to the master's degree, it does not seem to have been the custom at all in the studium of Bologna. Furthermore, such an arrangement would have jarred with Silvestro's seniority over Giorgio da Casale. Silvestro mentions in the *Additiones in Capreolum,* also published in April 1497 and as an appendix to the *Compendium,* that when he was composing it he did not have access to the works of Peter Aureolus.[45] This suggests that he was not at the time in a major academic center.

Wherever it was that Silvestro served as bachelor of the *Sentences* during 1495–97, his doing so *pro gradu et forma magisterii* was approved by the general chapter held in Ferrara in 1498 under Master General Gioacchino Torriani. It is perhaps instructive that the general chapter at the same time approved the exercise of the office by Giorgio da Casale, whom we have seen doing so during this biennium in Bologna. The general chapter also gave formal permission, "licensed," both Silvestro and Giorgio to proceed to the examination for the degree of master of theology.[46]

Even though so little can be discovered about it, Silvestro's term as bachelor of the *Sentences* is especially noteworthy insofar as it saw the appearance of his first publications: the *Compendium dialectice* (1496) and the *Opus in Capreolum* (1497). The first of these was published in Venice in June 1496 by Otto da Pavia. It was dedicated to Angelo Faella da Verona, who had been regent master when Silvestro began to teach in Bologna and who would be elected vicar general of the Congregation of Lombardy a very short while after the work's publication. We have already seen that its content comprises the substance of Silvestro's logic course taught in the Bolognese studium during 1489–91.

The *Compendium* consists of two parts. The first part is divided into three books, each of which deals with one of the three kinds of being of reason (*ens rationis*) consequent upon each of the three operations of the mind. The first book is concerned with that kind of being of reason which follows the act of simple apprehension. It consists of four tracts. The first tract, of four chapters, deals with terms common to both first and second intentions. The second tract, of eight chapters, deals with terms of second intention or predicables: *universal, genus, species, specific difference, property,* and *accident.* The third, of four chapters, deals with some terms of first intention or predicaments: *substance, quantity, relation,* and *quality.* The fourth, of twelve chapters, deals with the theories of supposition, ampliation, restriction, and appellation. The second book is concerned with that kind of being of reason which follows the act of judgment. It consists of three tracts. The first, of nine chapters, deals with categorial propositions. The second, of seven chapters, as well as the third, of ten chapters, deal with hypothetical propositions. The third book is concerned with that kind of being of reason which follows the act of reasoning. It consists of three tracts. The first, of nine chapters, deals with the theory of consequences. The second, of six chapters, considers the syllogism. The third, of nineteen chapters, considers primarily insolubles and obligations. The probably facetious remark with which Silvestro concludes his treatment of insolubles is worth recording: "An vero his modis vere solvantur insolubilia Deus gloriosus novit." The second part deals with a series of difficulties that emerge from the exposition presented in the first part.

Silvestro's *Compendium dialectice* has not as yet received from scholars the attention that it deserves. Besides some recent, occasional references,[47] there is only an entirely unsatisfactory page by Carl Prantl.[48] Yet it is one of the earliest logic text books that we have and its peculiarities make it worthy of further study. It might be particularly instructive to compare it closely with contemporaneous logic texts that hailed from the same context, the studium generale in Bologna or some other studium of the Lombard Congregation: Savonarola's *Compendium logice* (1488, first published 1492), Paolo da Soncino's *Super artem veterem* (1486, first published 1499), Crisostomo Iavelli's *Compendium logicae isagogicum* (ca. 1508, first published 1540).

The *Opus in Capreolum* was published in Cremona in 1497 by Carlo dei Darlieri. It consists of two distinct parts known as the *Compendium Capreoli* and the *Additiones in Capreolum*. The first part is prefaced by a dedicatory letter "ad magnificum ac generosum equitem aureum Johannem Portensem seniorem, nobilem Vincentinum" and a letter to the reader; but neither of these are by Silvestro himself.

Silvestro was extremely dissatisfied with this edition and on several occasions expressed his disappointment. Some two years after its publication he apologized to his readers for it and disclaimed significant portions of it in the preface to the *Apologia in dialecticam suam* (1499).[49] He also expressed the hope that the printer might still put things right. More than twenty years later, in the inventory of his works at the end of the *Conflatum* (1519), he still complained about it and claimed that it had been spoiled by another Dominican and shortened by the printer, who had also refused to print a third part consisting of *notabilia*.[50]

The *Compendium Capreoli* is a long digest of John Capreolus's *In IV Sententiarum*. It was not Silvestro's first summary of Capreolus's great work, for he had previously composed a shorter one, but only for his personal use.[51] Later Silvestro would continue to attempt to improve the work, but this did not result in any new edition.[52] As a mere summary of Capreolus's *Defensiones,* the *Compendium* lays no claim to theological originality.

Far more interesting is the *Additiones,* in which Silvestro complements Capreolus's treatments of particularly controversial issues with the opinions of other authors. Silvestro's avowed intention is to make clearer the opinions and conclusions of Aquinas on these matters by means of comparisons, and only secondarily of reporting those of others. The work is of particular interest as a guide to what must have been the most debated issues within the scholastic tradition, and especially the Thomistic School, at the close of the fifteenth century. The additions range over the entire field of scholastic philosophy and theology and number over two hundred.

The *Additiones* displays Silvestro's remarkable mastery of an extremely wide range of scholastic literature. During the course of what is, comparatively, a short work, he refers to the opinions of more than forty authors. These include the great and well-known names of scholasticism: Anselm, Richard of St. Victor, Alexander of Hales, Robert Grosseteste, St. Bonaventure, Henry of Ghent, Godfrey of Fontaines, Scotus, Giles of Rome, Peter Aureolus, William of Ockham, Gregory of Rimini. They also include lesser figures. The Dominicans mentioned include John Quidort of Paris, Thomas Anglicus, John Regina of Naples, Hervaeus Natalis, Pierre de la Palu, Durandus of Saint Pourçain, Robert Holkot, Anthony Carlenis (Archbishop of Amalfi), Peter of Bergamo, and Dominic of Flanders. The Franciscans include Francis Mayronnes, Francis of Marchia, Walter Chatton, Adam Wodeham, Peter Filargio of Candia (Pope Alexander V), and Anthony Andres. The Augustinians include Alphonsus Varga of Toledo, Bernard Oliveri, Gerard of Siena, Michael of Massa, and Thomas of Strasbourg. Finally, several rather obscure authors are also invoked: Alexander of St. Alipio, James of Apanis, Simon Terriate, and a certain Foresta.

The *Additiones* seems to have had a wide circulation and to have earned Silvestro a considerable reputation as a speculative theologian, especially in Germany. Andreas Bodenstein von Karlstadt cited it five times in his *Distinctiones Thomistarum* (1508).[53] Konrad Wimpina referred to it on several occasions in the *Epithoma . . . circa Sententiarum librum interpretando* (1508).[54] Johannes Eck, whose personal library contained both the *Compendium* and the *Additiones*,[55] cited the latter several times in the *Chrysopassus* (1514)[56] and again in his *Defensio* (1518) against Karlstadt, where he enumerated Silvestro in a list of "boni et sancti theologi."[57]

The *Opus in Capreolum* is cited by Silvestro, along with the *Rosa aurea* (1503), *Commentaria in sphera ac theoricas planetarum* (1514), and *Summa silvestrina* (1515), in his *Replica* (1518) against Luther so as to justify his claim that he enjoyed a greater reputation as an author than Luther even in Germany.[58] In the same place he adds the information that the *Opus* was employed as a text book at the University of Leipzig, which had a chair devoted to the doctrines of Capreolus.[59]

During the summer of 1497, Silvestro left wherever it was that he had served as a bachelor of the *Sentences* and journeyed to the south of France. As far as we know, this was the only time in his life that he traveled outside Italy. He went to the Dominican convent of Saint Maximin, almost two-thirds of the way along the road from Cannes to Marseille, to make a pilgrimage to the nearby shrine of St. Mary Magdalen, the Sainte Baume, which was a dependency of that convent. He tells us that he did so in order to fulfill a vow, but of this we know neither the cause nor the occasion.[60] The experience had a remarkable impact upon him and we know of it from two accounts. The first is in Latin and appears in the *Rosa aurea,*[61] which was first published in 1503 but had been completed several years earlier. The second is the derivative and expanded account, in the vernacular, in the *Vita de la seraphina e ferventissima amatrice de Jesu Christo Salvatore sancta Maria Magadalena,* which was, however, published earlier, in 1500.[62]

Silvestro's pilgrimage had nothing unusual about it. The Congregation of Lombardy, and indeed the entire Dominican Order at the time, had great devotion to St. Mary Magdalen, whom it considered one of its principal saintly patrons. This was so much the case that even as observant a congregation as that of Lombardy would approve an ordination at its chapter held in Bologna in 1510 that allowed individual friars to keep money personally not only, as was customary, for the odd book and the occasional call at a public bath, but also in the case that a friar "vult ire ad Magdalenam."[63] As the frequenting of *meretrices* is likely to have been frowned upon in such an observant congregation, the sense of this ordination cannot be called into question.

Devotion to St. Mary Magdalen, and the connected pilgrimage to the Sainte Baume, the almost inaccessible cave where she was supposed to have spent her final years, was by no means limited to the friars of the Dominican Order at the beginning of the sixteenth century. Indeed, it was at the time a phenomenon of great, perhaps exaggerated, importance. It was also especially popular with the nobility and the rich; Isabella d'Este, Marchioness of Mantua, for example, would make the pilgrimage in 1517.[64] One wonders whether Silvestro's *Vita,* obviously written with such an audience in mind and published at the very beginning of the century, was a cause, or a result, of the devotion's remarkable diffusion among the princely families of northern Italy.

One has the impression that Silvestro was not only edified by the pilgrimage but that he also thoroughly enjoyed it. He resolved to do it again if he ever had the chance to do so.[65] He certainly attempted to convince his readers to undertake it and concluded his account in the *Vita* with a few practical travel tips: he indicated both the sea and the mountain routes that could be taken to arrive at the Sainte Baume and, perhaps on the basis of his own experiences, praised the quality of the taverns that a traveler was likely to encounter.[66] But the most important result of Silvestro's pilgrimage was his assembly of materials on the legend of St. Mary Magdalen that he employed to compile his work. In the *Vita* he mentions the question that he first posed to the keeper of some of this material, the sacristan at the Sainte Baume: what was the *fundamento* of the legend?[67] Nothing if not consistent, Silvestro would make an analogous request for *fundamenta* more than twenty years later at the beginning of his first work against Luther, the *Dialogus* (1518).

Silvestro's *Vita* reproduces two very old but quite distinct traditions of the legend of St. Mary Magdalen.[68] The first, originating in Marseille and Provence, deals with the arrival of St. Mary Magdalen and her companions in Marseille after leaving the Holy Land and focuses on their subsequent conversion of the surrounding region to Christianity. The definitive redaction of this tradition, at least in Dominican literature, was in the *Legenda Aurea* of James of Voragine (d.1298). Silvestro was evidently well acquainted with this source and was also familiar with the versions of this tradition transmitted by Vincent of Beauvais, Pietro Calò, and St. Antoninus of Florence.

The second tradition is specifically Dominican in its preoccupations. Dealing with the presence of the Friars Preachers in Saint Maximin and at the Sainte Baume, it is fundamentally an attempt to justify the possession of these two sanctuaries by the Dominicans as opposed to their original custodians, the Benedictine monks of the Abbey of St. Victor in Marseille. The attempted rationalization of the situation appeals not only to the dispositions in this regard decreed by Charles II of Anjou in 1295, but also to an order supposedly imparted by Magdalen herself within the course of an apparition to that king. It is especially the content of this second tradition with which Silvestro was provided by the sacristan of the Sainte Baume in response to his request for the *fundamento*. It is very likely that the sacristan allowed him to consult a manuscript which is still extant and is currently preserved in the Bibliothèque Nationale in Paris. It contains the *Liber miraculorum beatae Mariae Magdalenae* of Jean Gobi (d.1328) along with several additional accounts.[69]

Silvestro's particular achievement is that his *Vita* was the first work on St. Mary Magdalen in which these two distinct traditions were brought together and synthesized. It is remarkable, however, that he introduces his work, whose contents must be described as literally fabulous, with critical remarks about the naiveté of previous authors as well as his intention to write only what was certain.[70] It is somewhat reassuring that, many years later, in the inventory of his works that accompanies the *Conflatum* (1519), Silvestro confessed that, although he had employed only the most reliable sources, he had always been rather skeptical about some of the material that he had gathered.[71] But by then, of course, the critico-historical examination of the legend of St. Mary Magdalen had already begun with the publication of Jaques Lefèvre d'Étaples's *De Maria Magdalena et triduo Christi disceptatio* (Paris and Hagenau, 1518).[72] There is no evidence, however, that Silvestro was familiar with this tract.

The *Vita* seems to have been very popular. Its first edition, dedicated to Adriana da Thiene and published in Bologna by Giovanantonio de' Benedetti in 1500, was immediately followed by another edition by Caligola de' Bazalieri which appeared in Bologna in 1501 and was probably pirated. A further edition was advertised on the title page of Silvestro's *Opere vulgare* (Bologna, 1501) but did not, in fact, appear in the book; it did appear, though, in the second edition of the *Opere vulgare* published in Milan in 1519. A final, posthumous edition in modernized Italian appeared in Florence in 1592.

The Latin account in the *Rosa aurea* concludes with some Latin verses in praise of St. Mary Magdalen attributed, by Silvestro, to Petrarch. The *Vita,* on the other hand, concludes with an Italian *canzone* in praise of the saint composed by Silvestro himself. It is one of the few examples that we have of his skill at versifying and it was reprinted separately by Giovanni Maria Crescimbeni in 1711.[73] Furthermore, Silvestro's *Vita* might have provided the material basis for Matteo Bandello's verses dedicated to St. Mary Magdalen.[74]

Regent Master in Bologna

After the pilgrimage to the Sainte Baume, Silvestro returned to Bologna and this time it was at the age of forty-two and as the climax of the academic career that he had commenced in 1471 and had been expressly in the making since 1487. The general chapter held in Ferrara in June 1498 assigned Silvestro as regent master of the Bolognese studium generale, in succession to Giovanni Cagnazzo da Taggia, for the two academic years 1499–1500 and 1500–01.[75] But he would hold the office for a triennium, since the general chapter held in Rome in 1501 reappointed him to the post for the academic year 1501–02 as well.[76]

These two appointments of Silvestro as Bolognese regent master were, however, mere formalities. In virtue of a privilege granted by Pius II to the

Congregation of Lombardy on 1 November 1464, the masters general and the general chapters were obliged to appoint as regent masters in Bologna whomsoever was presented by the vicar general of the Congregation.[77] Responsibility for Silvestro's first appointment is to be ascribed, then, to Vicar General Angelo Faella da Verona, whom we have seen to have been regent master in Bologna when Silvestro was appointed master of studies there in mid 1489 and to whom Silvestro had dedicated the *Compendium dialectice* in 1496. Responsibility for Silvestro's continuing in the office during 1501–02 pertains to Vicar General Giacomo da Pavia.

Rather unusually, Silvestro's appointment as regent master in June 1498, although not his taking possession of the office in mid 1499, actually preceded his graduation as a master of theology. Silvestro graduated in the Faculty of Theology of the University of Bologna on 18 September 1498.[78] It is not known who were his examiners or even who was his promoter at the *examen rigorosum* that, since this was customary, was probably held in the "old sacristy" of the Cathedral of San Petronio. But it is very likely that his predecessor as regent master, Giovanni Cagnazzo, played a prominent role in the proceedings, and perhaps it was he who, at the conclusion of the ceremony, presented Silvestro with the doctoral ring and placed the magisterial biretta on his tonsured head. Nor is anything known, not even a scrap of the menu, of the festive banquet that would have been held immediately afterwards in the refectory of the convent of San Domenico. A few days after the merrymaking, Silvestro was also aggregated as a member of the theological faculty's *collegium doctorum*.

The Faculty of Theology of the University of Bologna had been founded by Pope Innocent VI on 30 June 1362, long after the opening of that university's other faculties almost two centuries earlier.[79] But even then, unlike the other faculties, the faculty of theology was not constituted as a teaching institution comprising a number of chairs, but solely as an examining body. This was the case, as well, with the theological faculties of other Italian universities such as Padua, Pavia, Ferrara, Florence, and Parma. Very little theological instruction was in fact given within the various Italian universities from the fourteenth to the sixteenth century. In the few cases where this did take place, it was through chairs or lectorships of theology or Sacred Scripture within the faculties of arts as in Padua, Pavia, and Ferrara.

The Faculty of Theology of the University of Bologna was an association of masters of theology presided over by the bishop of Bologna, who was the chancellor of the university and, *eo ipso*, of each of its faculties. In official academic activities the bishop of Bologna was normally substituted by his vicar general, who held the office of university vice-chancellor. This association, or *collegium doctorum*, was empowered by papal authority to examine candidates for the degree of master of theology and to confer it upon those who were successful.

The association often included some eminent ecclesiastics, especially the generals of the mendicant orders, as honorary members. Its ordinary members were mostly drawn from the professors, in the first place the regent masters, of the studia generalia of the religious orders and other theological colleges in Bologna. At the end of the fifteenth century there were about twenty such schools and it was in these that the actual teaching of theology was carried out. It was also in these that usually the candidates for the master's degree had previously matriculated, studied as *studentes formales,* served as masters of studies, biblical bachelors, and as bachelors of the *Sentences, pro gradu et forma magisterii.*

These schools, loosely integrated within the theological faculty, were not all of equal importance. The most significant were the studia generalia of the mendicants: Dominicans, Franciscans, Augustinians, Carmelites, and Servites. Of these, the most influential was the Dominican studium generale in the convent of San Domenico. The seals and registers of the theological faculty were kept in the sacristy of its conventual church, and its public lectures attracted numerous external students. It was famous for its rigorous academic standards and, since the time of Pietro da Bergamo, had been the center of a renewed, living Thomistic tradition.

Furthermore, the convent of San Domenico enjoyed great prestige in its own right, for it probably had been founded at St. Dominic's own instigation around 1218 and its church contained his monumental tomb. It was also one of the principal foyers of the movement of reform. Indeed, when it accepted the reform in 1426, it was the first convent endowed with a studium generale to do so. It was also the site of the Bolognese tribunal of the Inquisition; it housed the chancery of the vicar general of the Congregation of Lombardy and possessed an exceptional library.[80]

The fact that in September 1498 Silvestro did not merely graduate as master of theology but was also aggregated as a member of the theological faculty's *collegium doctorum* needs to be appreciated. It meant that, undoubtedly because of the appointment as regent master in San Domenico, he became one of the small proportion of masters who were fully incorporated into the faculty: he acquired the right to present and examine candidates for the master's degree, to fully participate in all the faculty's activities, and to serve in its offices of dean and vice-dean.

Silvestro was extremely successful as regent master during 1499–1502. Leandro Alberti, who was one of his students at this time, stresses Silvestro's great learning. He also praises his pedagogical skills, which, he tells us, gained Silvestro a great following and something only rarely accorded to a professor: the undivided attention of his students.[81] Another of Silvestro's students at this time, the German Dominican Judocus Pistoris, would write, a few years later in 1510, an annotation in the copy of the 1508 edition of Silvestro's *Rosa aurea* that he had just bought for the library of his convent in Warburg. Judocus reveals his obvious pride at having been one of Silvestro's students and stresses that Silvestro had been a rigorous and demanding teacher, had asked him to assist him with the composition of the work, and moreover, had shown him many personal kindnesses.[82]

Silvestro's academic activities as a member of the theological faculty's *collegium doctorum* included serving twice as the faculty's dean, during the first quarter of 1500 and that of 1502, and once as its vice-dean, during the second quarter of 1501.[83] He is recorded as presiding as dean of the faculty, or as assisting as a member of the *collegium,* at at least twelve magisterial graduations.[84] On 9 March 1502, while serving his second term as dean, Silvestro summoned the members of the faculty and presented to them vernacular renditions of the *Pater Noster,* the *Credo,* and the *Ave Maria.* He argued that many pious persons had asked him that the faculty examine and approve these translations in the interest of those who were too ignorant to use the Latin versions. At Silvestro's request, the faculty unanimously approved the proposal.[85]

As regent master in its studium generale, Silvestro was ex officio a member of the house council of the convent of San Domenico. His regular participation in its deliberations is witnessed by his signature which accompanies, along with those of the other councillors, the minutes of its sessions recorded in the convent's still extant *Liber consiliorum.*[86] These signatures, taken with those which date from his subsequent priorship of San Domenico during 1510–12, seem to be Silvestro's only autographs that we still have. They display a nervous, untidy hand.

During his term as regent master, Silvestro was particularly active as an exorcist. In the *De strigimagarum daemonumque mirandis* (1521) Silvestro recalls how, at this time, he freed from demonic possession a Bolognese noble woman who had been possessed for a decade or so as the result of a spell cast on her by an apparently well-known witch whom he calls Cimera. He also tells us that this witch had been previously burnt by his predecessor as regent master, Giovanni Cagnazzo, who was the inquisitor in Bologna at this time.[87] The witch's name was, in fact, Gentile Cimitri, and her trial and execution, which took place in 1498, are well documented.[88] It is probable that, as regent master, Silvestro was often called upon to participate in the juridical processes that preceded such executions. In the light of his experiences as an exorcist, Silvestro composed and published, in Bologna by Caligula de' Bazalieri, a manual for exorcists, the *Tractatulus de diabolo*

(1502), which would eventually be reprinted by Girolamo Menghi in Bologna in 1573.

But Silvestro's first publication during his regency was the *Apologia in dialecticam suam*.[89] Published in Bologna in 1499 by Ugo Ruggeri, it was dedicated to the regent master's students in the Bolognese studium generale—a matter that has been already discussed. The *Apologia* was Silvestro's response to the criticisms that had been made of the *Compendium dialectice* (1496). We do not know who Silvestro's critics were, but their objections are mentioned in the tract's preface. The first is that Silvestro treated suppositions before propositions, and his reply is that he did so because supposition is a property of simple terms although it is only exercised within propositions. Another is the obscurity of the text because of its brevity. Silvestro retorts that its seeming obscurity is due to its originality, which made it unpalatable to those interested only in the repetition of the sophistries of the Terminists or the "same old stuff" of the Realists. Silvestro claims that his critics were not sufficiently familiar with the works of Aquinas, Capreolus, Hervaeus Natalis, and other Thomists. He replies to the accusation that he had plagiarized his treatment of insolubles and obligations from Albert of Saxony by pointing out that it is not customary to name one's sources. Finally, he concedes that his treatment of intentionality had been too brief and promises to devote the *Apologia* to a thorough discussion of this issue, which, he asserts, had not been explicitly dealt with even by Aquinas.

The *Apologia* has four parts. The first presents eighteen distinctions and sixteen definitions, which taken together correspond to a primer of Thomistic philosophical logic. The second assembles citations from Aquinas on the issue of first and second intentions and shows how they can be the subject of diverse interpretations. The third is a lengthy summary of Hervaeus Natalis's *Liber de intentionibus*.[90] The fourth part outlines the differences between Capreolus and Hervaeus on intentions and attempts to reconcile them. Silvestro, however, ultimately opts for the position of Hervaeus. Finally, he concludes with a brief reference to the differences between the Terminists and the Thomists.

In the *Apologia* Silvestro proposed an interpretation of the distinction between the act of understanding and the formal concept—an interpretation which was subsequently generally criticized by his contemporary Thomists. Silvestro argued that these two elements, postulated by the Thomistic account of knowledge, are not really distinct but only according to different modes of signification.[91] Silvestro's stand would be attacked by Cajetan, Francesco Silvestri, and Crisostomo Iavelli.[92] The works of the last two appeared too late for Silvestro to be able to respond to them, but he forcefully replied to Cajetan's critique in the *Conflatum* (1519).[93]

The great bulk of Silvestro's literary production during 1499–1502 took the form of numerous hagiographical and spiritual tracts composed in the vernacular and all published in Bologna by Giovanantonio de' Benedetti. The most significant of these was the *Vita de Sancta Maria Magdalena* (1500) that we have already considered. Other works published during 1500 were: *Esortazione al coniugo spirituale, Il modo di contemplare Dio, Trialogo chiamato Filamore, Refugio de sconsolati,* and *Devota meditatione.* During 1501 he published: *Scala del sancto amore, Sommario per confessarsi,* and *Vita e conversione sancta del beato Iacobo.*[94] In 1501 he also published the *Opere vulgare,* which is a collection of most of these tracts previously published separately.

Several of these tracts were subsequently republished during Silvestro's life and often they were republished elsewhere than Bologna. The *Opere vulgare,* for example, was republished in Milan in 1519, and there is a late edition of the *Sommario per confessarsi* which was published in Rimini and, although it is not dated, refers to Silvestro as Master of the Sacred Palace. A few of these works also enjoyed posthumous editions: the *Trialogo chiamato Filamore,* for example, was republished in Florence in 1572 by Serafino Razzi.

These works are, all in all, neither striking nor particularly original: the *Scala del sancto amore,* for example, is clearly derivative of Henry Suso's *Horologium sapientiae.* They do seem, however, to have enjoyed a remarkable popularity and to have met a demand for material of this kind in the vernacular. It is noteworthy that the specimen of the Milanese edition of the *Opere vulgare* (1519) preserved in the Biblioteca Vallicelliana in Rome was the personal copy of St. Philip Neri.[95]

For Silvestro these tracts might have represented, most of all, exercises in public relations and propaganda on behalf of the Congregation of Lombardy, for they are invariably dedicated to notables and most often noble women: Bartolomeo Ghislardo, Adriana da Thiene, Camilla Sforza d'Aragona, Theodorina Spinola. They are, nonetheless, of considerable interest in their own right, since they reveal the kind of spiritual themes that a sophisticated, professional theologian on the eve of the Reformation deemed suitable for "consumption" by the pious, lay audience for which they were primarily intended.

While there is little need to discuss each of these tracts separately, it will be worthwhile to consider briefly at least the *Scala del sancto amore,* which, insofar as it is by far the longest and reproposes many of the spiritual themes dealt with by the other, far shorter tracts, can be taken as representative. The *Scala* is, in fact, rather long for a work of its kind, for it occupies 190 of the 304 tightly printed, double-columned pages of the Milanese edition of the *Opere vulgare.*

The *Scala* is divided into three books. Although it is fundamentally a compilation of several minor tracts ranging from simple instructions on methods of prayer to popularized philosophical and theological disquisitions, the *Scala* possesses an overall unity insofar as it is a structured portrayal of the dynamics of the spiritual growth of the soul. The soul is represented as ascending a nine-stepped ladder of divine love. This ascent finds its point of departure in the promptings of *synderesis:* the soul's innate, intuitive capacity for the discernment of moral values. It finds its fulfilment in the soul's spiritual marriage with Divine Wisdom. Each of the three books commences with a chapter which presents a vision that encapsulates the content of the entire book and in the subsequent chapters deals, along with several digressions, with three steps of the ladder of divine love.

The first book comprises nine chapters, preceded by an introduction which dedicates the work to Theodorina Spinola and other friends and benefactors of the Congregation of Lombardy. The introduction presents as well the protagonists of the first book: Lady Synderesis; Fortunato, a seven-year-old child whose ascent of the ladder of divine love commences in the first chapter with a vision of both the ladder and Synderesis; Deodato, a disciple of Aquinas who, on Synderesis's behalf, instructs Fortunato through the remainder of the book. It also points out that the first set of three steps of the ladder deal with natural, created love, the second set with supernatural, partly created and partly uncreated love, and the third set with divine, entirely uncreated love. Deodato's teaching commences in the second chapter, where he outlines the different powers of the soul. He then distinguishes between good and disordered love (chap. 3), presents simplified, supposedly Aristotelian arguments for the immortality of the soul (chap. 4), discusses the resurrection of the dead (chap. 5), considers the limitations of human happiness in this life (chap. 6), explains the significance of the vision presented in the first chapter (chap. 7), outlines the first three steps of the ladder (chap. 8), and concludes by stressing the importance of a firm faith based on hope, humility, and constant prayer (chap. 9).

The second book comprises ten chapters. The opening chapter presents Fortunato's vision of the Church Militant and indicates the fourth step of the ladder. It is followed by an exposition of the fifth and sixth steps (chap. 2). The remaining eight chapters constitute a mariological tract that is largely derived from the *De laudibus,* which in Silvestro's time was generally attributed to Albert the Great. It deals with the Virgin Mary's life (chap. 3), her sufferings during the passion of Jesus (chap. 4), her principal joys and sorrows (chap. 5), the twelve privileges associated with her virginal state (chap. 6), the references made to her by various sybils and prophets (chap. 8), her principal virtues (chap. 9), and her spiritual advice to Fortunato (chap. 10).

The third book comprises eleven chapters and their content is largely borrowed from Suso. In the first chapter Fortunato, who has just turned thirteen, enters the Dominican Order, assumes the religious name of Amadio, and falls in love with Divine Wisdom, who appears to him. Divine Wisdom then instructs Amadio on the principal way of achieving union with God: meditation on the passion of Jesus (chaps. 2–3). The meditation is then extended so as to consider within the context of Jesus' passion the role of the Virgin Mary (chap. 4) and our own sufferings in this life (chap. 5). In the two following chapters Divine Wisdom continues to instruct Amadio on the techniques of prayer (chap. 5) and spiritual conversation (chap. 6). Divine Wisdom then discloses to Amadio her identity with God (chaps. 7–8) and outlines the seventh and eighth steps of the ladder (chaps. 9–10). The final chapter indicates the ninth step: union with God through true friendship and symbolized by spiritual marriage to Divine Wisdom.

It must be stressed that, all in all, the religiosity that the *Scala* and Silvestro's other spiritual tracts inculcate is neither as "precious" nor as "visionary" as the preceding very brief outline of the *Scala* might lead one to believe. Silvestro constantly insists that the spiritual growth of the soul is not the exclusive prerogative of cloistered members of religious orders but is possible for all properly disposed Christians. Moreover, it is achieved primarily by a very "down to earth" forbearance with the trials and tribulations of everyday life, the practice of the basic Christian virtues, and, most of all, fidelity to a routine of simple, daily prayers.

Venice and Padua

Silvestro left Bologna soon after terminating his triennium as regent master, around the middle of 1502. His precise movements during the second half of that year are, though, nearly impossible to make out because of two almost contemporaneous events: an appointment as regent master in Venice and a call to the University of Padua. Both of these would soon lead nowhere, but for a while they seem to have had him almost at the end of his tether and running around helter-skelter. On 17 May 1502, Master General Vincenzo Bandello appointed Silvestro regent master in the studium of the convent of Santi Giovanni e Paolo in Venice.[96] The nomination was accompanied by the injunction that Silvestro arrive in Venice within ten days. The appointment was envisaged as lasting until the next general chapter and, as that chapter was due to be held in Milan in May 1504 (it was actually held in May 1505), it covered the biennium 1502–04.

The appointment of Silvestro, by then a very prominent friar of the Observant Congregation of Lombardy, as regent master in the studium of the largest, richest, and most important convent of the unreformed Province of St. Dominic is surprising. It must have been intended as the first move of an attempt to reform Santi Giovanni e Paolo planned by the master general. In fact, a year later, Vincenzo Bandello brusquely incorporated Santi Giovanni e Paolo in the Congregation of Lombardy.[97] The attempt, though, must have failed, for, besides the decree of incorporation, there is no evidence that the projected reform ever took place.

The *Liber consiliorum* of the Venetian convent does not list, although it was customary to do so, the friars present at the meetings of the conventual council for the period from 8 November 1501 to 16 December 1504.[98] This is unfortunate, because the regent master in a convent was an ex officio member of its council, so that, if the friars had been listed, it would have been possible to determine just when Silvestro first filled the office. An entry in the *Liber consiliorum* dated 26 September 1502, concerning the duties and the renumeration of the regent master, gives the impression that by then the office was vacant.[99] A further entry, dated 3 October 1502, records the decision made by the council to petition the master general and the provincial for the appointment of a regent master. The reason given for the petition was that "master Silvestro had said that he wanted to go to Bologna and then on to Padua and had left it to the council to settle the matter of a regent."[100] Silvestro clearly was not present at this meeting of the council as the entry refers to a statement made by him sometime earlier. It is likely, then, that Silvestro held the office of regent master in Santi Giovanni e Paolo for a few months at the most and that he resigned it when he received the call to the University of Padua.

Leandro Alberti, who makes no mention of Silvestro's appointment in Venice, claims that Silvestro was called to Padua just after he had ended the period as regent master in Bologna.[101] This certainly makes sense because Silvestro himself tells us, in the dedication to Cardinal Niccolò Fieschi which prefaces the *Malleus contra Scotistas* (1514), that he was called to the University of Padua by the Doge Leonardo Loredan and the Venetian Senate to lecture in metaphysics.[102] And, in fact, the chair of metaphysics *in via Thomae* in the university's faculty of arts had become vacant with the death of its incumbent, Vincenzo Merlino da Venezia, in July 1502.[103] But there is no trace whatsoever of Silvestro's presence and professorial activity in Padua in the university's records or elsewhere.[104] Moreover, the university's records are explicit that the chair of metaphysics *in via Thomae* was filled almost immediately after Merlino's death, in August 1502, by Girolamo di Ippolito da Monopoli, who would hold it until 1518.[105]

Silvestro makes a further remark about the matter in the concluding paragraph of the *Malleus*. He tells us that he had first composed the work at the time when he was concerned about the prospect of going to Padua and wanted to be prepared for the doctrinal conflicts characteristic of its university.[106] Silvestro's apprehension is understandable. If he had been appointed to the chair he would have succeeded a series of brilliant teachers: the famous Francesco Securo da Nardò, who held the chair from its foundation in 1465 till his death in 1489; Valentino da Camerino, who held it during 1489–94; Cajetan, who filled it temporarily during 1494–95; Vincenzo Merlino, who held it during 1495–1502. Upon him would have fallen the onus of living up to the tradition that they had established and defending Thomism from its most sophisticated adversaries. As his *concurrens* he would have had the long-standing holder of the chair of metaphysics *in via Scoti,* the Conventual Franciscan Antonio Trombetta (1436–1515), who was the greatest Scotist of the time. Furthermore, the chair of natural philosophy was held by the famous Pietro Pomponazzi, who had as his *concurrens* Tiberio Baccilieri (1461–1511), a disciple of the Bolognese Averroist Alessandro Achillini (1463–1512).

Silvestro does not claim, in either of his references in the *Malleus,* that he was actually appointed to a position in the University of Padua. He merely says that he had responded to a call to go there and had tried to prepare himself beforehand. Silvestro must have spent a short period indeed in Padua, perhaps as little as a few weeks; it is certain that he never held the chair of metaphysics *in via Thomae* in its university. It might be that Silvestro's call to Padua envisaged from the first only a temporary and short-term appointment. This would not have been unusual. For example, G. Contarini cites an old chronicle that mentions that in June 1494 the holder of the chair of metaphysics *in via Thomae,* Valentino da Camerino, asked for a leave of absence of one month and to be temporarily replaced by another master because he had been elected provincial of the Roman Province.[107] The friar chosen as Valentino's replacement was Cajetan, who, as Valentino could not subsequently return to Padua, continued as *locum tenens* for the rest of that academic year, 1494–95. The chair was then permanently filled, at the beginning of the following academic year in late 1495, by Vincenzo Merlino. That Silvestro went to Padua on the basis of a similar temporary arrangement is rendered plausible by the fact that during the last few months of his life Vincenzo Merlino was very ill and did not teach at all but spent his time away from the university convalescing in the convent of Santi Giovanni e Paolo in Venice.[108]

But it is more likely that Silvestro's call to Padua originally envisaged him as the future incumbent of the chair of metaphysics *in via Thomae* and that nothing came of it because of subsequent opposition to his appointment. This seems to be intimated by Silvestro himself with a remark in the preface to the *Malleus*. Silvestro refers to certain *Patres* who were opposed to his appointment. He also makes a classical allusion which gives the impression that he believed that he had been denied the chair, despite the fact that he deserved it, because these "fathers" were aware that there was some hostility toward him.[109] The "fathers" in question are most likely the Venetian senators who were so styled. Those who were hostile to Silvestro's appointment were probably the conventual friars. The chairs of theology and metaphysics *in via Thomae* at the University of Padua had been always the preserve of friars from the unreformed provinces. The friars of the Province of St. Dominic in particular would surely have resented the intrusion of a friar of the Congregation of Lombardy and would have remonstrated about it with the Venetian senate.

Return to Bologna

After the disappointing, frustrating Venetian and Paduan episodes, Silvestro returned to Bologna sometime during the second half of 1502. He would remain there for some six months, until his election as prior of Santa Maria delle Grazie in Milan in the middle of 1503. This brief interlude represented the first spell in many years, and never to be repeated thereafter, when he did not hold a significant academic or administrative position. Silvestro, nonetheless, used this time well, for during it he finally published the *Rosa aurea*.

The *Rosa aurea* was published in Bologna in March 1503 by Benedetto di Ettore and is dedicated to Count Ludovico da Thiene. We have seen already that the work was begun a little after 1482 as well as the circumstances that led to its conception. We have also seen that the work was many years in the making and that Silvestro continually added to it new material: the section on St. Mary Magdalen, for example, could only have been inserted after Silvestro's return from Saint Maximin in late 1497. Nonetheless, it was completed by 1500, since Silvestro tells us that he corrected its final version during that year.[110]

It has been claimed that the Bolognese, 1503, edition of the *Rosa aurea* was its second edition since it was, supposedly, first published in Hagenau in 1500.[111] This suggestion bases itself exclusively on the mention of such an edition by Hain, who seems to have simply followed Panzer on this.[112] But this is probably erroneous, because no specimen of such an edition is to be found. Furthermore, it is unlikely that the first edition of one of Silvestro's works, at a time when he was not yet internationally known, would have been published outside Italy. It seems most likely that Panzer misread a specimen of the Hagenau edition of 1508. One of Silvestro's most popular works, the *Rosa aurea* had at least nineteen editions during the sixteenth century.

After the preface, which was discussed in a previous context, the work comprises four tracts. The first deals with the rules which govern the interpretation of Sacred Scripture. It presents a detailed discussion of the various senses of Scripture: literal, allegorical, moral, and anagogical. Silvestro stresses the primacy of the literal-historical sense.

The second tract, which is by far the longest, is devoted to the exposition of the Gospels of each Sunday of the year and those of weekdays, as well as Sundays, of Advent, Lent, the octave of Christmas, and that of Easter. This exposition is geared to the needs of preachers. Each of the Gospel passages is expounded according to each of its four senses. Silvestro's presentation avoids the speculative questions of scholastic theology. While references to Aquinas and Peter Lombard are not uncommon, Silvestro constantly appeals to the Fathers of the Church: Ambrose, Augustine, Basil, Chrysostom, Cyril, Gregory the Great, Gregory Nazianzen, Hilary, Jerome, John Damascene, Leo, Origen, Remigius, and Theodore are repeatedly cited. Their great antagonists, Apollinaris, Arius, Eutiches, Marcion, Nestorius, Pelagius, Sabellius, Tatian, Valentinus, the Ebionites, and the Manichees are all identified and their heresies rebutted. The works of Bede, Eusebius, and Josephus as well as those of some early medieval authors such as Rhabanus Maurus and Alcuin are also frequently cited. But, of late medieval authors, it is the *Magister Historiarum*, Petrus Comestor, and the Franciscan biblical commentator Nicholas of Lyra who are invoked most often. In the determination of the literal sense Silvestro is often guided by the Hebrew and Greek texts of the Scriptures and on occasion he refers explicitly to the Greek text of the New Testament established by Cardinal Bessarion.

The third tract comprises two parts. The first part offers sixty-eight *quaestiones pertinentes* corresponding to the Gospels of each Sunday and some major feast days. They deal with speculative theological issues which represent, however, *materia praedicabilis*. In these questions, while appeals to the authority of the Fathers are not absent, it is often the different doctrinal stances of Aquinas and Scotus that are at stake and the authorities most invoked are usually Thomists such as Capreolus and Hervaeus Natalis. Questions 30–34 are of particular interest: Silvestro presents a lengthy discussion of the famous theological dispute over the Precious Blood which bitterly opposed Dominicans and Franciscans during the fifteenth century. A valuable part of this account is the integral reproduction of the determination of the issue presented to Pius II by three eminent masters of the Bolognese studium: Giacomo da Brescia, Gabriele da Barcellona, and Vercellino da Vercelli.

The second part of the third tract comprises sixty-five *quaestiones impertinentes,* which are in effect difficult cases of conscience. The authorities introduced in this part are largely canonists and compilors of *summae de casibus:* "Archidiaconus" (Guido da Baisio, Archdeacon of Bologna), "Archiepiscopus" (Antonino Pierozzi, Archbishop of Florence), "Hostiensis" (Card. Enrico Bartolomei da Susa, Bishop of Ostia), "Panormitanus" (Nicola Tedeschi, Archbishop of Palermo), Pierre de la Palu, Raymond of Peñafort, and many others.

The majority of the cases deal with various economic practices of the time and the extent to which they might be tainted with usury. Some of the issues, though, seem a little out of place. *Casus IV,* for example, addresses the issue whether women who wear braids made out of other people's hair sin mortally and Silvestro concludes that this is not necessarily so. *Casus X* is of particular interest, for it deals with indulgences and Silvestro enunciates in it what he believes to be the fundamental principle at stake, thereby anticipating by many years the essential point of his later *Dialogus* (1518) against Luther's Ninety-five Theses: "In doctrina ecclesiae nulla falsitas continetur, et ipsa debet esse regula fidei nostrae."[113] *Casus LXIII* reproduces a letter of Pietro da Bergamo in which Pietro recounts being present at a disputation held in the Bolognese studium attended by many renowned masters: Gabriele da Barcellona, Vercellino da Vercelli, Angelo da Nirdono, Antonio da San Germano, Domenico da Catalonia, and Giovanni da Calopia.

The fourth tract contains sermons for special feasts. It is supplemented by a *tabula* coordinating the contents of the *Rosa aurea,* which follows the liturgical calendar of the rite peculiar to the Dominican Order, with the calendar of the Roman Rite. Despite its many interesting elements, the *Rosa aurea* has so far been the object of only very limited scholarly attention.[114]

III PRIOR AND VICAR GENERAL, 1503–1515

Prior in Milan, Verona, and Genoa

 During 1503–08 Silvestro held the post of prior, or superior, in three convents of the Congregation of Lombardy. The legislation of the Congregation prescribed that a friar could exercise the office of prior for only a biennium and could not be his own immediate successor in it in the same house. Leandro Alberti tells us that Silvestro served as prior in Milan, Verona, and Genoa.[1] Silvestro's first election as prior in 1503, at the age of forty-seven, represented the beginning of an administrative career in the Congregation which lasted for a dozen years, until late 1515.

The Milanese convent of which Silvestro was elected the eighteenth prior sometime during the first half of 1503[2] was Santa Maria delle Grazie, which had belonged to the Congregation of Lombardy since it was founded as a reformed house in 1459.[3] Silvestro must have been elected to the office after 22 June when the previous prior, Onofrio da Parma, was absolved from office and confirmed by Master General Vincenzo Bandello as vicar general of the Congregation.[4] At the end of the biennium 1503–05 Silvestro was elected prior of the convent of Sant'Anastasia in Verona and at the end of the biennium 1505–07 he was elected prior of the convent of Santa Maria di Castello in Genoa. Silvestro completed only half of his prioral term in Genoa because on 19 May 1508 he was elected vicar general of the Congregation of Lombardy.

The only account of Silvestro's activities as Milanese prior concerns solely some material improvements of the convent that he brought about. Santa Maria delle Grazie's magnificent church had been built previously thanks to the munificence of Lodovico Maria Sforza. Silvestro desired to leave some mark of his own on the Milanese convent, but he probably realized that he had little hope of competing with his immediate predecessors, who only a few years earlier had commissioned Da Vinci to decorate the refectory with the Last Supper and Bramante to build the church's cupola as well as one of the convent's five cloisters. Nonetheless, he managed to convince his "singolarissimo padrone," Bishop Etienne Ponchier of Paris, who was then passing through Milan, to pay for a new water font where the brethren could wash their hands before entering the refectory. From the same benefactor he also obtained sufficient additional funds to complete the sacristy cupboards for which purpose Master General Bandello had previously remitted an initial donation. Unlike Da Vinci's disintegrating fresco, Silvestro's font and cupboards are still in fine shape. Finally, Silvestro had some of the convent's waste area cleared and turned into a lawn where the friars could frolic during their recreations.[5]

Nothing is known of Silvestro's activities as prior of Sant'Anastasia in Verona. This convent had been founded before 1260 and the friars commenced the construction of its large gothic church by the end of the thirteenth century. Pope Nicholas V had conceded it to the observant Dominicans in 1449 at the request of the Venetian Doge some ten years before the formal establishment of the Congregation of Lombardy by Pius II.[6]

During his priorship of Sant'Anastasia, Silvestro attended the general chapter held in the unreformed convent of Sant'Eustorgio in Milan in May 1505 as the definitor of the Province of Scotland.[7] An entry in Ambrogio Taegio's *Chronicae Ampliores* explains this curious situation. Master General Bandello, a former member and twice vicar general of the Congregation of Lombardy, had seized the opportunity provided by the high incidence of absenteeism at the general chapter and "stacked" it by filling the vacancies with friars largely drawn from the Congregation.[8] Perhaps Bandello wished to ensure that the general chapter would be as supportive as possible of his plans for the further spread of the reform.

The very lengthy *Acta* issued by this general chapter are prefaced by a letter in which Bandello laments the dissolute state of the order that he had personally witnessed during his preceding visitation of almost all the order's provinces.[9] They also contain numerous ordinations, declarations, and commissions which, taken together, constitute a thorough plan for the order's reform.[10] Furthermore, they praise effusively the Congregation of Lombardy and expressly proclaim Bandello's intention to extend the reform to other convents.[11] It seems that Sant'Eustorgio itself was to be one of the first targets of the master general's reforming zeal.[12] Nonetheless, nothing came of all this, probably because of Bandello's early death in August 1506. It might well be, though, that Silvestro remembered Bandello's unfulfilled hopes when, as we shall see, some five years later and after his election as vicar general of the Congregation, he would himself attempt to reform Sant'Eustorgio.

An informative reference to Silvestro, while he was prior in Verona, was made by Alberto da Castello in the second edition of the *Chronica brevissima* (1506).[13] Alberto stresses Silvestro's intense literary as well as administrative labors. It is also of interest insofar as it reveals that several of his works were already circulating in manuscript form long before they were printed several years later. The "summa de casibus" mentioned by Alberto is surely to be identified with the *Summa silvestrina* (1515) and the "impugnationes Scoti" with the *Malleus contra Scotistas* (1514). Probably connected with these works is Silvestro's application at this time for a privilege from the Venetian college of printers in support of which he submitted a *testamur* by another Dominican who had been appointed by the master general to examine his works.[14]

We are informed a little better about Silvestro's activities as prior in Genoa. The oldest Dominican convent in Genoa, San Domenico, which no longer exists, was founded in 1222 and in Silvestro's time belonged to the unreformed Province of St. Peter Martyr.[15] The convent of which Silvestro was elected prior in 1507 was Santa Maria di Castello. Originally founded as a house of secular canons, it had been granted to the observant Dominicans by Eugene IV in 1443.[16]

In 1507 Silvestro delivered a series of Lenten sermons in Santa Maria di Castello which was eventually published as *Quadragesimale aureum* (1515).[17] The work is dedicated to the Genoese and it praises their city highly.[18] Of the fifty-four sermons that make up the work, sermon 17 is perhaps of greatest interest, for it deals with the situation in Genoa itself.[19] Silvestro traces the history of Christianity in that city and points to the many occasions when the Republic had manifested its loyalty and devotion to the Holy See by appropriate military and political actions. But he employs these very positive evaluations of Genoa as contrasts with its contemporary situation. Silvestro then focuses on the sins of the Genoese and his catalog of their failings is a valuable social-historical document. He condemns as all too common the tolerance shown to Jews, blasphemy, feuds and the thirst for revenge, the injustices that follow from the corruption of judges and magistrates, sodomy, incest, fornication, abortion, and infanticide. He parades these as the sins of the majority rather than a minority of Genoa's citizens. Silvestro concludes the sermon by warning the Genoese about what the future has in store for them if they do not mend their ways. He predicts that if such horrendous crimes are not punished by the Genoese themselves, God Himself will intervene and undoubtedly do so very soon. It is intriguing that while Silvestro has no qualms about predicting the most dire consequences, he stresses that he is no prophet and has no desire to be taken for one.[20] It is quite likely that he was keen not to be mistaken for another Savonarola.

A specifically prioral activity that Silvestro engaged in at this time was the reception of novices into the order. During his priorship in Genoa, he received at least ten novices in Santa Maria di Castello, between March 1507 and May 1508.[21] And by this time Silvestro's considerable reputation as a wise and efficient administrator resulted in his being entrusted by higher authorities with the adjudication of disputes. Two instances of this pertain to this period. On 18 December 1507 he was appointed by the order's vicar general, Tommaso De Vio, to settle a litigation between the convents of Taggia and Albenga.[22] The details of the case as well as the satisfactory resolution of the conflict are reported in Niccolò Calvi's *Chronica conventus Tabiensis*.[23] A little later, on 24 February 1508, Silvestro pronounced a definitive judgment on a dispute between a lay person, Oberto D'Auria, and the prior of the Carthusian monastery of S. Bartolomeo di Ripariolo. He had previously been appointed the judge in this affair by Julius II in a brief dated 9 February 1508.[24] The documentation, which is still preserved in the archive of Santa Maria di Castello, has been published in its entirety by A. Vigna.[25]

At the beginning of the document recording the judgment pronounced by Silvestro on the second case he styles himself "Magister Silvester de Prierio, sacre theologie doctor, iuris canonici peritus, prior monasterii, per priorem soliti gubernari, Sancte Marie de Castello." The qualification "juris canonici peritus" was the equivalent, in the terminology of the early sixteenth century, to that of "jurisconsultus." Both expressions were classicizing ways of designating the academic degree of doctor of laws. But there is no evidence that Silvestro ever undertook formal study in a faculty of law or acquired such a qualification. Perhaps this self-description indicates that Silvestro had by then earned some kind of recognition of his special competence in matters canonical. By this time Silvestro had already completed the *Summa silvestrina,* which had been many years in the making and which already enjoyed a certain diffusion in manuscript form. Silvestro's remarkable mastery of canonical literature and issues displayed by this work might well have been already generally appreciated and, perhaps, in some way publicly acknowledged.

Vicar General

On 19 May 1508 Silvestro's term as prior of Santa Maria di Castello was interrupted by his election as the vicar general of the Congregation of Lombardy at its chapter held in Mantua.[26] Leandro Alberti does not fail to mention this important appointment.[27] Silvestro succeeded Andrea Porcellaga da Brescia (d.1508) and was confirmed in office by the newly elected master general, Tommaso De Vio, on 10 June 1508.[28]

Meanwhile Cajetan had made a strikingly rapid career after leaving Padua in mid 1495. He lectured in several minor, northern Italian convents until he was appointed to the chair of theology *in via Thomae* in the University of Pavia in 1497. He held this post, though, for only one academic year (1497–98). He subsequently lectured in the convents of Sant'Apollinare in Pavia (1498–99) and Santa Maria delle Grazie in Milan until he was called to Rome in 1501 and appointed procurator general by Master General Vincenzo Bandello. On 20 August 1507, after the death of Master General Jean Cleree, Pope Julius II named him vicar general of the order. In 1508 he was elected master general—largely at the insistence of Cardinal Oliviero Carafa, the order's cardinal protector, who presided at the elective general chapter held in Rome during June of that year. On account of his creation as cardinal by Pope Leo X on 6 July 1517, Cajetan would later resign the office of master general in early 1518.

Silvestro served as vicar general during the biennium 1508–10. His successor would be Eustachio Piazzesi da Bologna, who was elected on 20 April 1510. But Silvestro remained in effective control of the Congregation until Cajetan confirmed Piazzesi's election on 1 May 1510,[29] since it was the custom of the Congregation of Lombardy for the retiring vicar general to remain in charge until his successor's election was confirmed by the master general. The office of vicar general of the Congregation of Lombardy was an extremely powerful administrative position in the order and was subject only to that of master general and to the general chapters. At the time of Silvestro's election the Congregation seems to have comprised some forty major houses having the juridical status of convents or priories and several smaller, dependent houses or vicariates. It seems likely that during his term of office Silvestro exercised authority over a membership of well over a thousand friars.

Most important of all, the vicar general of the Congregation of Lombardy, unlike the provincials of the unreformed, conventual provinces, had become, by the end of the fifteenth century, virtually independent of even the master general in very many matters. On several issues he could by-pass the master general's authority altogether and had direct access to the Holy See since he was represented by a procurator of his own in the Roman curia. This exceptional situation was the result of the fact that the Roman Pontiffs had granted many privileges and graces to the Congregation since its foundation in 1459 so as to ensure the survival and foster the further expansion of the reform. The popes had so favored the Congregation because they were concerned about the frequent election of masters general drawn from the ranks of the conventuals, who were not likely to be entirely sympathetic to the reform in general and to the Congregation in particular. Furthermore, masters general who had been drawn from the ranks of the observants and favored the reform had also granted many graces and privileges to the Congregation of Lombardy over the years. These were meant to protect it from the interference of the provincials of the unreformed provinces within whose territories the Congregation had its houses and, as well, whose houses were the targets of the reform movement.

The history of the Congregation involved, consequently, a series of struggles between it and successive masters general who resented and resisted the papal curtailment of their authority. It also involved frequent conflicts with the provincials of the unreformed provinces who objected to the encroachments of the Congregation into their territories. By the time of Silvestro's election as vicar general in 1508 these graces and privileges were so well established as to be virtually unassailable. Indeed, just a short time before his election, the authorities of the Congregation published a collection of its privileges and graces in the form of a small manual. This work, known as the *Liber Privilegiorum,* appeared in Milan in February 1507 and Amedeo Vigna suggested that it was compiled by Sebastiano Maggi.[30]

Nevertheless, shortly after Silvestro's election, Master General Cajetan did manage to have one of the Congregation's most important privileges revoked. It had been granted to the Congregation by Alexander VI on 23 January 1494 and it prescribed that no friar could leave the Congregation of Lombardy and enter an unreformed province without the permission of the vicar general.[31] Cajetan felt that this was contrary to his prerogatives as master general and appealed to Pope Julius II, who issued a bull on 3 August 1508 stating that the master general could accept under his jurisdiction any friar whomsoever he wished.[32] In other words, a master general thereafter would not need the prior consent of a vicar general before transferring elsewhere a friar of the Congregation. There seems to be no trace of Silvestro's reaction to this diminution of his authority, but it would surely have been a source of friction between him and Cajetan.

Silvestro himself, in his capacity as vicar general, managed to obtain two privileges *oraculo vivae vocis* from Julius II on 3 February 1509 through the mediation of Cardinal Bernardino Carvajal.[33] One of these is of little interest, for it concedes no more than the permission to anticipate by one hour the time of the friars' main meal during times of fasting. The other is of greater significance since it concerns the procedure to be followed in the introduction of the reform into common-life houses and witnesses to Silvestro's preoccupation with the matter. But, besides the notorious affair of Sant'Eustorgio in Milan, which will be considered below, we do not know of any attempt to extend the reform during Silvestro's vicarship.

Silvestro did not leave Genoa immediately after his election as vicar general but seems to have continued in residence there for a few months. Thus, on 17 September 1508 he received three further novices into the order at Santa Maria di Castello.[34] Silvestro did not have a fixed residence during his term as vicar general, even though the chancery of the office was in San Domenico in Bologna, but, rather, was constantly on the move between the various houses of the Congregation. The prefaces to both the *Libellus de sublevatione morentium*,[35] published in early 1509, and the *De expositione misse*,[36] published later during that year, indicate his residence as then being in Santa Maria delle Grazie in Milan.

These two works are Silvestro's only publications during his term as vicar general. The *Libellus de sublevatione morentium* was published by Angelo Brittanico in Brescia and is dedicated to Bartolomeo Ghislardo, an official of the Commune of Bologna. It is a book of comfort for the dying. The *Tractatus de expositione misse, seu de immolatione spiritalis agni et sacrificio novae legis* was published by Gotardo da Ponte in Milan and is dedicated to Cardinal Louis d'Amboise, Bishop of Albi. The work is divided into two books, the first of which comprises twenty-eight chapters. The first twenty-six of these are devoted to an exposition of the Roman Order of the Mass while the last two deal with the differences between the Roman and the Ambrosian rites. The second book comprises four chapters which consider practical questions concerning the matter, the minister, the use, and the effects of the sacrament of the Eucharist.

Silvestro's continuous travel as vicar general is illustrated well by three letters sent by him to the Marchioness of Mantua, Isabella d'Este-Gonzaga, during a period of a little more than two weeks at the end of June and the beginning of July 1508. Sometime earlier, Isabella had contacted Silvestro and asked for permission to visit the Dominican monastery of San Vincenzo in Mantua and to hold private conversations with some of the nuns. Silvestro replied, granting the request and forwarding the appropriate letters patent, on 26 June from Reggio Emilia.[37] Silvestro wrote again to Isabella on 1 July, remarking about the previous letter "non so se quella lhabbia receputa," this time writing from Parma.[38] The letter of 26 June must have gone astray, for Isabella wrote again to Silvestro and repeated the request. Silvestro replied on 11 July, expressing "admiratione considerando la negligentia del portatore de le nostre lettere le quale fureno scripte a xxvii del passato" and forwarding a new set of letters patent, from Brescia.[39]

Unfortunately, almost nothing can be discovered about Silvestro's day-to-day administration of the Congregation. The register that would have been kept by his secretary, Gregorio da Vogonia, recording the patent letters by means of which he promulgated his official acts, such as assignments of the friars subject to him, is lost. Furthermore, there is no record of the ordinations that he is likely to have made at the chapter of Mantua in 1508 at which he was elected. Similarly, nothing is known of his performance at the following chapter held in Reggio Emilia in 1509. The *Acta* of both of these chapters are not extant. It might be mentioned at this point that it was the custom of the Congregation of Lombardy to hold a chapter or legislative assembly every year. Of the seventy-two chapters held during the juridical existence of the Congregation (1459–1531) we still have the *Acta* of only approximately a third. But even these records are incomplete, for they do not contain the entirety of the original *Acta* but only the ordinations: none of them contain, for example, the customary initial list of the participants at the chapters or the concluding list of the assignments of friars to different houses and works.

Silvestro himself is likely to have attended the chapters held during 1500–03 as a master of theology, those of 1504–08 as conventual prior, those of 1509 and 1510 as vicar general, and those of 1511–15 once again as prior. Before becoming a master of theology in late 1499, and thereby acquiring the right to participate in the Congregation's assemblies, he might well have attended some previous chapter as the *socius* of the conventual prior of the house to which he was assigned. But of all this, almost nothing is known because of the lack of extant documentation. Silvestro's final act as vicar general was to preside at the chapter held in Bologna in April 1510 which elected Eustachio Piazzesi as his successor.[40] At this chapter he made eleven ordinations which were subsequently confirmed by Piazzesi before the end of the chapter and of which a record still survives.[41] These are of certain interest, for they are typical of the ordinations of other chapters as well and show the usual, disciplinary preoccupations of the vicars general.

The first two ordinations concern purely formal questions: the ordinations of previous chapters are to be considered still in force unless expressly repealed and the instructions issued by a vicar general at a chapter bind both priors and their subjects under pain of a penance. The third concerns sins and faults that may be absolved only by conventual priors: those which incur excommunication, open insubordination, theft and the witholding of money, libidinous acts with oneself or another. The fourth proscribes undue contacts between friars and nuns. The fifth returns to the problem of friars who withhold or fail to render due account of monies. The sixth deals with friars who brawl and physically harm one another. The seventh concerns friars who are fugitives from the Congregation. The eighth condemns blaspheming. The ninth prohibits the eating of meat. The tenth prescribes that no friar may exercise the office of confessor in any particular monastery of nuns for longer than a biennium. The eleventh orders that the ordinations be read publicly in every convent of the Congregation at least twice every year.

As vicar general, Silvestro was also entrusted by Master General Cajetan with the most diverse tasks. On 28 January and 4 February 1509, Cajetan commissioned him to deal with matters concerning Dominican monasteries in Pisa[42] and Milan.[43] Probably in continuity with these injunctions we find Silvestro aggregating to the order the tertiaries of the Monastery of San Lazzaro in Milan soon after.[44] Far more significantly, only a week after having confirmed Silvestro's election as vicar general, Cajetan appointed him inquisitor in Brescia, Crema, and other localities in their vicinities. Furthermore, on 14 March 1510, only a few weeks before the end of Silvestro's term as vicar general, Cajetan entrusted him with the task of reforming the convent of Sant'Eustorgio in Milan. But both of these are matters that deserve separate treatment.

Inquisitor in Brescia and Crema

Master General Cajetan appointed Silvestro inquisitor in Brescia, Crema, and their surrounding districts on 17 June 1508.[45] Silvestro would hold the position until he was replaced in it by Giorgio Cacatossici da Casale on 5 August 1511 and promoted to the more important inquisition of Milan, Lodi, and Piacenza. Silvestro's appointment to an inquisitorial post is not unusual; if anything, it is surprising that he had not been nominated to such an office much earlier.

Since approximately the end of the thirteenth century the Dominicans exercised an almost complete monopoly of inquisitorial tasks in northern Italy. The only significant exceptions were the inquisitions in the republic of Florence and in some localities of that of Venice, such as Padua, which were entrusted to the Franciscans. The Inquisition, by Silvestro's time, was organized in districts which corresponded to the territories of one or more dioceses, and each of these was endowed with a tribunal presided by a chief inquisitor. Although appointments to inquisitorial posts were normally made by the Dominican master general, the inquisitors exercised powers delegated to them by the Holy See and were generally independent of their local Dominican superiors such as the priors of the houses in which they resided.[46]

By the end of the fifteenth century, with the spread of the Dominican reform and the concomitant expansion of the Congregation of Lombardy, most inquisitorial districts in northern Italy had come under the control of that congregation. The only major inquisitions still entrusted to the conventual provinces of St. Peter Martyr and St. Dominic were those of Milan, Parma, and Ferrara. The Congregation of Lombardy attempted to seize control of the inquisition of Milan in 1511 but was only temporarily successful since, as we shall see, the reform of the convent of Sant'Eustorgio which housed the Milanese tribunal failed. But it managed to take over the inquisitions of Parma and Ferrara with the annexation and reform of those two cities' convents in 1507 and 1518.[47]

A result of the Congregation's heavy commitment to inquisitorial tasks was that the studium generale in San Domenico in Bologna became, de facto if not by design, Italy's principal nursery of would-be inquisitors. During Silvestro's time the regent masters of the Bolognese studium were invariably appointed inquisitors at the end of their regencies. On occasion, they were even appointed inquisitors immediately after their graduation as masters of theology and continued to serve as such while acting as regents. Such cases were very common and it will suffice to mention two examples. Giovanni Cagnazzo da Taggia, Silvestro's predecessor as regent master in Bologna, was appointed inquisitor in Bologna at the same time as he was appointed regent master in 1494 and filled the office till 1513. Giorgio Cacatossici da Casale, Silvestro's successor as regent master in Bologna, was appointed inquisitor in Piacenza and Cremona in 1502 at the very beginning of his regency in Bologna and held the post until he succeeded Silvestro in Brescia and Crema in 1511.[48] Furthermore, it was not merely a matter of supplying masters of theology for the official posts of inquisitors. The Congregation of Lombardy had also to provide the inquisitors with vicars and other assistants who, at least in the principal inquisitions, were quite numerous. For example, the inquisitor in Como had at least ten vicars at the beginning of the sixteenth century.[49]

I have not been able to discover any trace of Silvestro's activities during his triennium as inquisitor in Brescia and Crema. The entry on Silvestro in the chronological catalog of inquisitors compiled by Domenico Francesco Muzio in the eighteenth century and which based itself on then extant inquisitorial archives does not yield, in his regard, any information that is not admittedly derived from printed sources such as Fontana and Quétif and Échard.[50] To a certain extent this lack of information is not surprising, for the bulk of the day-to-day work associated with the post would have been done by vicars or assistants since Silvestro held it concurrently with that of vicar general of the Congregation of Lombardy and, from the middle of 1510, with those of prior and regent master in Bologna.

The principal occupation of inquisitors in northern Italy during the century or so before the Reformation was not the prosecution of heretics— at least in the conventional sense. Of the various heretical sects that had proliferated in northern Italy during the previous centuries—Cathars, Patarines, Dulcinians, and Fraticelli of various hues—only the Waldensians had not been completely extirpated by then. These, isolated in their remote valleys in the Duchy of Savoy, were generally left alone after their exchange of external conformity for freedom of conscience in the treaty of Pinerolo, which concluded the crusade launched against them by the Duke of Savoy in 1484. They would only become again a direct concern of the Inquisition in 1532, after their formal adhesion to the Protestant Reformation at their Synod of Chanforan.

Rather, the inquisitors focused their attention on the members of what they held to be a new heretical movement. This was the "sect of the witches" whose adherents were held to be apostates from Christianity insofar as they were supposed to have renounced their baptismal vows and to have made a pact with the devil, whom they worshiped. They were also supposed to participate in the orgiastic sabbath (*ludus, giuoco della donna*), to which they gathered by nocturnal flight, and to indulge in various practices harmful to humans, especially children, as well as animals and harvests (*maleficia*).[51]

The phenomenon of sorcery had been of only minimal concern to the medieval church. There had been some sporadic persecutions and a very limited number of papal declarations encouraging such hostility, of which Gregory XI's bull *Vox in Rama* (1233), Alexander IV's bull *Quod super nonnullos* (1258), and John XXII's bull *Super illius specula* (1320) are the most noteworthy. But, all in all, sorcery was considered to be a symptom of superstition rather than heresy, and inquisitors had, accordingly, taken little interest in it: Bernard Gui's famous *Practica inquisitionis* (ca. 1323), for example, makes only a passing mention of it.[52]

Any tendency toward the identification of sorcery with heresy had been contained by the prestige of the famous *Canon Episcopi* (ca. 900). Traditionally, but falsely, ascribed to the Council of Ancyra (ca. 380), this decree had characterized as mere illusions (albeit possibly of diabolical origin) the prodigious effects supposedly wrought by the sorcerers and, indeed, had qualified as heretics whosoever believed in their reality. It had been followed in this by such authoritative texts as Gratian's *Decretum* and Peter Lombard's *Sentences* and, subsequently, by Thomas Aquinas.[53]

But the situation gradually changed during the last quarter of the fourteenth and the first half of the fifteenth centuries as the result of two fundamental innovations. First, the *Canon Episcopi* was reinterpreted in such a manner as to subvert its principal thesis. Second, certain practices which were formerly dismissed as superstitious began to be condemned as manifestations of heresy. An influential example of the beginnings of the first innovation is provided by the *Directorium inquisitorum* (ca. 1378) of Nicholas Eymerich, the Grand Inquisitor of the Kingdom of Aragon,[54] and an important case of the intentional accumulation of supposed examples meant to lend credence to the reality of the sorcerers' fabrications is provided by Johann Nider's *Formicarius* (ca. 1437).[55] The second innovation was first publicized by the Dominican inquisitor in Carcassone, Jean Vinety, in the *Tractatus contra daemonum invocatores* (ca. 1450).[56]

It was the subsequent, general acceptance of the combination of these two innovations, and the consequently inevitable appropriation by the inquisitors of sorcery-heresy as one of their due concerns, that resulted in the identification of witchcraft properly speaking, that is, as a diabolically inspired heretical movement with the specific characteristics mentioned above. The extent to which the identification of witchcraft in this special sense was the product of the imposition of categories invented by the inquisitors themselves upon the previous, comparatively innocuous medieval sorcery, is still a controversial, open question. Whatever the case, it also unleashed the great witch-hunt of the following three centuries or so. Indeed, inquisitors at the beginning of the sixteenth century, such as Silvestro, believed that, precisely as a heretical movement or sect, the phenomenon of witchcraft had begun only a little before the promulgation of Innocent VIII's bull *Summis desiderantes affectibus* on 5 December 1484. This conviction became itself, in turn, an argument against the relevance of the *Canon Episcopi:* the sorcerers that it spoke of, the invokers of Diana and Herodiades, were not the same as the witches of the new sect, the serfs of Satan.

The northern Italian Dominican inquisitors' preoccupation with witchcraft was not entirely of their own devising. That it was at least partially is evident from such works as the *Lamiarum sive striarum opusculum* and the *Opusculum de striis* (both ca. 1460, although first published 1490) by Girolamo Visconti (d. ca. 1478), who served for many years as provincial of the Province of St. Peter Martyr.[57] But it was largely transmitted to them by their German Dominican confreres, such as Nider, and was confirmed especially by the publication in 1486 of Heinrich Kramer's and Jakob Sprenger's *Malleus maleficarum.*[58]

In view of Silvestro's subsequent authorship of a manual against witchcraft, the *De strigimagarum daemonumque mirandis* (1521), which will be considered later, the question arises whether as inquisitor in Brescia and Crema he personally participated in the prosecution of witches. Of this, I have not been able to find any evidence. In all his works, there is only one reference which indicates, perhaps, that Silvestro was present at an execution at this time,[59] and it must be remembered that he was not loath to report his personal experiences in his writings. The possibility, however, cannot be excluded. It is known that in 1510 some sixty presumed witches and wizards were burnt by the inquisitors in the Val Camonica, which fell within the territory of Silvestro's inquisition of Brescia.[60]

The conception of witchcraft that would have guided him by this time is clear, for it is delineated in the entry "Haeresis III" in the *Summa silvestrina* (1515, but completed by 1506). Silvestro's discussion focuses on the problem of the interpretation of the *Canon Episcopi* and stresses that the adherents to the new sect of the witches cannot be identified with the sorcerers mentioned by it. He then emphasizes the reality of the witches' pact with the devil and their performance of *maleficia*. He is particularly concerned to explain the possibility of their participation at the sabbath as well as their nocturnal flight to it, although he concede that at times this is merely imagined by them during sleep. He concludes that the inquisitors have the right to prosecute witches, not because of their real or imaginary participation at the sabbath, since this could be motivated solely by lasciviousness, but because they are manifestly proponents of heresies.

Silvestro complements his analysis with an anecdote which is worth dwelling on, for it shows that there was resistance to the prosecution of witches even among the friars and reveals the extreme passions that the issue must have aroused.[61] He recalls an incident that had taken place at the chapter of the Congregation of Lombardy held in Piacenza in 1503 and he is probably writing as a witness since he was entitled to attend the chapter as a master of theology. He tells us that a "major superior of a certain order of mendicant friars" bitterly attacked the local inquisitor during the chapter over his prosecution of witches and pompously invoked the *Canon Episcopi* while doing so. He adds that it was said at the time that this major superior did so because he had been unduly influenced by the parents of a young woman whom the inquisitor had recently burnt as a witch. The inquisitor in question, who is not named by Silvestro, was probably Giorgio Cacatossici da Casale, who had been appointed to the inquisition of Piacenza in 1502 and very quickly acquired a reputation as an extremely zealous prosecutor of witches. The major superior is again not named by Silvestro, but the expression employed by Silvestro to refer to him makes it likely that he was a Franciscan. Silvestro concludes his account with a further remark which, for him, encapsulated the moral of the story: before the end of 1503 the major superior was set upon and viciously strangled by a large group of his own confreres.

There is another work by Silvestro that reveals his ideas on witchcraft at this time. Unlike the entry in the *Summa silvestrina,* it has not been previously noticed by scholars. It consists of a sermon, entitled "De strigibus," preached during the course of Lenten sermons delivered in Genoa in 1507 and later published as the *Quadragesimale aureum* (1515), which has been already mentioned.[62] Although the substance of this sermon is identical with that of the entry in the *Summa silvestrina,* of which it is a summary, its different literary genre and destination lend it a certain interest, for it reveals just what Silvestro was prepared to say about the matter from the pulpit.

Reformer of Sant'Eustorgio

The affair of Sant'Eustorgio began shortly before the end of Silvestro's term as vicar general of the Congregation of Lombardy and lasted for a little over two years. Accordingly, it continued to occupy him as he subsequently served as prior and regent master in Bologna during 1510–12. Nonetheless, it is convenient to deal with it in its entirety at this point. It consisted of an attempted reform by the Congregation of Lombardy of the convent of Sant'Eustorgio in Milan, which formed part of the unreformed Province of St. Peter Martyr. The convent of Sant'Eustorgio had belonged to the Dominican Order since 10 August 1220 and its basilica enjoyed great prestige since it contained the monumental tomb of St. Peter of Verona ("St. Peter Martyr"). The basilica also benefited from exalted patronage insofar as it was the burial church of important Milanese families commencing with the Visconti.[63] The convent was, furthermore, the seat of the Milanese tribunal of the Inquisition and for almost three centuries had housed an important studium.[64] It also possessed an exceptional library, as is shown by its inventory, compiled in 1494, which lists 797 volumes.[65]

A brief account of the Congregation of Lombardy's attempt to annex and reform Sant'Eustorgio has already been presented by Mortier.[66] But Mortier gives us only a curiously truncated version of the affair, omitting its background, the details of the sequence of events that constituted it, and, significantly, the attempted reform's conclusion in failure. Any attempt to reconstruct faithfully the affair is complicated by the often contradictory accounts presented by the relevant sources. These are, in the first place, the often cryptic references to it in the first register of Master General Cajetan.[67] Second, there is the account in the late-sixteenth-century chronicle of Santa Maria delle Grazie by Girolamo Gattico, written from the point of view of the friars of the Congregation of Lombardy.[68] Third, there is the account in the late-sixteenth-century chronicle of Sant'Eustorgio by Gasparre Bugatti, written from the point of view of the conventuals.[69] Finally, there are the transcriptions made by Giuseppe Allegranza in the eighteenth century of several unedited bulls of Julius II and Cardinal Mattias Shinner which had been overlooked by the editors of the fourth volume of the *Bullarium Ordinis Praedicatorum* (1732).[70]

The official beginning of the affair took place on 14 March 1510 when Cajetan exempted Sant'Eustorgio from any jurisdiction inferior to that of the master general—that is, his own—thereby, in effect, withdrawing it from the jurisdiction of the provincial of the conventual Province of St. Peter Martyr. By the same patent letter, Cajetan appointed as his personal vicar for Sant'Eustorgio the vicar general of the Congregation of Lombardy, Silvestro.[71] On the following day, 15 March 1510, Cajetan summarily incorporated Sant'Eustorgio in the Congregation of Lombardy.[72] At the same time, he entrusted the actual task of reforming Sant'Eustorgio to a commissioner in the person of the prior of San Marco in Florence, Giovanni Maria Canigiano. Cajetan, even at this early stage, had no hesitation about authorizing Canigiano, a former disciple of Savonarola, to have recourse to the secular arm if resistance to the reform was such as to warrant it.[73]

The initial problem is that of Cajetan's motives. Mortier, rather simplistically, presents the beginning of the affair as the result of Cajetan's enthusiastic zeal for reform. But Cajetan's attitude to the reform is a complicated, and indeed controversial, issue: no unqualified appeal to it is of much explanatory value. Gattico, on the other hand, is less sanguine about Cajetan's stance. He accounts for the move as being Cajetan's attempt to placate the resentment that had arisen in the Congregation of Lombardy as the result of his previous separation from it of the convent of Santa Maria della Quercia in Viterbo.[74] It was therefore, according to Gattico, the friars of the Congregation of Lombardy who really initiated the affair by asking to be allowed to annex Sant'Eustorgio as a kind of reimbursement. Cajetan's permission to them to do so was, then, not so much a matter of his enthusiasm for the spread of the reform, as a simple political expedient. Bugatti confirms that the affair began as the result of the intrigues of the friars of the Congregation of Lombardy, but attributes its original conception to Master General Vincenzo Bandello, a former member of the Congregation, who first devised it at the time of the general chapter of 1505 which had been held in Sant'Eustorgio.[75]

If both the Gattico and the Bugatti accounts of the affair are correct, with the initiative having been taken by the friars of the Congregation of Lombardy rather than Cajetan, then Silvestro, as vicar general, must have been the prime mover. There are indications that during his term as vicar general Sant'Eustorgio had become a haven for deserters from the Congregation of Lombardy and, as well, was torn by internal strife.[76] Silvestro probably felt that the time had come to do something about the situation and, seizing the occasion provided by the loss of the convent in Viterbo, pressured Cajetan about it.

Silvestro might well have been convinced of the feasibility of moving on Sant'Eustorgio because of the particular political situation in the Duchy of Milan at the time. The Duchy had been occupied by the French since 1499 and King Louis XII's viceroy in Milan during Silvestro's term as vicar general was Charles d'Amboise, the brother of the Bishop of Albi, Cardinal Louis d'Amboise. The latter had a reputation for fostering the Dominican reform in France and had taken a personal part in the attempted reform of Saint Maximin in Provence in 1505.[77] Silvestro might well have believed in the likelihood of French support in the matter of Sant'Eustorgio. That he consciously sought to win their favor is beyond doubt: it is evident from the dedication of his *De expositione misse,* published in Milan on 20 October 1509, to Cardinal d'Amboise.[78]

The reform of Sant'Eustorgio, which then housed a community of about sixty conventuals,[79] turned out to be a difficult task. Its inmates simply refused the alternatives that were proposed to them, of accepting the reform or transferring to some other unreformed convent, and stayed put. At this point, Silvestro ended his term of office as vicar general and was succeeded by Eustachio Piazzesi on 20 April 1510. But this did not mean the end of his involvement in the affair.

Piazzesi must have decided that the only way to resolve the situation was, in line with the directives first issued by Cajetan, to appeal to the secular arm. But this help was not to be obtained immediately. According to Gattico, the eventual intervention of the French was secured by the machinations of Isidoro Isolani da Milano (d.1528).[80] Isolani was a former student of Silvestro in Bologna, as is indicated in the prefatory letter by Silvestro which accompanies Isolani's *De regum principumque institutis,* published in Milan a few years earlier.[81] Almost ten years later, Isolani would achieve a certain notoriety as the "ungennanter Cremonense" who published in Cremona the anonymous *Revocatio Martini Lutheri Augustiniani ad Sanctam Sedem* (1519).[82] At the time of the outbreak of the affair of Sant'Eustorgio, Isolani was a lecturer in theology in Santa Maria delle Grazie.

Isidoro Isolani, who had enjoyed the favor of the French since the time that he delivered an *oratio* in praise of Louis XII on the occasion of that king's first entry into Milan, went to Brescia to see Charles d'Amboise and pleaded with him to intervene. D'Amboise responded by writing letters to two French cardinals then in Milan requesting them to pressure Milan's archiepiscopal vicar general to use his influence so as to convince the conventuals to accept the reform. But the vicar general, who sympathized with the conventuals, refused to act as requested. At that point Isolani wrote a letter to Louis XII which he had delivered to him by Guillaume Petit, a fellow Dominican and close friend who was the king's confessor and Inquisitor General of the Kingdom of France. Louis XII then wrote repeatedly to Goffredo Carli, the president of the Milanese senate, ordering him to assist the friars of the Congregation. Carli finally did so by providing Piazzesi with an armed force which violently expelled the still resident conventuals from Sant'Eustorgio on 10 July 1510.

There are several documented expressions of the gratitude to Carli felt by the friars of the Congregation, who, thanks to his intervention, managed to seize control of Sant'Eustorgio. One of these is the dedication to Carli which prefaces Tommaso Radini Tedeschi da Piacenza's *Sideralis Abyssus,* first published in Milan in 1511.[83] This is an especially interesting text, for it is the only evidence that we have of Radini Tedeschi's presence in Sant'Eustorgio at this time. This might well have been the occasion of Radini Tedeschi's first encounter with Silvestro. As will be seen later, Radini Tedeschi would eventually become Silvestro's vicar as Master of the Sacred Palace and his assistant in the chair of theology at the University of Rome.

The Congregation of Lombardy was in full control of Sant'Eustorgio from 10 July 1510 and we find Cajetan on 4 August reiterating his incorporation of that convent in the congregation and, undoubtedly at the Congregation's request, providing for the establishment in it of a studium generale patterned on that of Bologna.[84] The Congregation's possession of Sant'Eustorgio was ratified by Julius II, at the insistence of Cardinal Oliviero Carafa, in a bull issued on 13 August 1510.[85] Silvestro himself, although by this time he was serving as prior and regent master in San Domenico in Bologna, continued to be involved with Sant'Eustorgio: on 10 December 1510 Cajetan gave him permission to transfiliate to it from San Domenico in Savona if he wished to do so.[86]

But the Congregation's effective control of Sant'Eustorgio did not mean the end of the matter. The expelled conventuals, who enjoyed considerable support in Milan because of influential family connections, refused to accept the new state of affairs. Cajetan certainly made some provisions for their welfare, but these were conditional upon their desisting from their opposition to the reform.[87] Furthermore, he nonchalantly left the matter to the discretion of the friars of the Congregation.[88] Accordingly, Sant'Eustorgio's former residents took it upon themselves to appropriate and alienate some of the convent's possessions.[89] They also persisted in various forms of protest and even misdemeanor in Milan and tended to congregate, without permission, in the area of the Porta di Ticino near Sant'Eustorgio.[90] Some even forged the general's patent letters as a means of attempting to return to their convent.[91]

The expelled conventuals, with the support of the governor of Milan, Giovanni Trivulzio, decided to send their own representatives to France to plead their cause before Louis XII. To respond to this the friars of the Congregation sent further representatives of their own, including Isolani and Matteo Bandello. Gattico claims that at this point, toward the beginning of 1511, Louis XII, realizing the impossibility of any peaceful reconciliation of the two parties, decided that the only solution was the reestablishment of the situation that had held before the beginning of the affair.[92] But, on this point, Gattico is surely mistaken, for the friars of the Congregation remained in full control of Sant'Eustorgio throughout 1511 and well into 1512. The evidence for this is plentiful. There are, in the first place, the continuing references in Cajetan's register to the taking of disciplinary measures against the expelled conventuals who were continuing to cause havoc in Milan and to plot for their reentry into their convent.

On 13 February 1512 Silvestro himself was commissioned by Cajetan to take severe measures against such recalcitrant friars, and his authority was extended to deal not only with the expelled conventuals loitering in Milan but also to include the convent of San Tommaso in Pavia.[93] The cause of this was an attempt made by the expelled conventuals to storm and reoccupy Sant'Eustorgio with the assistance of a large group of armed student friars from the conventual studium generale in Pavia, who were led by their regent master, Vincenzo Dodo da Pavia, and his predecessor, master Gioacchino Beccaria da Pavia.[94] The attempt was foiled by the timely intervention of the French and its instigators punished.[95] A further, connected injunction to deal with the expelled conventuals was given by Cajetan to Girolamo Fantoni da Vigevano, regent master in Sant'Eustorgio, and Damiano Crasso da Rivoli, the provincial of St. Peter Martyr, as late as 29 May 1512.[96]

But the most important piece of evidence is Cajetan's continuing provisions for the studium generale in Sant'Eustorgio, modeled on that of Bologna, that he had founded on 4 August 1510. On 5 August 1511 he assigned Girolamo Fantoni as regent master, Francesco Silvestri as bachelor of the *Sentences,* and Isidoro Isolani as master of studies for the academic year 1511–12.[97] On 19 June 1512 he assigned Vincenzo Colzado da Vicenza as regent master and Francesco Silvestri for a second year as bachelor of the *Sentences* for the academic year 1512–13, as well as Crisostomo Iavelli da Casale as bachelor of the *Sentences* and Bartolomeo Spina da Pisa as master of studies for the academic year 1513–14.[98] Obviously, the friars of the Congregation of Lombardy were in full control of Sant'Eustorgio as late as mid 1512 and, moreover, they were convinced that they were there to stay.

The loss of Sant'Eustorgio by the Congregation of Lombardy happened unexpectedly, toward the end of June 1512. It was the result of a radical turn in the broader political situation. As a consequence of the successes of the forces of the Holy League during the first half of 1512, the French gradually evacuated Lombardy. After the defeat of the French at the battle of Pavia on 14 June, Julius II's Swiss mercenaries, who were commanded by Cardinal Mattias Shinner and who might have included Ulrich Zwingli as a chaplain,[99] entered Milan on 20 June. The conventuals then immediately reoccupied Sant'Eustorgio and, in their turn, violently expelled the friars of the Congregation of Lombardy.[100]

Cajetan's reaction to this turn of events was instantaneous. On 4 July he ordered the conventuals who had reoccupied Sant'Eustorgio to leave the convent and relinquish it to the Congregation within six hours of their reception of his letter and under threat of excommunication.[101] Furthermore, with the support of the new cardinal protector of the order, Niccolò Fieschi, he obtained a brief from Julius II on 6 July addressed to Cardinal Shinner. In this brief the pope instructed Shinner to expel the conventuals, if need be with the help of the secular arm, and restore Sant'Eustorgio to the Congregation of Lombardy.[102]

But Cardinal Shinner, rather than enforce the bull of Julius II without further ado, decided to have the entire case reexamined and summoned both parties to appear before him. Shinner subsequently delegated the power to conduct the inquest and adjudicate in the matter to Giovanni Angelo Arcimboldi.[103] But a new and decisive element entered at this point in the form of a petition presented to Shinner by a large number of Milanese nobles who were unequivocally in favor of the conventuals.[104]

The petition of the Milanese nobles was, in effect, a severe indictment of the behavior of the friars of the Congregation of Lombardy who had established themselves in Sant'Eustorgio. The petition accused these friars of having taken over the convent and expelled the conventuals primarily in order to acquire its income. It scolded them for setting a bad example by taking over Sant'Eustorgio when they already possessed a more than adequate and, indeed, imposing convent of their own, Santa Maria delle Grazie. It accused them of having squandered Sant'Eustorgio's income during their occupancy without fulfilling any of the obligations attached to that income, which was mainly in the form of Mass legacies. It claimed that they had practically pillaged Sant'Eustorgio and alienated some of the most precious possessions with which it had been endowed by many noble families, especially the Visconti who had their family tombs in its basilica. Finally, it praised the original occupants for having lived no less religiously than the friars of the Congregation and without the hypocrisy of the latter. The petition concluded with a plea to Cardinal Shinner that the conventuals be allowed to return to Sant'Eustorgio and be protected from any further harassment by the friars of the Congregation.

Cardinal Shinner concluded that the brief of Julius II was not to be enforced since it must have been motivated by a false representation to the pope of the entire situation. Obviously not concerned about the sensitivities of either Cardinal Fieschi or Master General Cajetan, Shinner described the brief of Julius II as having been obtained by stealth. In his own brief, dated 9 September 1512, Cardinal Shinner ordered the restoration of Sant'Eustorgio to the conventuals and its reintegration within the Province of St. Peter Martyr.[105]

A second brief of Cardinal Shinner, dated 9 October 1512, is the last extant document concerning the affair, and it does not fail to mention Silvestro.[106] This brief was issued in response to a complaint by the newly returned conventuals that the friars of the Congregation had despoiled the convent both during their occupancy and upon their final departure.[107] Shinner ordered the restitution of the goods that, according to the representations of the conventuals, had been stolen and alienated by "a certain Silvestro da Prierio" and some other friars "so called of the observance." Be that as it may, by the end of 1512 the affair of Sant'Eustorgio was definitively over.

Regent Master and Prior in Bologna

The end of Silvestro's term as vicar general of the Congregation of Lombardy was immediately followed by his return to the studium generale in Bologna to serve for a second term as its regent master. Master General Cajetan had decided Silvestro's appointment to the post on 2 January 1509, while Silvestro was still vicar general.[108] Cajetan's intervention had probably been sought by the superiors of the Congregation, for it seems that they could not decide between Silvestro's candidature and that of Giorgio da Casale, since Giorgio's appointment to the post had been proposed by the general chapter of Rome, 1508. Cajetan's resolution of the matter was accepted and Silvestro subsequently held the office during the academic year 1510–11. As regent master in Bologna, Silvestro succeeded Eustachio Piazzesi da Bologna, who replaced him as vicar general.

The records of the Bolognese studium list Silvestro as the regent master for two academic years: 1511–12 as well as 1510–11.[109] But this is erroneous. During the second year of this biennium, the office of regent master was held by Giorgio Cacatossici da Casale, as is evident from an entry in Cajetan's register, dated 5 August 1511.[110] It is also proved by an entry in the *Liber consiliorum* of the Bolognese convent dated 6 November 1511: in it Giorgio da Casale's signature is accompanied by the qualification "magister regens."[111] It is instructive that Cajetan's appointment of Giorgio da Casale as regent master took place on the same day as that of Silvestro as inquisitor in Milan, Piacenza, and Lodi. Clearly, Cajetan must have felt that Silvestro could not possibly carry out contemporaneously the three offices of regent master, inquisitor, and, as we shall see presently, also prior in San Domenico, and relieved him of that of regent master.

During this year as regent master Silvestro had serving under him as bachelor of the *Sentences* Vincenzo Colzado da Vicenza and, as master of studies, Girolamo Fornari da Pavia. The most significant of the *studentes formales* in Bologna at this time was Bartolomeo Spina da Pisa. All of these men would, a few years later, be among the principal Dominican antagonists of Pomponazzi during the famous affair that arose from the Mantuan philosopher's denial that Aristotle had taught the immortality of the soul. Their connection with Silvestro, who by that time would be serving as Master of the Sacred Palace, is not to be discounted as the motive behind their interventions against Pomponazzi. But this is a matter that will be considered in detail below. Other than Silvestro's participation at a magisterial graduation on 25 November 1510, there are no traces of his activities at this time as a member of the theological faculty of the University of Bologna.[112] But it is recorded that Cajetan commissioned him to examine some friars of the Province of St. Peter Martyr for the rank of Preacher General.[113]

Leandro Alberti tells us that after Silvestro's appointment as regent master he was also elected prior of the convent of San Domenico, in which the Bolognese studium generale was located.[114] Silvestro held the post for two years, during 1510–12, and some of his properly priorial activities are recorded in San Domenico's *Liber consiliorum*. There are five relevant entries and they are of interest insofar as they reveal the kind of pragmatic, day-to-day issues that he had to deal with as prior. The first, dated 10 July 1511, considers the opportuneness of accepting a Mass legacy offered to the convent of San Domenico by Giovanna Ludovisi-Bolognini, the daughter of the late Giovanni Ludovisi and widow of Ludovico Bolognini.[115] The second, dated 6 November, records Silvestro's decision to melt superfluous church plate, so as to avoid being forced to alienate conventual property or dismissing junior friars, in order to pay some pressing debts.[116] The third, dated 16 January 1512, records Silvestro receiving a novice into the order.[117] The fourth and fifth, both dated 12 April, return to minor matters of economic administration.[118]

In a work published a decade later, the *Errata et argumenta* (1520), Silvestro mentions that during his priorship of San Domenico he had performed some function in the presence of Pope Julius II.[119] But this claim is difficult to account for. Julius II had certainly visited San Domenico on

17 February 1507 when, to commemorate the event, a suitably inscribed, still surviving column topped with a statue of St. Dominic was erected in one of the convent's courtyards. Julius II subsequently passed through Bologna on at least two further occasions: in late September 1510 and early February 1511. These two dates certainly coincide with Silvestro's priorship, but of an additional visit by the pontiff to San Domenico there seems to be no record and, of course, such a visit is not necessarily implied by Silvestro's statement. It is a pity that we have no account of their meeting, for it is possible that by this time Silvestro had started harboring the hope of being called to some position in Rome—a wish that, as we shall see, he would first express openly in 1513.

Inquisitor in Milan, Piacenza, and Lodi

While serving as both regent master and prior in San Domenico in Bologna from the middle of 1510, Silvestro continued in the post of inquisitor in Brescia and Crema until he was replaced by Master General Cajetan with Giorgio da Casale on 5 August 1511. But, on the same day, Cajetan appointed him to the more important inquisition of Milan, Piacenza, and Lodi.[120] It is not known for precisely how long Silvestro held this post, for Cajetan's second register (1514–18), which might have recorded the appointment of his successor, is lost. Domenico Francesco Muzio does not name, in his *Tabula Chronologica*, a successor to Silvestro until 1520 with the nomination of Gioacchino Beccaria da Pavia.[121] But it is impossible that Silvestro continued in the post until then, and especially after his appointment as Master of the Sacred Palace and his move to Rome at the end of 1515. The imprimatur in a work by the Servite friar Girolamo di Amedeo da Lucca, written against Pomponazzi and published in Milan on 9 May 1518, names Martino Giustiniani da Genova as the then inquisitor in Milan and Crisostomo Iavelli da Casale in Piacenza and Cremona.[122] It is probable that Silvestro stopped being inquisitor in Milan by the end of 1512, when the convent of Sant'Eustorgio in Milan, which housed the tribunal of the Inquisition, was restored to the conventuals of the Province of St. Peter Martyr.

There seems to be no extant documentation of Silvestro's activities as inquisitor in Milan, Piacenza, and Lodi. This is unfortunate because, as with his period as inquisitor in Brescia and Crema during 1508–11, it is not possible to determine whether he played an active role in the prosecution of witches. But it is not surprising: the archives of the Milanese inquisition were completely destroyed in 1788.[123]

Vincenzo Maria Fontana (1675) asserts, however, that Silvestro's appointment was principally motivated by Cajetan's wish to have an eminent theologian in Milan since at that time the anticouncil of Pisa had just decided to transfer its sessions to that city.[124] Fontana makes the further claim that Silvestro certainly lived up to Cajetan's expectations, for he brought about the collapse of that *conciliabulum* at its first attempt to meet in Milan. Silvestro supposedly achieved this by persuading the Milanese clergy to close their churches and suspend the celebration of all sacred rites on the occasion of the solemn entry into Milan of the participants at the anticouncil which took place on the feast of St. Ambrose (4 January 1512), Milan's patron saint. The result of this was such tumultuous rioting on the part of the Milanese populace that the "council fathers" immediately took flight and, to Julius II's great delight, never reassembled thereafter.[125]

But Fontana's account is pure fiction. He seems to have composed a Milanese script that, *mutatis mutandis,* is a remarkable carbon copy of the sequence of events that had in fact taken place in Pisa a few months earlier. The *conciliabulum* did manage, after all, to hold the last five of its eight sessions in Milan, with the final assembly taking place on 21 April 1512. Fontana's account is no more to be believed than his allied, entirely unfounded claim that Julius II rewarded Silvestro, for his supposed part in the collapse of the anticouncil of Pisa-Milan, by summoning him to Rome and appointing him Master of the Sacred Palace in 1512.

It has also been claimed that Silvestro's ecclesiological tract *De papa et eius potestate,* eventually published by Rocaberti (1695),[126] was first composed at this time and directed precisely against the pretensions of the anticouncil.[127] But, as Ulrich Horst has pointed out, this tract is simply an excerpt from Silvestro's *Summa silvestrina,* which although it was first published in 1515, had been completed by 1506.[128] Perhaps, however, a separate edition of the tract was published at that time and with that motive in mind. After all, Erasmus would later refer, in a letter to Jacob Hochstraten of 1521, to works by Silvestro, as well as Cajetan, that had been unfavorably judged by the theological faculty of the University of Paris some years earlier and it is likely that he had such a separate edition of this tract in mind.[129]

Prior in Cremona

At the end of his biennium as prior in Bologna, around the middle of 1512, Silvestro was elected prior of the convent of San Domenico in Cremona for the biennium 1512–14. This convent was founded in 1283 when the bishop of Cremona, Cacciaconti Sommi, had given the Dominicans the church of Sant'Agnese and during the first half of the fourteenth century the friars built the much larger church of San Domenico. The convent was reformed and aggregated to the Congregation of Lombardy in 1484.[130] Although Leandro Alberti makes no mention of his appointment, Silvestro's priorship of the Cremonese convent is indicated by the catalog of the priors of San Domenico from 1308 to 1737 compiled by Ermenegildo Tedeschini and is also mentioned in the list of priors published by Pietro Maria Domaneschi in 1768.[131] Both of these authors had as their source the convent's then still extant *Liber consiliorum.*

Silvestro's presence in Cremona at this time is also mentioned by Silvestro himself in the two different prefaces of the *Commentaria in spheram ac theoricas planetarum* published in Milan by Gotardo da Ponte in July 1514. There are two versions of this work, and they are identical except for their prefaces. The preface of the first version is dedicated to Cardinal Christopher Bainbridge and is dated 31 June 1513;[132] it is here that Silvestro first expresses his desire to be given a Roman post.[133] The preface of the second version is dedicated to Cardinal Niccolò Fieschi and is dated 31 June 1514.[134] Silvestro must have managed to interrupt the work's printing and change the dedication of at least some of its copies a little before the death of Cardinal Bainbridge on 14 July 1514.

The *Commentaria* consists of two distinct parts of equal length. The first, the *In spheram,* was written, as we have already seen, many years earlier when Silvestro had taught astronomy in Mantua around 1482. The second part, the *In theoricas planetarum,* was written much later, certainly after 1510. It is an exposition of Georg Peuerbach's *Theoricas planetarum.* The *In theoricas planetarum* would be published separately in Paris by Michel Leslencher in 1515. It appears within an edition of Peuerbach's tract which is accompanied by reprints of an exposition by Francesco di Capua da Manfredonia and Jaques Lefèvre d'Étaples's *Astronomicon theoricum corporum coelestium,* as well as Silvestro's own commentary.

During his time in Cremona Silvestro had previously published a piece of hagiography written in the vernacular. *La sacra hystoria de sancta Agnese de Montepoliciano* was published in Bologna by Gerolamo de' Pelati in January 1514. This Italian text was not composed by Silvestro himself, for it was a translation by another Dominican, a certain Andrea da Pisa, of Silvestro's Latin original.

Other than the publication of these works, we know little of Silvestro's activities during his spell in Cremona. We do know, though, that Vicar General Giorgio da Casale entrusted to him, on 11 March 1513, the task of founding a house of Dominican tertiary sisters in Soncino.[135] Furthermore, there is a letter, dated 22 June 1513, from Silvestro to the Marquis of Mantua, Francesco II Gonzaga. It deals with the matter of a dispensation to be obtained from Master General Cajetan so as to allow a daughter of the marquis and Isabella d'Este, Ippolita Gonzaga (1501–70), who was a novice in the Dominican monastery of San Vincenzo in Mantua, to anticipate her religious profession. The letter, which expresses Silvestro's support for the dispensation, reveals his presence on that date in the convent of Santa Maria degli Angeli in Mantua.[136]

Domaneschi mentions, on the basis of a document in his time still present in the archive of San Domenico, that Silvestro assisted the convent later while serving as Master of the Sacred Palace.[137] In 1500 a certain Filippo Tinti had bequeathed a legacy to the convent of Cremona for the building of a small convent and church, which was to be staffed by eight priests, in the village of Azzanello. Julius II permitted the friars of Cremona to found this convent, Santa Maria della Consolazione, on 31 March 1506. But Tinti had attached to the bequest the condition that the convent's construction had to be completed within a specified period of time. Because of various reasons it was not possible to meet this deadline and, in 1518, the Cremonese friars appealed for support to their former prior. Silvestro subsequently approached Leo X, who at his insistence, granted the convent of Cremona an extension of time to complete the project.

Prior in Venice

Around the middle of 1514, following the end of his priorship of Cremona, Silvestro was elected prior of the convent of San Domenico di Castello in Venice. This house, which belonged to the Congregation of Lombardy, was entirely independent of the convent of Santi Giovanni e Paolo, which formed part of the unreformed Province of St. Dominic, and where Silvestro had been appointed regent master in 1502. Unlike the latter, which is still one of Venice's most prominent monuments, the convent of San Domenico di Castello no longer exists, for it was demolished at the turn of the eighteenth century. A small convent, San Domenico di Castello was founded in 1317 as a dependency of Santi Giovanni e Paolo thanks to a bequest left by the Doge Marino Giorgio in 1312. It became an independent house in 1391 when Bl. John Dominici was appointed its prior and started there the movement of reform within the Dominican Order in northern Italy, which eventually led to the establishment of the Congregation of Lombardy by Pius II in 1459.[138]

Silvestro's priorship in Venice was meant to last for the biennium 1514–16. This appointment is, once again, not mentioned by Leandro Alberti, but it is clearly indicated in the *incipit* of Silvestro's *Quadragesimale aureum* (1515), where Silvestro is described as the then prior of San Domenico di

Castello.[139] Silvestro's priorship is also confirmed by Altamura (1677)[140] and is listed as well in the catalogs of the priors of San Domenico di Castello published by Giovanni Domenico Armani (1729) and in that of Flaminio Cornelio (1749).[141] We can be certain, though, that Silvestro did not complete the entire period of his term as prior in Venice, for at the end of 1515 he was appointed Master of the Sacred Palace and moved to Rome either at that time or at the beginning of 1516.

It is curious that both Armani and Cornelio, who based their catalogs on the then still extant *Liber consiliorum* of San Domenico di Castello, claim that Silvestro's term as prior during 1514–16 was his second term in that office.[142] They assert that Silvestro had served a previous term as prior there during 1508–10. But this cannot possibly have been the case since during that biennium Silvestro served as vicar general of the Congregation of Lombardy. They both refer to the *Liber consiliorum* as simply listing Silvestro as the then prior without further ado. It is plausible, then, that Silvestro had indeed been elected prior of San Domenico di Castello at that time but did not in fact accept the office because of what must have been his simultaneous election as vicar general.

There is very little information on Silvestro's Venetian priorship. But both Armani and Cornelio mention one extremely interesting fact: Silvestro was instrumental in the acceptance by San Domenico di Castello's community of Bartolomeo Spina da Pisa as a *filius* of that convent on 1 January 1515.[143] They both also mention, but this is of little interest, Silvestro's acceptance of the religious profession of another friar, a certain Lorenzo da Bergamo, on 11 January of that year.[144]

During his priorship of San Domenico di Castello, Silvestro continued his impressive record of publications. The most significant of these was the monumental *Summa summarum, quae silvestrina dicitur.* Its actual date of publication remains uncertain, for while the bulk of the work is indicated as being printed in Bologna by Benedetto di Ettore in March 1514, its table of contents indicates as its date of publication April 1515. It is dedicated to Leo X. A work of massive proportions, comprising 680 folios, it has been described as the greatest achievement of the Bolognese printing industry during the sixteenth century.[145]

The Genoese Dominican historian Giovanni Maria Borzino (d.1696) informs us, in his *Memorie Genovesi Domenicane,* that in his time the autograph of the *Silvestrina* was still in Santa Maria di Castello in Genoa and that it indicated 1506 as the year of its completion.[146] Borzino refers to this manuscript in his *Nomenclator filiorum conventus S. Mariae de Castello* as well. There he adds the information that it was accompanied by a collection of supplementary notes, which had never been published, in which Silvestro sought to reply to the criticisms of the *Silvestrina* that had appeared in the contemporary *Summa Tabiensis* (1516) compiled by Giovanni Cagnazzo da Taggia.[147]

The *Silvestrina* is a vast encyclopedia of moral theology and canon law comprising 715 entries arranged in alphabetical order. It was written as an aid to confessors in the light of Silvestro's opinion that previous such works presented conflicting resolutions on far too many issues. Silvestro's work is, in effect, a synthesis of all its most important precedents. At its beginning, Silvestro lists all the authors that he has consulted and lists 48 theologians, 113 jurists, and 18 authors of analogous *summae de casibus*. Although the *Silvestrina* is fundamentally a compilation, it has been argued that it also displays considerable originality.[148]

Its very size, though, seems to have generally daunted contemporary scholarship. Its ecclesiological entries have received some attention on account of Silvestro's involvement in the Luther case, and its entry on witchcraft is regularly cited by scholars interested in the history of that phenomenon. Otherwise, except for some occasional references to some of its discussions of business ethics,[149] it has been completely neglected. This is in marked contrast with the great diffusion that it enjoyed during the century following its publication: the *Silvestrina* was by far Silvestro's most popular work and had at least forty editions before the end of the sixteenth century. It was much admired by Silvestro's contemporaries. Johannes Cochlaeus, for example, while a student of law in the University of Bologna, mentioned it in a letter to Willibald Pirckheimer dated 28 May 1517 and in a further letter to Pirckheimer dated 5 July 1517, indicated it as his favorite work of its kind.[150]

The *Malleus in falsas assumptiones Scoti contra divum Thomam in primo sententiarum,* usually referred to simply as the *Malleus contra Scotistas,* was published in Bologna by Benedetto di Ettore in September 1514. But as its colophon tells us, it had been completed many years earlier in 1503. It had represented Silvestro's attempt to prepare himself for the doctrinal controversies that he would have had to deal with if he had indeed been appointed, in late 1502, to the chair of metaphysics *in via Thomae* at the University of Padua. It is dedicated to Cardinal Niccolò Fieschi, the then cardinal protector of the Dominican Order.

The *Malleus* is a critical examination of Scotus's commentary on the first book of Peter Lombard's *Sentences.* In it, Silvestro seeks to refute the criticisms that Scotus had presented in his work of the doctrines of Aquinas. Silvestro claims that Scotus's criticisms are largely founded upon false assumptions. Silvestro himself describes the work as a mere collation and digest of the works of other authors.[151] Indeed, it seems to be largely derivative of Thomas Anglicus's *Liber propugnatorius* (composed ca. 1315).[152] Despite their consequent lack of originality, Silvestro would nonetheless consider his discussions of several speculative issues in the *Malleus* as definitive. In later works, especially the *Conflatum* (1519), Silvestro often referred the reader back to the *Malleus*.

Although it was published in Venice by Lazzaro dei Soardi in September 1515, the *Quadragesimale aureum* was first composed in 1507. It comprises a series of Lenten sermons preached in Santa Maria di Castello in Genoa during that year and is dedicated to the citizens of Genoa. Its most interesting sermons, those dealing with the sins of the Genoese and calling for their repentance and with the sect of the witches, have been discussed already. A curious fact, perhaps worthy of mention, is Silvestro's employment in the course of one of the sermons, of several sophisticated, logical paradoxes that he had first discussed in the *Compendium dialectice* (1496). One wonders what was made of it all by what must have been, at least at that point, a truly penitent congregation.

The Office

Silvestro's term as prior of San Domenico di Castello in Venice, which was due to expire halfway through 1516, was interrupted toward the end of 1515 when Pope Leo X appointed him to a chair of theology at the University of Rome and, shortly after, to the office of Master of the Sacred Palace. In the latter post he succeeded Giovanni Rafanelli da Ferrara, who had died sometime earlier that year.[1] Silvestro was the first Master of the Sacred Palace to be drawn from the ranks of the Congregation of Lombardy.

Silvestro was now almost sixty years old, and the move to Rome that the appointment occasioned represented the beginning of a new, and final, phase of his life. Silvestro would serve as Master of the Sacred Palace until his death in 1527 and through the course of three pontificates: the greater part of that of Leo X, the entirety of that of Adrian VI, and almost the first half of that of Clement VII.

The history and character of the office of Master of the Sacred Palace is inextricably woven with that of the Studium Romanae Curiae.[2] This peculiar academic entity must not be confused with the theological school attached to the Lateran Basilica and founded by Honorius III in accordance with the directives for the establishment of cathedral schools issued by the Fourth Lateran Council in 1215. Authors who have argued for the identification of these two institutes have tended to do so in order to defend the traditional, but unfounded, claim that the first Master of the Sacred Palace was St. Dominic.[3] Nor is the Studium Romanae Curiae to be confused with the University of Rome, the Studium Urbis founded by Boniface VIII in 1303 and later usually referred to as the Gymnasium Romanum and, more popularly, as the Sapienza.

The Studium Romanae Curiae was founded by Innocent IV, in Lyon, in late 1244 or early 1245. Its most striking characteristic, which justifies its distinction from the two other institutes just mentioned, was that it was not necessarily a Roman institute, in the sense of being located in Rome. It was an institute that was attached precisely to the papal curia, no matter where it happened to be at any particular time. It was originally an itinerant school which formed part of the "sacred apostolic palace" in the sense of the curial establishment in general and moved with it as it traveled from place to place. It only settled definitively in Rome with the papacy's final return from Avignon during the pontificate of Martin V (1417–31).

The Studium Romanae Curiae did not seek to meet the educational needs of any particular place, but those of the numerous clergy attached to the papal curia as officials, retainers, or simply camp-followers of one kind or another. It imparted instruction in theology, canon law, and civil law and comprised the two faculties of sacred theology and *utriusque juris*. It enjoyed the status of a recognized studium generale or university of the same rank as those of Paris and Bologna from at least the beginning of the fourteenth century. It was empowered to confer the various degrees leading up to and including those of Master of Theology and Doctor in Canon and Civil Law.

It is also important not to confuse the Studium Romanae Curiae with the various *studia curiae* of the mendicant religious orders. The Dominicans, Franciscans, Augustinians, Carmelites, and so on often employed the expression "studium curiae" to designate their own houses of studies located in the particular place where the Roman curia happened to be at any one time without, though, implying any kind of identity between these and the Studium Romanae Curiae itself. The designation of a friar belonging to one of these orders as a "lector," "regens," or "magister curiae" does not necessarily mean, then, that that friar held the position of Master of the Sacred Palace.

The Master of the Sacred Palace was precisely the regent master of the faculty of theology of the Studium Romanae Curiae. The employment of the title itself of "Master of the Sacred Palace" to designate this regent master seems to date from 1343, and it is from a little before this time that he began to enjoy the status of a curial official properly speaking. As a curial official, of ever increasing importance, the Master of the Sacred Palace tended, during the course of the fourteenth and fifteenth centuries, to be less and less involved in the normal, day-to-day teaching activities of the Studium Romanae Curiae and, eventually, lectured solely to assemblies of members of the papal court. He did, nonetheless, always maintain exclusive rights in the Studium Romanae Curiae in the institution of bachelors of the *Sentences* and magisterial graduations. He also gradually became the curial official considered most authoritative on doctrinal matters. As such, he became, in effect, the pope's personal theological counselor. He was quite often appointed to preside over theological commissions instituted to deal with particularly thorny doctrinal issues. At times, he took the initiative in addressing controversial questions and, accordingly, acted as an inquisitor.

Over the years the Master of the Sacred Palace was also entrusted with some routine chores within the papal household. He was charged with the selection of preachers for papal functions, such as solemn liturgies and consistories, and the prior vetting of their sermons. He was even burdened with the surveillance of the orthodoxy of curial officials. At times, he was also called upon to act as the pope's representative and was sent as a legate on important diplomatic missions. On such occasions he had the right to nominate a substitute who could exercise his rights and fulfill his duties in the Studium Romanae Curiae. It is not surprising, therefore, that although the office became very early and traditionally the preserve of Dominican friars, appointments to it were always made personally by the pontiff rather than by the Dominican master general.

Only a few years before Silvestro's appointment, the position of Master of the Sacred Palace became an exclusively curial one. That is, the last tenuous links with effective university lecturing, by virtue of being the regent master of the theological faculty of the Studium Romanae Curiae, were abolished as the result of the suppression of that institute. This took place either a little before or just after the beginning of the pontificate of Leo X in 1513 and as the result of that pope's, or his predecessor's, wish to bolster the lot of the newly established faculty of theology of the Sapienza. The Master of the Sacred Palace did not, thereafter, automatically become a professor in that faculty in virtue of his office. When Silvestro himself was appointed to a chair of theology at the Sapienza in 1515 it was, as we shall see, before his appointment as Master of the Sacred Palace and not in succession to his predecessor in that office, Giovanni Rafanelli, but to Nikolaus von Schönberg, who had held the chair since 1510.

Only a few months before Silvestro's appointment another onerous task was apportioned to the Master of the Sacred Palace. In conformity with the decree *Inter sollicitudines* promulgated by Leo X on 4 May 1515 during the tenth session of the Fifth Lateran Council, the Master of the Sacred Palace was appointed book censor for Rome with the duty of examining all proposed publications to which he was to grant or deny the imprimatur.

In Silvestro's particular case, and at the personal behest of Leo X, to the office of Master of the Sacred Palace was also added that of Roman Inquisitor, with the responsibility of overseeing the Roman tribunal of the Inquisition.[4] But of the details of Silvestro's handling of the latter post nothing is known. The convent of Santa Maria sopra Minerva, where the tribunal was located, seems to have gone unscathed during the Sack of Rome so that the tribunal's archive probably survived that event.[5] But whatever documentation it might have contained concerning Silvestro's term of office would have been destroyed when the Roman populace stormed and set fire to the palace of the Holy Office on 18 June 1559 immediately after the death of Paul IV, to say nothing of the later vicissitudes suffered by the archive of that Roman Congregation.

At the Court of Leo X, Adrian VI, and Clement VII

Leo X's bull nominating Silvestro Master of the Sacred Palace is still preserved in the Vatican Secret Archive and is dated, from Bologna, 16 December 1515.[6] The claim, first made by Fontana and repeated by Quétif and Échard,[7] that Silvestro was named Master of the Sacred Palace as early as 1512 by Julius II as a reward for his supposed part in the collapse of the anticouncil of Pisa-Milan, is mistaken.

The bull of 16 December would not have taken Silvestro by surprise. As Leandro Alberti, who may have been an eyewitness, tells us, the matter had been decided a few days earlier, sometime between 11 and 13 December, when Silvestro had met Leo X at San Domenico in Bologna.[8] Leo, who was then in Bologna to meet Francis I, had gone with the king of France to venerate the relics of St. Dominic preserved in the Chapel of the Ark in the church of San Domenico. It is interesting to notice that a member of the papal retinue was Lancelotto de' Politi (1484–1553), at the time a lay professor of law at the Sapienza and a consistorial advocate. Two years later, Politi would enter the Dominican Order in San Marco in Florence and take the religious name Ambrogio Caterino. He would subsequently become one of Silvestro's most faithful supporters in the struggle against Luther and one of Cajetan's bitterest antagonists on doctrinal issues.[9]

The entire Dominican community of San Domenico would have assembled to welcome such distinguished personages, and many friars from other convents, especially the priors, would have traveled to Bologna to be present at such an event. It would have been surprising if Silvestro, the then prior of San Domenico di Castello in Venice, had not been there himself. Silvestro must have met the pontiff and on that occasion Leo X would have informed him of his intention to appoint him Master of the Sacred Palace. Leandro Alberti claims that Cajetan played a certain role in the pope's decision, but he also seems concerned to stress that Leo X had arrived at it quite independently. Indeed, there was quite a background to Silvestro's call to Rome which had been some years in the making and went back to at least 1513. But, as it is primarily connected with Silvestro's contemporaneous appointment to a chair of theology at the Sapienza, it will be best to deal with it at a later point.

Silvestro would have arrived in Rome, then, either at the very end of 1515 or, perhaps, right at the beginning of 1516. Because of the immense prestige attached to the office that he filled, his authority would be appealed to, thereafter, not only in Rome but from the most distant quarters. An example of this is provided by Konrad Köllin, a German Dominican and professor in the theological faculty of the University of Cologne. In the preface to a work published in Cologne in 1518, Köllin stresses that Silvestro had thoroughly examined and approved the text before its publication.[10]

There is an informative account of Silvestro which coincides precisely with the period immediately following his appointment as Master of the Sacred Palace. It is the entry on him in the third edition of Alberto da Castello's *Chronica brevissima* (1516).[11] Alberto emphasizes particularly that Silvestro continued to be heavily committed to the publication of new works despite his many duties. Indeed, as well as his four polemical works against Luther, Silvestro would publish two major works during his term as Master of the Sacred Palace: the first volume of the *Conflatum ex. S. Thoma* (1519) and the *De strigimagarum daemonumque mirandis* (1521). But these important works need to be discussed in their particular contexts. He also published a new edition of the *Opere vulgare* (1519) and a brief manual for confessors, to which it will be opportune to return toward the end of this section.

Silvestro spent the years 1516–21 entirely in Rome, although he might have traveled to Genoa in the middle of 1516 when, along with his nephews Aurelio and Silvestro, he transfiliated to the convent of Santa Maria di Castello. Giovanni Maria Borzino claims that while in Rome Silvestro insisted on residing in the convent of Santa Sabina on the Aventine.[12] This house, which had belonged to the Dominicans since St. Dominic's time, had been reformed and annexed to the Congregation of Lombardy by Sixtus IV in 1482.[13] It briefly passed to the Tuscan-Roman Congregation founded by Alexander VI in 1496[14] to dilute the influence of Savonarola's Congregation of San Marco that it absorbed.[15] With the partial disintegration of that congregation, and immediately after the death of Master General Gioacchino Torriani, Santa Sabina was reunited with the Congregation of Lombardy by the order's vicar, Vincenzo Bandello, in 1500.[16] The only extant chronicle of Santa Sabina which deals with this period gives the impression that in Silvestro's time it enjoyed a well-ordered and reasonably prosperous existence that would only be shattered by the Sack in 1527.[17]

Borzino's claim is confirmed by Silvestro himself. In a remark in the *Conflatum,* Silvestro, while expressing his gratitude to Leo X for having appointed him Master of the Sacred Palace, states that one reason why he had decided to accept the office was that St. Dominic had been its first incumbent. He adds that, like St. Dominic, he also dwelt at Santa Sabina.[18] It is also understandable that Silvestro preferred to live in a house of the

Congregation of Lombardy rather than the principal Dominican convent in Rome, Santa Maria sopra Minerva, which, even though it was the residence of the order's master general and housed the Roman office of the Inquisition, belonged to the unreformed Roman province.

Silvestro spent at least the second half of 1521 and most of 1522 largely outside Rome. According to Fontana, he was appointed a papal nuncio by Leo X with the commission of promulgating in the courts of the Italian peninsula the bulls against Luther, *Exsurge Domine* (15 June 1520) and especially *Decet Romanum Pontificem* (3 January 1521).[19] It is not certain just when Silvestro left Rome, but an entry in the register of Jeronimo Peñafiel, procurator and vicar general of the order, gives the impression that he was in Perugia during May 1521.[20] Silvestro is thus likely to have missed the public burning of Luther's effigy which took place in the Piazza Navona in Rome on 12 June 1521 and was presided over by Girolamo Ghinucci and the Dominican Cipriano Beneto, who delivered an address. It is, perhaps, during this spell of travel throughout Italy that is to be situated Matteo Bandello's reference to meeting Silvestro in Milan and discussing with him, and some local notables, the matter of the Lutheran heresy, in the garden of the convent of Santa Maria delle Grazie.[21]

Silvestro returned to Rome only after the death of Leo X (1 December 1521) and the election of Adrian VI (9 January 1522). Fontana assures us that he was well received by the new pope, who endowed him with many benefices.[22] Thus he must have returned to Rome after Adrian VI's own arrival there, which took place on 29 August 1522. Silvestro continued as Master of the Sacred Palace throughout the pontificate of Adrian VI. Unfortunately there is no trace of his activities during this period other than his probable composition of a memorandum on church reform presented to Adrian late in 1522. This memorandum, *Consilium datum Summo Pontifici super reformatione ecclesiae,* has hitherto been attributed to Cajetan. It is a matter which deserves separate treatment and will be considered at a later stage.

A short while before the death of Adrian VI (14 September 1523), Isidoro degli Isolani delivered an inaugural lecture on the occasion of his inception as a *baccalaureus theologiae* in the theological faculty of the University of Bologna. In the lecture, dated 3 August 1523, Isolani explicitly mentions Silvestro as the current Master of the Sacred Palace.[23] There is also an entry in the register of Antonio Beccaria da Ferrara, vicar general of the order during 1521–23, which reports the permission granted to a lay brother (*conversus*) to enter the service of the Master of the Sacred Palace on 9 September 1523.[24] Although the entry does not mention Silvestro by name, it indicates the brother as being a certain Giovanni da Albenga. It would have been entirely appropriate for Silvestro to take as a domestic a friar originating from the same part of Italy as he did and from a town very close to the convent of Santa Maria di Castello in Genoa of which he was a *filius*.

Silvestro did not only survive Adrian VI but lived well into the pontificate of Clement VII (elected 19 November 1523). That Silvestro was still fairly active at least at the beginning of the pontificate of Clement VII is certain, for at that time he published a new manual for confessors, entitled *Brevissima practica,* and composed "gratia reformationis," which bears a dedication to that pontiff.[25] After this, however, there is no trace of his activities other than an incidental reference in a chronicle of Santa Sabina which mentions Silvestro's lease of a vegetable garden from that convent in 1524.[26] But, as we shall see, Erasmus would still be expecting correspondence from him in the middle of 1525. The question of Silvestro's few final years and of the date of his death deserves to be considered separately and I shall return to it below.

As Master of the Sacred Palace, Silvestro was assisted by a vicar in the person of the Dominican Tommaso Radini Tedeschi da Piacenza (1488–1527) from at least early 1519 and probably even earlier, since Radini Tedeschi is mentioned as such in the *De strigimagarum daemonumque mirandis* (completed 1520). Radini Tedeschi would be promoted Master of the Sacred Palace *supernumerarius* as the result of a dispute over ceremonial precedence halfway through 1521, during Silvestro's absence from Rome. But, inasmuch as I have written on Radini Tedeschi elsewhere, there is little need to consider him in detail in the present context.[27] In the preparation for publication of some of his works, Silvestro enjoyed especially the collaboration of another Dominican, Gaspare di Baldassare da Perugia (1465–1531), the professor of theology *in via Thomae* in the University of Padua during 1502–30. Once again, and for the same reason as Radini Tedeschi, there is no need to dwell on him in this work.[28]

During the little more than a decade that Silvestro was Master of the Sacred Palace he performed, in the first place, the routine chores attached to his office. He also held, from late 1515 till at least 1522, a chair of theology in the University of Rome, the Sapienza. Furthermore, he became embroiled in two famous Roman juridical processes, those of Reuchlin and Luther, and in a brief epistolary exchange with Erasmus—these are the matters for which, hitherto, he has been chiefly remembered. Yet, he also played a central role in the famous "Pomponazzi affair," which to be properly understood needs to be seen within the context of a long-standing theological feud with Thomas De Vio Cajetan. His last burst of energy was devoted to countering the supposed threat emanating from the sect of the witches. These, like his death, are all issues that need to be treated separately.

Silvestro's day-to-day tasks as Master of the Sacred Palace were principally of two kinds: the selection of preachers for papal liturgical functions (*coram papa inter missarum solemnia*) and consistories, along with the prior vetting of their sermons and the censoring of books. There is little need to enter into the generalities of these two matters for they have both been the subject of important, recent studies.[29] It will suffice to indicate the little that is known of Silvestro's own handling of these duties.

As J. W. O'Malley has shown, the prerogative of choosing preachers for papal functions was firmly in the hands of the Master of the Sacred Palace at least by the time that the Papal Masters of Ceremonies Agostino Patrizi and Jacob Burchard presented their *De caerimoniis curiae Romanae libri tres* to Innocent VIII in 1488. The provision that he was to inspect the preachers' sermons before they were actually delivered occurred as early as in a bull of Eugene IV (1431–47) and was repeated thereafter by his successors on an almost regular basis and, not least, by Leo X, the pontiff who appointed Silvestro as Master of the Sacred Palace.[30]

Silvestro's performance in this work seems to have been conscientious on the whole. The only source that we have on the matter are the *Diaria Leonis X, 1513–21* composed by Paride de Grassi, the Papal Master of Ceremonies during the pontificates of Julius II and Leo X. De Grassi refers to Silvestro only a few times and almost invariably in a disparaging manner. But it must be remembered that the extremely finicky De Grassi bothers to mention Silvestro only on those few occasions when his handling of the task left something to be desired, and not at all on what must have been the very many times when it was entirely satisfactory and beyond reproach.

On the second Sunday of Advent, 1517, De Grassi records how, after a long and tedious sermon, Leo X asked him to remind Silvestro that sermons were not to be longer than fifteen minutes. Later that year, on the feast of St. John the Evangelist (27 December), De Grassi took it upon himself to reprimand Silvestro for allowing a sermon which was more pagan than Christian in content to be preached by a student from Narni, even though Leo himself had tended to be patient and tolerant and made little fuss over it. Silvestro must have taken to heart Leo's insistence on the length of sermons for, on 1 January 1518, he prohibited the delivery of a sermon by a preacher who refused to shorten it, and, in this, he was fully supported by the pontiff. On Ascension Thursday, 1518, Silvestro made his excuses to De Grassi after a particularly unsatisfactory sermon and claimed that it was different from the sermon that had been submitted to him previously. Silvestro was forced to apologize once again to De Grassi almost two years later, on Ash Wednesday, 1520, when the preacher delivered another excessively long sermon. De Grassi's final reference to Silvestro finds him at his most indignant and in this, for once, Leo fully shared his misgivings. It seems that on the feast of St. Stephen (26 December), 1520, Silvestro allowed a thirteen-year-old boy to deliver the sermon. As O'Malley has observed, this was quite consonant with the practice of the time. Yet, Leo reacted sharply and commanded De Grassi to inform Silvestro that he would be punished if a similar situation were ever repeated.

The earliest evidence of a clear papal policy with respect to the censorship of books seems to be Innocent VIII's bull *Inter multiplices* of 17 November 1487. The pontiff, while stressing the great utility of the art of printing, points to the possibility that it might also be perversely employed as an instrument directed against right morals and the doctrines of the Catholic faith. Accordingly, after threatening appropriate spiritual and financial sanctions against those printers who acted in such a manner, the pontiff prescribes that, henceforth, printers must acquire appropriate licenses for their publications from their local bishops or experts appointed by them. In the city of Rome itself, proposed publications are to be submitted to the Master of the Sacred Palace, who is named as the proper authority for the release or withholding of licenses.

Nonetheless, there are very few traces of the Masters of the Sacred Palace's activities in this regard in the quarter century or so following Innocent VIII's bull. Only a few of the very many books published in Rome during this period mention expressly that such a license had been procured. Perhaps Innocent VIII's prescriptions remained largely a dead letter. Whatever the case, the issue of censorship seems to have been taken far more seriously after the promulgation of Leo X's decree *Inter sollicitudines* on 4 May 1515 during the tenth session of the Fifth Lateran Council. This decree, like Innocent VIII's bull, entrusted the matter to the Master of the Sacred Palace so far as the city of Rome itself was concerned.

Several books printed in Rome during 1515–27 bear witness to Silvestro's activities as a book censor, since they expressly mention that the required license for publication had been obtained from him. There is no need to list all of these, but two such cases deserve to be considered for they either resolve or raise other issues. The first is Gregorius de Gengyes's *Decalogus de sancto Paulo primo heremita,* published in Rome by Antonio Blado on 29 November 1516. The work mentions that it had been revised by Silvestro. This makes sense of Quétif and Échard's evidently mistaken attribution to Silvestro himself of a similarly entitled work of which, in fact, there is no trace.[31] The second is Giovanni Battista Avveduti's *Prophetia sive Divina Institutio,* published in Rome by Iacopo Mazzochio supposedly during July 1515. Its imprimatur mentions Silvestro as the then Master of the Sacred Palace. But this is irreconcilable with the fact that Giovanni Rafanelli was then still the Master of the Sacred Palace and, indeed, we find him mentioned as such in a supposedly subsequent edition of the same work. It is also incompatible with the fact that Silvestro was only appointed Master of the Sacred Palace in December 1515.

To make sense of this curious situation, M. G. Blasio has suggested that Silvestro probably began to act as some kind of vice-master of the Sacred Palace during Rafanelli's term of office.[32] But this suggestion cannot be reconciled with Silvestro's tenure of the priorship of San Domenico di Castello in Venice until at least his meeting with Leo X in Bologna in December 1515. It is much more likely, then, that the edition of the *Prophetia* which bears Rafanelli's license is its first edition, while the edition bearing Silvestro's imprimatur is a subsequent one and its date 1515 a mere typographical error.

Professor at the Sapienza

While serving as Master of the Sacred Palace, Silvestro also held a chair of theology at the Sapienza. He succeeded in this post Nikolaus von Schönberg, who had held the chair since 1510 and resigned it in order to enter the service of Cardinal Giulio de' Medici. It might be that Silvestro had sought an academic post in Rome for quite some time, for he had certainly expressed the desire to be called to Rome as early as 1513. The dedication to Cardinal Christopher Bainbridge ("Cardinalis Angliae") of the *Commentaria in spheram ac theoricas planetarium,* published in 1514 but composed during the previous year, contains an explicit avowal of this.[33] But the wish is not repeated in the dedication of the same work addressed to Cardinal Niccolò Fieschi and written in 1514.

What is extremely controversial is the chronology of Silvestro's appointment to the chair at the Sapienza. Quétif and Échard claimed that Silvestro was appointed to the post by Julius II in 1512 and actually filled it thereafter.[34] But, from what we have seen of Silvestro's life, it is obvious that they erred. Michalski, who has been followed on this by almost all subsequent authors, concluded that Silvestro was only called to Rome to fill this position at the beginning of the academic year 1514–15 and actually commenced doing so at that time.[35] But, for the same reason as Quétif and Échard, Michalski is surely also wrong. Yet, Michalski based his conclusion on two supposed pieces of evidence that merit examination. I shall deal with the least important first.

Michalski pointed out, correctly, that it was precisely from the middle of

1514 that Silvestro began to style himself "sacrae theologiae professor" in the titles and prefaces of his publications. The first instance of this designation occurs in the *Commentaria in spheram ac theoricas planetarum,* published in July 1514. It also appears in the *Malleus contra Scotistas,* published in September 1514, and in the *Summa silvestrina,* published in March 1514/ April 1515. But the designation does not appear at all in the separate Paris edition of the *In theoricas planetarum,* which appeared in late 1515, nor in the *Quadragesimale aureum,* published in September 1515. If Michalski's inference were correct, one would have to conclude that Silvestro held the chair at the Sapienza during the academic year 1514–15 but not during the academic year 1515–16.

Michalski's argument is unfounded, however, since the three designations "magister," "doctor," and "professor" were synonymous in Silvestro's time and they did not necessarily imply anything at all about actually holding a university chair. In Silvestro's three letters to Isabella d'Este, written in 1508 when he was vicar general and did not hold any academic post, he styled himself "sacrae theologiae doctor" in the letters of 27 June and 11 July, and "sacrae theologiae professor" in the chronologically intermediate letter of 1 July.[36] Furthermore, in the three entries in the *Liber consiliorum* of San Domenico in Bologna dating from Silvestro's priorship there during 1510–12, he invariably styled himself "sacrae theologiae professor."[37]

Michalski's more important piece of supposed evidence is the testimony of Leandro Alberti, who indicates Silvestro's call to the Sapienza by Leo X as taking place in 1514.[38] Of course it could be, as has been suggested by U. Bubenheimer, that Alberti (or his printer) simply made a mistake.[39] But, it should be noticed, Alberti does not say that Silvestro actually moved to Rome and began teaching at the Sapienza in 1514. He tells us only that, having been impressed by Silvestro's learning and, perhaps more importantly, influenced by the two cardinals acting on Silvestro's behalf, Bernardino Carvajal ("Cardinalis Sanctae Crucis") and Domenico Grimani, Leo X in 1514 *called* him to teach in Rome.

It should also be noticed that Alberti's statement contains a reference to the fact that Silvestro's appointment to the Sapienza involved an appropriate emolument. It might just be that with this remark Alberti, perhaps inadvertently, furnishes a clue which enables us to make sense of the situation. It is well known that by the end of 1514 the papal finances were under severe stress due to the notorious prodigality of the first two years of Leo X's pontificate. It is possible, therefore, that although Leo X might have called Silvestro to the Sapienza as early as 1514, nothing came of it because of financial considerations. Perhaps Alberti's "Romam . . . statuto stipendio accivit" is not to be understood as saying, as one might assume at first sight and as seems to have been concluded by some authors, that Silvestro was called to Rome in 1514 to commence teaching "with the customary stipend" but, rather, that he was only to take over the chair "once the matter of the stipend had been settled."

Be that as it may, there is certainly no mention of Silvestro in the roster of the professors at the Sapienza for the academic year 1514–15 first published by F. M. Renazzi (1803).[40] Furthermore, when the *Summa silvestrina* was published in April 1515, it was Silvestro's first work dedicated to Leo X. If Silvestro had indeed commenced teaching at the Sapienza in 1514, he could not have omitted some expression of gratitude for the appointment or at least some mention of the event. But the dedication bears no trace of this. Perhaps the dedication was Silvestro's oblique reminder to Leo X that the matter of the stipend had still to be settled. On the other hand, Silvestro's dedication to Leo X in the *Conflatum,* published in 1519 but completed in 1516, does include an appropriate expression of gratitude for the appointment to the Sapienza.[41]

The matter of the necessary financial provision, if it was indeed this that was the issue, must have taken some time. Hence, Silvestro had no hesitation about accepting his election as prior of San Domenico di Castello in Venice in the middle of 1514. He would hardly have done so if he had been sure that the matter was being taken care of, let alone if he had been already occupying the chair at the Sapienza. The issue must only have been finally resolved following Giovanni Rafanelli's death in 1515, which made possible Silvestro's appointment as Master of the Sacred Palace.

There is another contemporary source, besides Alberti, which refers to Silvestro's teaching at the Sapienza, and Michalski was not familiar with it. It is the entry on Silvestro in the third edition of Alberto da Castello's *Chronica brevissima* (1516) mentioned above.[42] Alberto gives no indication that Leo X's call and the commencement of Silvestro's lecturing at the Sapienza happened before his appointment as Master of the Sacred Palace. Furthermore, Silvestro himself tells us, in the dedication to Leo X in the *Conflatum,* that he was made Master of the Sacred Palace immediately after being appointed to the Sapienza.[43]

I would suggest, then, that when Silvestro met Leo X in Bologna around 11–13 December 1515, the pontiff informed him that the matter of his appointment to the Sapienza had finally been settled because it was his intention to appoint him, as well, to the office of Master of the Sacred Palace, which had become vacant with the death of Giovanni Rafanelli. Thus appointed on 16 December, Silvestro probably began teaching at the Sapienza only after taking over the exalted office and moving to Rome at the very end of 1515 or the beginning of 1516. One wonders if for the quite distinct position as professor at the Sapienza Silvestro received a further stipend in addition to that which was due to him as Master of the Sacred Palace. Perhaps the Apostolic Camera's financial worries were slightly alleviated by the adroit filling of two posts, previously held by different men, with a single man who was payed a single stipend.

Because of his missions outside Rome during 1521–22 and, later, because of his deteriorating health, Silvestro after a while probably relinquished his duties at the Sapienza as much as the routine chores of the office of Master of the Sacred Palace. The *De strigimagarum daemonumque mirandis* (1521) mentions a substitute for Silvestro in the post at the Sapienza as well. It is the same Tommaso Radini Tedeschi who assisted Silvestro in his duties as Master of the Sacred Palace. Radini Tedeschi is described as being, by November 1520, the *protolector* at the Sapienza.[44] Silvestro, then, probably no longer taught at the Sapienza after the end of the academic year 1519–20, and if this is correct it means that he had only done so for five academic years. Even during this period the bulk of the teaching might well have been done by Radini Tedeschi, who had been on the staff of the Sapienza since 1515. Whatever the case, Radini Tedeschi is likely to have definitively succeeded Silvestro in the chair at the Sapienza by 1522 at the latest: in the title of his *Oratio in Philippum Melanchthonem* (1522) Radini Tedeschi styled himself a full professor (*docens ordinarius*) at the Sapienza.[45]

There are certainly very few traces of Silvestro's academic activities at the Sapienza. The most interesting material is that presented by U. Bubenheimer in his study of Andreas Bodenstein von Karlstadt. Karlstadt published in 1520 a work entitled *Von Bepsticher heylichkeit* in which he related his experiences as a participant in a theological disputation held at the Sapienza early in 1516.[46] Karlstadt claims that on that occasion he entered into conflict with a "theologian and monk" whom he does not name. Karlstadt is very critical of the referent of this description. He accuses him of having attacked him for appealing to the authority of Sacred Scripture in the course of the disputation and blames the pope for allowing such an "unchristian teacher" to lecture in Rome. In a sentence earlier in the passage in question, Karlstadt had explicitly criticized the Master of the Sacred Palace as unlearned and as wholly lacking knowledge of the Bible. In a subsequent passage Karlstadt explicitly identifies the "theologian and monk" of the disputation with the Master of the Sacred Palace.

But is Karlstadt talking in this context about Silvestro, as Bubenheimer has suggested? Of course he might well be, and Bubenheimer's identification is fairly plausible, particularly in the light of his assembly of further likely references to Silvestro in Karlstadt's other works. But the matter is not as certain as it might appear to be at first sight. At least the possibility remains that Karlstadt's antagonist in the disputation was not Silvestro but Radini Tedeschi.

Bubenheimer has noticed that Karlstadt often speaks in the plural of "the Masters of the Sacred Palace" and concludes that Karlstadt did so in order to polemicize against the office as such. After all, according to Bubenheimer, it is wholly improbable that Karlstadt did not know that there was only one Master of the Sacred Palace.[47] But, during Silvestro's term of office, there were at first *de facto* two and there would be *de jure* two from mid 1521, as we have seen, and, to turn Bubenheimer's insight against his conclusion, it is entirely unlikely that Karlstadt did not know it.

Furthermore, the accusation of a gross ignorance of Sacred Scripture does not fit Silvestro well, with his many years of teaching and authorship of the *Rosa aurea*, even when allowance is made for the fact that Karlstadt's representation in 1520 of an event which had taken place in 1516 was probably colored by his intervening adhesion to Lutheranism. On the other hand, none of Radini Tedeschi's works reveals any serious familiarity with the Bible and in 1516 at the age of twenty-eight he would have been only at the beginning of his theological career. It is instructive that as close a friend of Radini Tedeschi as Leandro Alberti admitted that he was a much better orator and poet than theologian.[48]

One of Silvestro's students at the Sapienza during the academic year 1515–16 was the German Dominican Johann Host von Romberg. In 1524 Host prepared a new edition of Johann Fabri's *Malleus in haeresim Lutheranam* to which he added a preface. In it, Host refers to his experience as a student at the Sapienza and praises Silvestro in an effusive manner.[49] Perhaps Silvestro never did lose that capacity for efficacious and entertaining teaching that Leandro Alberti had mentioned as being one of his most remarkable and praiseworthy characteristics many years earlier.

Reuchlin

Immediately upon his arrival in Rome to take up the post of Master of the Sacred Palace in late 1515 or the beginning of 1516, Silvestro was thrust into a famous case that had been already quite a number of years in the making: that of the celebrated German humanist and hebraist Johann Reuchlin.[50] The case had its antecedents in the anti-Semitic tracts published by the Jewish convert Johann Pfefferkorn between 1507 and 1509, arguing for the wholesale destruction of Jewish literature. On 19 August 1509 Pfefferkorn had managed to obtain an imperial mandate permitting him to confiscate and destroy all Jewish works directed against the Christian faith and contrary to Jewish law itself. But on 10 November 1509 the Emperor Maximilian appointed Archbishop Uriel von Gemmingen of Mainz to look into the matter and obliged him to consult the universities of Mainz, Cologne, Heidelberg, and Erfurt as well as several authorities, including the Dominican inquisitor in Mainz, Jakob Hochstraten, and the scholars Victor Karben and Johann Reuchlin. A third imperial mandate, dated 16 July 1510, directed the archbishop of Mainz to procure written opinions from all of these. Reuchlin's was the only opinion which advocated a moderate attitude in the matter of the destruction of Jewish works.

Pfefferkorn interpreted Reuchlin's opinion as a personal attack and published in 1511 the *Handspiegel,* in which he accused Reuchlin of having been corrupted by the Jews. Reuchlin responded soon after with the publication of the *Augenspiegel.* This work provoked a great deal of controversy and was relayed by Pfefferkorn to Jakob Hochstraten. It was then submitted by Hochstraten for examination to the theological faculty of the University of Cologne, which delegated the task to two Dominican theologians, Arnold von Tungern and Konrad Köllin. Their verdict was such that the emperor prohibited Reuchlin's work on 7 October 1512.

In 1512 Reuchlin published a further work in which he renewed his attack on Pfefferkorn, and Pfefferkorn responded to it with the *Brandspiegel.* Reuchlin then returned to the attack with the *Defensio Joannis Reuchlin contra calumniatores suos Colonienses* (1513), which was directed against the Cologne theologians, as well as Pfefferkorn, and was summarily ordered to be destroyed by the emperor. Hochstraten, who meanwhile had sought further opinions from the universities of Louvain, Mainz, Cologne, and Paris, opened a formal inquisitorial process at this point and summoned Reuchlin to appear before him in Mainz in September 1513.

Reuchlin then appealed to Leo X, who entrusted the matter to the bishop of Speyer, who in turn delegated it to Canon Truchsess. Truchsess, a disciple of Reuchlin, decided in favor of the *Augenspiegel* and demanded the condemnation of Hochstraten. Hochstraten in turn appealed to Leo X, who turned the affair over to Cardinal Domenico Grimani, who, on 8 June 1514, summoned both parties to appear before him in Rome. Reuchlin, on account of his advanced age, was allowed to be represented by a procurator.

Although Hochstraten was already in Rome at the time of Grimani's summons, the opening of the juridical process was repeatedly postponed. It appears that this happened because of pressures exerted by Reuchlin's many influential friends in the Roman curia, and even despite repeated interventions against Reuchlin by Cardinal Carvajal. It is instructive that the two cardinals most involved in the case at this stage, Grimani and Carvajal, are the two cardinals mentioned by Leandro Alberti as being Silvestro's most influential patrons in Rome.

The longer the case dragged on, the more people seem to have intervened, either for or against Reuchlin. Both the Emperor Maximilian and Erasmus interceded with Leo X in favor of Reuchlin, while the Archduke Carl and King Francis I of France clamored against him. Eventually the commission handling the affair concluded that the time had finally come to pronounce a definitive decision. By this time Silvestro had become Master of the Sacred Palace and might well, though it is not certain, have formed part of the commission. After four indecisive sessions the commission decided, in a fifth session held on 20 July 1516, that the consultors should set their verdicts in writing. It seems that a large majority of the consultors was in favor of Reuchlin.

At this point Leo X employed Silvestro to communicate to the commission a decree *de supersedendo,* that is, a decree which suspended the trial and postponed, once again, a final judgment on the matter. Hochstraten then left Rome, without having obtained the condemnation of Reuchlin that he had sought. It is interesting that on 11 August 1519 Erasmus would write to Hochstraten and chide him for supposedly being opposed to the works of Reuchlin on the basis that they had been judged adversely by the University of Paris while he was not opposed to, but indeed appreciated, the works of his fellow Dominicans, Agostino Giustiniani, Cajetan, and Silvestro, works which had also been unfavorably received in Paris.[51] Reuchlin was finally condemned, and Hochstraten completely rehabilitated, by Leo X only as late as 23 June 1520.

During the six years from 1514 to 1520 that the Roman juridical process against Reuchlin lasted, the case had become internationally famous and Reuchlin had gained ever increasing support from the German humanist circles. It is likely that these interpreted the Reuchlin case, probably incorrectly, as an attack on the German humanist movement. These circles produced a substantial amount of literature on the case, especially in the form of published correspondence.

It is this partisan literature, overwhelmingly in favor of a Reuchlin presented as a champion of German humanism and often defamatory in character, that is almost the only source that we still possess on the Reuchlin case. Furthermore, more often than not, the accounts of the details of the case provided by this literature are seriously inconsistent. As a consequence of this, both the number and the identity of the consultors involved in the commission, as well as the number of votes for and against Reuchlin, cannot be determined with precision. For example, Bernard Adelmann von

Adelmannsfelden, in a letter to Willibald Pirckheimer dated 15 August 1516, claimed that eighteen consultors had voted in favor of Reuchlin and eight against him. Ulrich von Hutten, in the expanded edition of the *Epistolarum obscurorum vivorum* (1517), claimed that eighteen were for Reuchlin and seven against him. Reuchlin, in his own account published in *Actis iudiciorum* (1518), held that, with the exception of three abstentions and a null vote, all the consultors had voted in his favor.

There are several references to Silvestro in this literature and it does not treat him kindly. On several occasions it repeats the claim that Silvestro alone supported Hochstraten, which in terms of the reports of the voting that we have just seen could not possibly have been the case. One of the most unpleasant references to Silvestro is in Adelmann's letter to Pirckheimer mentioned above. It reports that Silvestro had the reputation of being an evil man entirely lacking in conscience and possessing a trouble-making disposition. Adelmann also claims that it was Silvestro who took the initiative and personally convinced Leo X to issue the decree *de supersedendo.*[52]

Silvestro's involvement in the Reuchlin case clearly harmed, justly or otherwise, the high reputation that he had previously enjoyed in Germany on account of his literary works. As such it would adversely affect his involvement in the case of Martin Luther. Luther himself, in his *Responsio* (1518) to Silvestro's *Dialogus* (1518), would make several pejorative references to Silvestro's treatment of Reuchlin. He even accused him of persecuting Reuchlin in order to enhance his career and curry favor with the pope. Silvestro replied to these accusations, in the *Replica* (1518), and insisted that Reuchlin had not just been an object of Dominican persecution but had aroused the opposition of great universities such as those of Paris and Cologne. Furthermore, Silvestro accused Luther of being entirely uninformed about the real character of his participation in the case, which, he stressed, was that of a just and merciful man.[53]

The Feud with Cajetan

The enmity between Silvestro and Cajetan that I shall now discuss came to the fore during the famous Pomponazzi affair. But it was not caused solely by their diverse interpretations of Aristotle on the complex matter of the immortality of the soul. What stood between them was a deep, long-standing divergence on a wide range of speculative issues in both philosophy and theology.

These doctrinal contrasts might have been exacerbated by a degree of resentment and even envy on Silvestro's part. We have seen how Silvestro and Cajetan had known each other since at least 1488, when for a few months and for the only time in their lives they resided in the same house in Bologna, with Cajetan very much the junior. Thereafter each had gone his own way in every sense possible. Silvestro made a grinding, comparatively slow career within the narrow confines of the Congregation of Lombardy. Master of theology in 1499 at the age of forty-two and vicar general in 1508 at the age of fifty-one, he was finally called to Rome to become Master of the Sacred Palace in 1515 at the age of fifty-nine—an old man by the measures of the sixteenth century. Cajetan, on the other hand, who never worked within his own Province of the Kingdom of Naples, was created a master of theology by the master general's fiat in 1494 at the age of twenty-five and after an accelerated course of studies was called to Rome as procurator general in 1501 at the age of thirty-two, was elected master general in 1508 at the age of thirty-nine, and was created a cardinal by Leo X in 1517 at the age of forty-eight. But then, Silvestro might have pondered, a Mazzolini from the rustic hamlet of Priero never had the well-placed family connections, such as that with Cardinal Oliviero Carafa, enjoyed by Tommaso de Vio.

Yet, whatever the case about Silvestro's personal grudges, it was Cajetan's supposed failure to adhere to the authentic doctrines of Aquinas that he would set out to take to task. In this he would not be alone, since, despite many nineteenth- and twentieth-century Neo-Thomists' representation of Cajetan as the classical commentator on Aquinas and a paradigm of fidelity to his doctrines, very few of his contemporary Thomists looked kindly on his many singular opinions. Indeed, among Cajetan's Dominican, doctrinal antagonists are to be counted not only the notoriously anti-Thomist Ambrogio Caterino, but also all the leading representatives of the Thomism of his generation: Silvestro himself, Cajetan's own teacher in Padua Valentino da Camerino, Francesco Silvestri, Crisostomo Iavelli, Bartolomeo Spina, Gaspare da Perugia.

Perhaps even this doctrinal confrontation was really forced upon Silvestro and not of his own making, for it seems that it was Cajetan who fired the first shots in their speculative skirmishes. As early as 1499 Cajetan had criticized some of Silvestro's opinions on business ethics while ascribing them to an "egregius doctor in theologia."[54] He then presented further, anonymous critiques of Silvestro, directed against the doctrines of the *Additiones in Capreolum* (1497) and the *Apologiam in dialecticam suam* (1499), in his great commentary on Aquinas's *Prima Pars,* which was completed in 1507.[55] The date is significant, for it was precisely at this time that Silvestro commenced working on the *Conflatum ex. S. Thoma.*

The first volume of the *Conflatum* was published in Perugia in 1519. It was printed by Girolamo di Francesco Cartolario, the nephew of Gaspare di Baldassare da Perugia, professor of theology *in via Thomae* at the University of Padua. Gaspare, who was charged by Silvestro with the routine tasks of preparing the *Conflatum* for publication, was a veteran adversary of Cajetan. Sometime toward the end of the 1490s, Gaspare had composed a work in defense of his former teacher Paolo Barbo da Soncino. The *Apologia Pauli Soncinatis olim magistri sui* is, unfortunately, not extant. But we do know that it was directed against Cajetan. Cajetan had previously written a critique of Soncinas's commentary on Aristotle's *Metaphysics* which is itself now lost and which until very recently scholars mistakenly believed to be a commentary by Cajetan on Aristotle's work. Gaspare's *Apologia* must, then, have been a response to Cajetan's attack on Soncinas. Gaspare's speculative hostility to Cajetan might well explain his readiness to be of service to Silvestro.

The first volume of the *Conflatum* bears on its title page a woodcut of Aquinas with, at the bottom, representations of Silvestro in pious and studious poses, which are the only likenesses of him that we still have. Its introductory section includes a brief of Leo X dated 28 June 1516, a dedicatory letter by Silvestro to the pontiff, and one to Cardinal Niccolò Fieschi, the cardinal protector of the Dominican Order. It also includes a letter by Gaspare da Perugia to the Venetian nobleman Domenico Loredan and, after a lengthy table of contents, a further prologue by Silvestro. It is here that Silvestro tells us that he had commenced the *Conflatum* nine years earlier,[56] that is, since its first volume was completed early in 1516, precisely in 1507.

The *Conflatum* was conceived as a great anthology and digest of all Aquinas's works accompanied by a detailed commentary by Silvestro. It follows the thematic order of the *Summa Theologiae* and was originally meant to comprise four tomes corresponding to the Ia, the Ia–IIae, the IIa–IIae, and the IIIa of Aquinas's work. Silvestro tells us that by 1519 the anthology was completed to the point corresponding to the end of the IIa–IIae and the commentary to a point corresponding to almost the end of the Ia–IIae.[57] In the *Brevissima practica* (late 1523 or early 1524) he refers to his commentary on the IIa–IIae as complete.[58]

Of these completed parts of the *Conflatum* only a "small" portion was published in its first volume. This was the part corresponding to the first forty-five questions of the *Prima Pars* and, therefore, to only the first half of the first tome of the work as initially conceived. Nonetheless, some of the further, completed but never printed parts of the *Conflatum* do seem to have enjoyed a certain circulation in manuscript form. This was certainly the case with the part which was meant to be published in a second volume, corresponding to the material dealt with by Aquinas in the second half of the *Prima Pars* and, hence, to the second half of the first tome of Silvestro's original project. The second half of the *Prima Pars* contains Aquinas's discussion of the intellective soul. Accordingly, the unpublished, but circulating, second volume of the *Conflatum* must have contained Silvestro's own writings on the immortality of the soul, including his critique of Cajetan on this issue which would play a certain role, as we shall see, in his involvement in the Pomponazzi affair.

This unpublished second volume is mentioned by contemporary chroniclers such as Alberto da Castello and Leandro Alberti and is even cited often by later authors such as Mattia Gibboni da Aquario (d. 1591) and Giovanni Paolo Nazari da Cremona (d. 1641).[59] Giovanni Maria Borzino tells us that, in his day, this second volume was still in the library of the convent of San Domenico in Bologna.[60]

Silvestro stresses, as he had previously done in the *Additiones in Capreolum* some twenty years earlier, that his motive in composing the *Conflatum* is not that of self-glorification (*pace* Cajetan, one suspects) but of acquiring readers for Aquinas.[61] In his compilation of the anthology and digest of the parallel Thomistic texts, Silvestro is guided by the *Tabula aurea* of his former teacher Pietro da Bergamo and is particularly concerned to establish a sound text. To ensure this, he is meticulous with his precautions and turns often to the *originalia*.[62]

It is not clear precisely what Silvestro means by the expression "originalia" and perhaps all that he has in mind are simply the texts of Aquinas from which he copied his citations. But it is also possible that he means complete, manuscript redactions of Aquinas's works as opposed to partial, printed editions. Be that as it may, on several occasions his constant references to the *originalia* enable him to resolve some controversial problem of interpretation. A very interesting example of this is in his commentary on *Summa Theologiae*, Ia, q. 25, a. 1, ad 4um. Cajetan argues, in his own commentary on this text, that Aquinas contradicts himself here by offering two conflicting solutions. Silvestro, on the other hand, refutes Cajetan's reading by pointing out that a part of the received text did not appear in the *originalia* and must be a subsequent interpolation.[63] Since this point has not been recognized by the Leonine edition of Aquinas's works, one wonders about the manuscript material that was accessible to Silvestro and which is possibly no longer extant.[64]

A striking feature of Silvestro's commentary is its determined resistance to the recognition of changes and developments in Aquinas's thought proposed by other commentators. Whenever such supposed modifications are indicated by these commentators as being confirmed by divergences between Aquinas's early commentary on the *Sentences* and the later *Summa Theologiae,* Silvestro invariably appeals to the same explanation, borrowed from Pietro da Bergamo's *Ethimologiae* (*dubia,* 342, 721, 1208), in order to reject them. Silvestro argues that these divergences do not affect Aquinas's own thought because the positions presented by him in the commentary on the *Sentences* did not necessarily express his own views at all. Rather, when commenting on the *Sentences* Aquinas simply presented the then commonly accepted positions as a mere bachelor of the *Sentences* was expected to do. On the other hand, when Aquinas composed the *Summa Theologiae,* he invariably presented his own opinions as he was entitled to do since he was, by then, an experienced and celebrated master of theology.[65]

The most interesting features of the *Conflatum* are, however, Silvestro's many polemical discussions carried out in his commentary. These critiques, unlike those which appear in the *Additiones in Capreolum,* do not have as their primary concern the defense of Aquinas against the attacks issuing from competing scholastic traditions such as Scotism and Nominalism. Opponents such as Scotus, Durandus, Henry of Ghent, Aureolus, and Gregory of Rimini, among others, are indeed mentioned in the *Conflatum,* but their theses are usually quickly dismissed with a reference to the rebuttals offered by Capreolus and summarized in Silvestro's *Compendium Capreoli.* Rather, Silvestro's polemics in the *Conflatum* are primarily concerned with the defense of what he believes to be the authentic doctrine of Aquinas from erroneous interpretations proposed within the Thomistic School itself. This particular polemical preoccupation of the *Conflatum* is stressed by Gaspare da Perugia in his prefatory letter to Domenico Loredan.[66]

Especially interesting are Silvestro's evaluations of previous Thomists. For Silvestro the greatest Thomists are Hervaeus Natalis (d. 1323) and John Capreolus (d. 1444). Silvestro believes Hervaeus to be the superior of the two and invariably follows his interpretations on controversial issues rather than those of Capreolus. Nonetheless, Silvestro is not loath to acknowledge the great services rendered by Capreolus to the Thomistic School.[67] Furthermore, he usually defends Capreolus on those points where Capreolus is criticized by Cajetan.[68]

The principal target of Silvestro's polemics in the *Conflatum* is Cajetan, though in these critical discussions Cajetan is never mentioned by name except for one important reference.[69] Cajetan had argued in his commentary on Aquinas's *Prima pars,* q. 7, a. 4, that Aquinas had unwittingly entered into conflict with Aristotle by implicitly affirming the possibility of an actually infinite number of human souls. Aquinas, according to

Cajetan, had fallen into this error by mistakenly presuming that Aristotle had taught the immortality of the human soul while correctly recognizing that he had held the eternity of generation. For Cajetan, this error cannot arise once it is admitted that Aristotle had not, in fact, taught the immortality of the human soul. Silvestro summarily rejects Cajetan's argument by pointing out that, while Aristotle had indeed taught the immortality of the soul, it was Aristotle himself who had erred by advocating the eternity of generation. Silvestro insists that Aristotle is simply not to be followed on positions which are philosophically erroneous as well as against Christian doctrine. It is noteworthy that for Silvestro Aristotelianism and philosophical truth cannot simply be identified.

Cajetan is, instead, usually referred to by means of conventional expressions such as "quidam Thomistae" and "nonnulli Thomistae moderni." That Cajetan is indeed the referent of these expressions cannot be doubted, however, since Silvestro's criticisms invariably focus on explicit citations from Cajetan's commentary on the *Prima pars*. These criticisms of Cajetan are so preponderant a part of the *Conflatum* that it is evident that Silvestro's primary motive behind his composition of that work was the rebuttal of Cajetan's peculiar interpretation of Aquinas.

The points of conflict between Silvestro and Cajetan discussed in the *Conflatum* are so numerous that it is not possible to deal with them all in the present context. Three particular issues, though, are especially worthy of mention because of both the length and the asperity of Silvestro's critiques. These are the doctrine of analogy,[70] the nature of God's knowledge of future contingents,[71] and the nature of the distinction between a predicamental relation and its fundament.[72] I shall focus a little on this last matter because it represents the longest of Silvestro's polemical discussions in the *Conflatum* and illustrates rather well the "color" of Silvestro's attitude to Cajetan.

Cajetan had argued, in his commentary on the *Prima Pars,* that Aquinas undoubtedly teaches that a predicamental relation is always really distinct from its fundament. He also remarked that most of his contemporary Thomists failed to understand Aquinas on this point.[73] Silvestro, in the *quaestiuncula* that he devotes to the issue, argues, on the other hand and following Hervaeus Natalis, that Aquinas holds that a predicamental relation is not necessarily and always really distinct from its fundament. In the course of his long discussion he considers all the different interpretations proposed within the Thomistic School, expounds and defends the position of Hervaeus that he makes his own, and submits possible objections to it to a thorough scrutiny and refutation. It is in this context that he attacks Cajetan. He stresses that "despite some contemporary Thomists who have become, by the grace of God, very rapidly famous" he remains convinced of the correctness of Hervaeus's interpretation and will make it his business to destroy completely Hervaeus's critics. He explicitly cites Cajetan's claim that contemporary Thomists fail to understand Aquinas and exclaims: "I want to be numbered among these ignoramuses and will refute all the arguments [of the modern Thomists] and many others as well."

This feud between Silvestro and Cajetan continued long after the end of the Pomponazzi affair that will be considered separately in the next section, for the *Conflatum* only appeared in 1519. It would indeed last for many years, since it prolonged itself in the subsequent, continuing attacks on Cajetan's doctrines by Silvestro's disciples and sympathizers such as Bartolomeo Spina, Crisostomo Iavelli, and Ambrogio Caterino.

At least on one occasion, moreover, the feud manifested itself outside the narrow confines of speculative, Thomistic literature. When Cajetan resigned as Dominican master general in 1518, as the result of having been created a cardinal during the previous year, his successor was to be elected at the general chapter held in Rome in May of that year. It has been claimed that Silvestro was at first the leading candidate for the office.[74] Giovanni Maria Borzino asserts that Silvestro's chances were destroyed by Cajetan, who spoke against him at the general chapter because of their doctrinal conflicts.[75] Unfortunately, Borzino gives us no clue as to his sources.

Nevertheless, whatever the case about the mastership general, the feud between Silvestro and Cajetan may well have had another important, surely deleterious consequence. When, a short while after the general chapter of May 1518, the Luther case broke out, the two leading Roman theologians who were to be immediately involved in it, Silvestro and Cajetan, probably found it very difficult to act in unison, for it was precisely at this time that their feud became most intense within the context of the Pomponazzi affair.

Pomponazzi

The principal events which constituted the famous "Pomponazzi affair" will require only a brief recapitulation for they are well known.[76] The role played in it by Silvestro, however, has been generally overlooked.[77] Yet it is necessary for a full understanding of the affair to be aware of the central part played by him as well as to see it within the broader context of his conflict with Cajetan that has just been outlined.[78]

On 19 December 1513 the Fifth Lateran Council issued a decree condemning the Averroistic interpretation of Aristotle's *De Anima* which had affirmed the unicity of the human intellect (both passive and active) and the mortality of the individual human soul. The decree also prescribed that thereafter even teachers of philosophy who dealt with the matter were bound to present and defend the traditional Christian doctrine. It was because of the latter proviso that Cajetan, at the time Dominican master general but not yet a cardinal, voted against a part of the decree. Cajetan believed that this prescription blurred the distinction between philosophy and theology and threatened the autonomy proper to the natural philosopher.

In 1516 Pietro Pomponazzi, at that time professor of natural philosophy in the Faculty of Arts of the University of Bologna, published a treatise entitled *De immortalitate animae*. Pomponazzi claimed that the work's composition had been provoked by a question posed to him by one of his students, the Dominican Girolamo Natali da Ragusa: whether the position of Aquinas on the immortality of the soul corresponded to that of Aristotle. In his treatise Pomponazzi generally followed the position of Alexander of Aphrodisias and argued that the authentic teaching of Aristotle was that the individual human soul was of its essential nature mortal.

Pomponazzi was immediately attacked for holding this position by several philosophers and theologians, including Ambrogio Fiandino and Gaspare Contarini. He was attacked as well by the inquisitor in Bologna, Vincenzo Colzado da Vicenza, to mention just one of the several Dominicans who entered the fray in its early stages. Pomponazzi responded to these attacks by composing in 1517 and publishing early in 1518 a further tract entitled *Apologia*. At this point, and perhaps at the request of Leo X, as has been suggested, the famous Agostino Nifo intervened and composed the *De immortalitate animae libellus*. Pomponazzi then sought to reply to Nifo's attack by writing a third treatise, the *Defensorium*.

On 13 June 1518 Leo X demanded a retraction from Pomponazzi, but nothing came of this because of a swift intervention in Pomponazzi's favor by Cardinal Pietro Bembo. Nonetheless, when a little later Pomponazzi tried to publish the *Defensorium*, Giovanni Torfanni, the vicar of the inquisitor in Bologna, refused permission since the work was not accompanied by the refutation of mortality required by the ordinations of the Fifth Lateran Council. But it seems that Pomponazzi was either unwilling, or simply felt unable if he were to remain coherent, to write such a refutation. Instead Pomponazzi chose to write a highly complimentary letter to Crisostomo Iavelli da Casale, the regent master of the Dominican studium generale in Bologna, asking him to write an appropriate theological refutation of his position which could complement the text of the *Defensorium* and thereby render possible its publication. Iavelli replied to Pomponazzi with a letter accepting the task and in his *Solutiones* published a concise, theological refutation of Pomponazzi's position. This arrangement seems to have satisfied church authorities: Pomponazzi's *Defensorium* was published together with the *Solutiones* in 1519 and again in 1525.

Iavelli later published two further works in which he dealt with the matter of the immortality of the soul. In 1534 he published the *Quaestiones in III De anima* and in 1536 the *Indeficentia animae humanae*. In the second of these works Iavelli gave an account of the entire affair, reproducing Pomponazzi's letter to him and indeed recapitulating the entire Renaissance debate on the complex question of the immortality of the soul. He also examined the controversial interpretations of the Aristotelian text which had been proposed. In both works Iavelli did not hesitate to criticize Cajetan and to identify him as the ultimate source of the errors of Pomponazzi. Iavelli pointed out that Cajetan had himself argued, in his commentary on Aristotle's *De anima* completed in 1509 and published in 1510, that Aristotle had not taught the doctrine of the immortality of the soul.

Iavelli was not the first to link Pomponazzi and Cajetan and to impute to Cajetan the responsibility for the supposed errors of Pomponazzi. This had already been done openly by another Dominican, Bartolomeo Spina da Pisa. His attack on both Cajetan and Pomponazzi took the form of three tracts written during the second half of 1518: the *Propugnaculum Aristotelis de immortalitate animae contra Thomam Caietanum*, a critique of Cajetan's commentary on Aristotle's *De anima;* the *Tutela veritatis de immortalitate animae contra Petrum Pomponatium mantuanus*, directed against Pomponazzi's *De immortalitate animae;* and the *Flagellum in Apologiam Peretti*, a response to Pomponazzi's *Apologia.*[79]

What motivated Spina's attacks against Cajetan and Pomponazzi? Scholars who have dealt with this question have always answered it in terms of vague references to either Spina's conservative and reactionary temperament or his aggressive and mischievous personality. E. Gilson, while not proposing an alternative explanation, added a word of caution: "Nous sommes trop loin des événements pour juger en connaisance de cause."[80] Spina himself justified his attack by invoking his love for truth as well as his concern for those who were likely to be harmed by the pernicious thesis advocated by his two antagonists. He also protested his extreme reluctance at attacking Cajetan, whom he had praised less than a year earlier in the preface to his 1517 edition of Cajetan's commentary on Aquinas's *Summa Theologiae*, IIa–IIae.

Spina's attack on Cajetan provoked an immediate reaction from his religious superiors. Though written in late 1518, Spina's three tracts were not printed until 10 September 1519. A little less than two months later, on 24 October 1519, Francesco Silvestri da Ferrara, the then vicar general of the

Congregation of Lombardy to which Spina belonged, sharply reprimanded him for having written against Cajetan and for having published his tracts without first obtaining his permission. The copies of Spina's publication were confiscated.[81] But it was not Spina's arguments against Cajetan that Spina's superior found objectionable. After all, Francesco Silvestri himself had criticized Cajetan's position in his commentary on Aquinas's *Summa contra Gentiles* published only in 1524 but already completed by 1517.[82] But he had done so in a courteous manner, never naming Cajetan and employing the conventional formula "nonnulli Thomistae." It was the personal and bellicose nature of Spina's attack on Cajetan that Francesco Silvestri seems to have deemed offensive.

Nonetheless, even in the short run, the incident did no harm whatsoever to Spina's further career. He continued in his posts of conventual lector in the convent of San Domenico in Modena and as vicar of the inquisitor in Modena and Ferrara, Antonio Beccaria da Ferrara. Not long afterwards he was appointed bachelor of the *Sentences* in the Bolognese studium for the biennium 1524–26. During 1530–31 and 1532–33 he served as regent master in Bologna and spent the intervening year as assistant to Master General Paolo Butigella. Later he held the office of Provincial of the Holy Land, and from 1536 he filled the chair of theology *in via Thomae* in the University of Padua. In 1545 he was appointed Master of the Sacred Palace by Paul III. At the time of his death in 1546 Spina enjoyed a considerable reputation as a theologian and was one of the major personages at the opening session of the Council of Trent.

But Spina's spectacular later career must not make us lose sight of his modest status when he first launched his attack on Cajetan and Pomponazzi in 1518. At the time Spina held only the minor post of conventual lector in the convent of San Domenico di Castello in Venice and did not even have a university degree in theology. He was not a particularly significant person nor could he have possibly believed that he could directly attack Cajetan with impunity on the basis of his own standing. Is the audacity of Spina's attack against Cajetan to be explained, then, solely in terms of his supposed personality quirks? Could it not be, rather, that when Spina attacked Cajetan in 1518 he did so without hesitation because he was in fact acting on behalf of some more powerful person who, at the very least for the sake of decorum, could scarcely attack a cardinal openly?

The answer to this question is in a passage of the *Flagellum,* Spina's response to Pomponazzi's *Apologia.* In this passage Spina reacts furiously against a passage of the *Apologia* in which, according to Spina, Pomponazzi had attempted to bolster his case by claiming that the Master of the Sacred Palace, that is, Silvestro, was sympathetic to his position. In fact, in this passage of the *Apologia* Pomponazzi had said that he had tried to discover whether Silvestro had written against him as had been claimed by some Dominicans in Bologna. The result of this had been that Pomponazzi had been assured by master Johann Faber of Augsburg, a German Dominican then passing through Bologna after having spent some time in Rome, that Silvestro had not written against him. He had been informed, however, that Silvestro might have written against "some [Dominican] confrere" who had also argued that Aristotle held the opinion that the human soul was mortal.[83]

It is important to notice that this passage by Pomponazzi preceded Spina's literary intervention in the whole affair and is not as innocuous as it might appear to be at first sight. The reference to "some [Dominican] confrere" who, like Pomponazzi, held the opinion that Aristotle taught the mortality of the soul and against whom Silvestro might have written, can only be a reference to Cardinal Cajetan. Pomponazzi's reference to "some [Dominican] confrere" is both mocking and provocative. What Pomponazzi is really saying is that, despite all the threats made by the Bolognese Dominicans, Silvestro was in no position to move against him because he could not do so without implicating Cajetan as well.

In his reply to this passage Spina accuses Pomponazzi of lying about Silvestro's attitude. He praises Silvestro and stresses both his great learning and his zeal for the faith. He claims that Silvestro had not moved against Pomponazzi only because "many" held a similar position and not because he was sympathetic to it. Spina claims that in fact Silvestro abhorred Pomponazzi's writings and that Pomponazzi could discover this for himself if he examined Silvestro's works.[84] Silvestro's work that Spina must have had in mind here is the unpublished, but circulating, second volume of the *Conflatum*. It is instructive that in the course of this passage Spina refers to Silvestro as "my special teacher" and speaks of his works as something with which he was very well acquainted.[85]

Spina not only knew Silvestro well but was also particularly close to him. Spina had not always been a member of the Congregation of Lombardy; when he transferred to it from the Tuscan-Roman Congregation in 1509 he was received by Silvestro, who was then its vicar general. Spina subsequently studied in the Dominican studium in Bologna as a *studens formalis* during 1510–12 when Silvestro was serving both as prior of the convent of San Domenico and regent master in the studium. When Spina attacked Cajetan and Pomponazzi he was a member of the convent of San Domenico di Castello in Venice. Silvestro had been that convent's prior till December 1515 and had been responsible for Spina's affiliation with that convent in January 1515 and probably also for his appointment as its theological lector.[86] Finally, when Spina's three tracts were published in 1519 they were dedicated to Cardinal Domenico Grimani, one of Silvestro's great patrons in Rome.

Silvestro was also particularly close to Spina. There are three explicit references to Spina in Silvestro's works. The first is in the *Conflatum* (1519). This work is accompanied by a letter to the reader in which Silvestro presents an inventory of his previous works. In this context Silvestro tells us that he had entrusted the task of revising some of his very early works, such as the *Compendium dialectice* (1496), to his "beloved and very erudite disciple" Spina.[87] But Silvestro's two other explicit references to Spina are far more important because they occur within a lengthy discussion of the immortality of the soul. This is presented in the *De strigimagarum daemonumque mirandis* (1521). In some of this work's preliminary chapters, chapters 3–5 of its first book, Silvestro deals in turn with the issues of the immateriality and subsistence of the human soul, its immortality, and the authentic opinion of Aristotle on the matter. In chapter 5 Silvestro refers explicitly to the case of Pomponazzi and it is precisely in this context that he mentions Spina. This extremely interesting material has not been previously noticed by scholars who have dealt with the Pomponazzi affair.[88]

Silvestro's attitude to Pomponazzi is uncompromising. After accusing him of having distorted his words in the *Apologia,* he tells of his reaction on reading Pomponazzi's *De immortalitate animae* and of his conviction as to the harm that the work was likely to do. He praises the Venetian senate for having consigned the work to the flames, an example which he insists should have been followed everywhere. He praises his "most erudite and beloved son and disciple" Spina for having refuted the position of Pomponazzi and stresses that he had himself written against "that kind of position" even before Pomponazzi had composed the *De immortalitate animae.* Here Silvestro expressly refers to the unpublished, but circulating, second volume of the *Conflatum,* in which he must have attacked Cajetan on the immortality of the soul.[89] He concludes the fifth chapter by reiterating his claim that he had written on these matters even before Pomponazzi—a further reference to the second volume of the *Conflatum*—and his conviction that the position of Pomponazzi had been successfully refuted by Spina and by another of his former students, Girolamo Fornari da Pavia.[90]

This material warrants several remarks. First, since the *De strigimagarum daemonumque mirandis* was completed by 20 November 1520, these opening chapters must have been written at the same time or just a little after Spina's reprimand from Francesco Silvestri. Thus, when Spina was himself attacked for his polemics against Pomponazzi and Cajetan, Silvestro stood fully behind him.

Second, the point by point similarities between the passage on Pomponazzi in Silvestro's *De strigimagarum daemonumque mirandis* and the passage from Spina's *Flagellum* are too striking to be coincidental. They both contain expressions of anger at Pomponazzi's attempt to manipulate Silvestro's initial inaction for his own interests. They both insist on Silvestro's reaction of disgust and concern for the simple, which had been provoked by Pomponazzi's *De immortalitate animae*. They both refer to positions similar to that of Pomponazzi held by others before Pomponazzi—both implicitly referring to Cajetan. They both stress that Silvestro's authentic position can be discovered by reading his works—the second volume of the *Conflatum*. Furthermore, Silvestro's observation that Pomponazzi's work should not be entitled "on the immortality of the soul" but "on the mortality of the soul" is also found in the opening paragraph of Spina's *Tutela Veritatis*.[91]

Did Silvestro have Spina's works open in front of him while writing this passage of the *De strigimagarum daemonumque mirandis* or had Spina's tracts been simply an echo of Silvestro's words to begin with? Either way, one can hardly doubt that there must have been some kind of understanding between them, and the motive force behind Spina's attack on Cajetan and Pomponazzi is evident. It was not a matter, in the first place at least, of either an entrenched conservatism or of a naturally polemical disposition. Spina was simply acting on Silvestro's behalf in a conflict in which Silvestro himself could not become openly involved. The general scenario is clear. Silvestro had been opposed to the position of Cajetan since 1510 when it had first been proposed in his commentary on Aristotle's *De anima*. Sometime after this, and before the publication of Pomponazzi's *De immortalitate animae*, Silvestro wrote against Cajetan on this point in the second volume of the *Conflatum*. When in his capacity as Master of the Sacred Palace, inquisitor, and book censor in Rome Silvestro examined Pomponazzi's work in 1516, he must have looked upon it, correctly or otherwise, as the result of the influence of Cajetan. Yet, precisely because Cajetan was then Dominican master general he could not go so far as to condemn Pomponazzi's book outright.

What must really have provoked Silvestro's anger was Pomponazzi's attempt in the *Apologia*, completed on 23 November 1517 and published early in 1518, to manipulate his reticence so as to cast him as a sympathizer. Silvestro must have also found especially irritating Pomponazzi's obvious reference to Cajetan and his implicit reference to his own consequent impotence. Pomponazzi's remarks were particularly cutting in the light of Cajetan's elevation to the cardinalate in July 1517. At this point Silvestro is likely to have exerted his influence as Master of the Sacred Palace so as to induce Leo X to demand the retraction which was called for in June 1518 and which brought the entire Pomponazzi affair to its climax. Pomponazzi, however, was able to defuse the matter by securing the intervention of Cardinal Bembo. At this point Silvestro might also have convinced Agostino Nifo, who was at the time one of his colleagues at the Sapienza, to enter the fray with the *De immortalitate animae libellus,* but for this there is no evidence.

It was precisely at this point, sometime toward the beginning of the second half of 1518 and at a time when Silvestro's chances of taking radical steps against Pomponazzi must have seemed slim indeed, and, moreover, at the time when, if Borzino is to be believed, Cajetan had just spoiled Silvestro's chances of becoming master general, that Spina began to compose the three tracts which were published in 1519. But did Silvestro propose the attack on Cajetan and Pomponazzi to Spina or was it Spina himself who took the initiative, convinced that Silvestro would approve and indeed defend him if need be? If we are to believe Spina the latter would seem to be the case.[92] This might just be a classic example of protesting too much. Be that as it may, when Spina attacked Cajetan and Pomponazzi it was surely on Silvestro's behalf and Silvestro knew about it and supported him.

It is instructive, moreover, that Spina would continue his attacks on Cajetan long after the end of the Pomponazzi affair and even after Silvestro's death. He did so on a wide range of speculative issues and largely on behalf of Silvestro's doctrinal stand. His *Quaestiones tres de Deo contra Caietanum* (Venice, 1535), for example, represents the continuation of one of Silvestro's critiques of Cajetan presented in the *Conflatum.*[93] This controversy dealt with the extremely sophisticated, speculative issue of whether subsistence pertains formally to God's essence or to the three subsistent relations which constitute the three persons of the Trinity. Spina, following Silvestro, argues against Cajetan that subsistence pertains formally only to the three subsistent relations and not at all to the divine essence. That Spina's antagonism toward Cajetan was principally inspired by his loyalty to Silvestro was, moreover, widely acknowledged within the Thomistic School well into the seventeenth century.[94]

Luther

Silvestro's reputation as a theologian had been very high at the time of his appointment as Master of the Sacred Palace on account of his previous publications. In certain circles, especially in Germany, it was spoiled soon after by the supposed character of his participation in the juridical process against Reuchlin. But it is his involvement in the Luther case that, rightly or otherwise, has determined his reputation for posterity. This is the only aspect of his life that hitherto has received serious scholarly attention.[95] As there are already several accounts of the matter, the events in question will require only a brief summary.

Albrecht of Brandenburg, the Archbishop of Mainz and Magdeburg, first received Luther's Ninety-five Theses in early December 1517. He immediately sent them to the University of Mainz for examination and received a response in mid December. The Mainz theologians had refused to pass a judgment on the Theses, however, since they were canonically impeded from dealing with issues verging on the prerogatives of the Holy See and recommended that they be sent to Rome for examination. By this time, Albrecht had already also forwarded them, along with Luther's *Tractatus de indulgentiis,* to the Roman curia, which received this material during January 1518.

The Roman juridical process against Luther was probably opened in late May 1518. Although there is no evidence for this, it might have been initiated as the result of pressures emanating from the Dominican general chapter held in Rome during 23–31 May and attended by Hermann Rab, the provincial of the Province of Saxony and a friend and supporter of Johann Tetzel. Whatever the case, the matter was entrusted by Leo X to the jurist Girolamo Ghinucci, Bishop of Ascoli and an auditor of the Apostolic Camera.

Silvestro, as Master of the Sacred Palace, was asked to prepare a theological assessment of the Ninety-five Theses. There is no evidence that Silvestro had seen the tract before this, but it has been surmised that he might have done so as early as January.[96] His response took the form of the *Dialogus* which was published in Rome in June. When he was asked to intervene in the case Silvestro had been working on the *Conflatum,* more precisely on the commentary accompanying the selection of Thomistic texts corresponding to Aquinas's Ia–IIae.[97] It is clear that his first reaction was to consider the task as an unwelcome distraction from his great project. Accordingly, he composed the *Dialogus* in three days. This surprising rapidity need not be taken necessarily as a sign of either superficiality or irresponsibility, as has been done at times, for Silvestro remarked that since Luther had not furnished the *fundamenta* from which he had deduced his supposed *conclusiones,* he could do no more at that point, but was willing to reexamine the question and write at greater length once he was adequately informed.

On the basis of Silvestro's report, which accused Luther of heresy on at least five points, Luther was cited in early July to appear in Rome within sixty days of his reception of the summons. Both Silvestro's *Dialogus* and the citation were forwarded to Cajetan in Augsburg and reached Luther in Wittenberg on 7 August. Luther did not obey the summons but, instead, wrote a response to Silvestro which he published at the end of August. Silvestro then responded to Luther's *Responsio* with the *Replica* published in November. Luther retorted by reprinting Silvestro's *Replica* with a critical foreword in January 1519. Silvestro then published his *Epithoma* in late 1519, which was reprinted by Luther in June 1520 with a foreword, glosses, and a postscript. Finally, Silvestro had meanwhile published the lengthy *Errata et argumenta* in March 1520, to which Luther did not reply even though it seems that he was acquainted with it.

It is possible that Silvestro participated in the consistories of 7 January and 21 May 1520 and it is certain that he did so in that of 23 May, which dealt expressly with the case of Luther. It is probable that he also attended the consistory of 25 May, which considered the proposal of drawing up a bull against Luther's doctrines, and that of 1 June, during which *Exsurge Domine* seems to have been drafted. It is not known whether Silvestro was involved in the elaboration of the bull *Decet Romanum Pontificem* promulgated on 3 January 1521 with which Luther was excommunicated. Whatever the case, Cajetan's frustration with the results of all these proceedings is well known and, in effect, they reflected Silvestro's rather than his own tactical stand on the matter.

Silvestro was also responsible for the original involvement of Girolamo Aleandro in the Luther affair. Silvestro had been commissioned by Leo X to select a suitable orator for the public consistory of 9 January 1520 which marked the reopening of the juridical process against Luther, which had been in abeyance since the time when Luther had been summoned to Rome. Silvestro chose Aleandro, who had held the post of Vatican librarian since 27 July 1519 and had previously been for a number of years in the service of Cardinal Giulio de' Medici. As is evident from Aleandro's letter to Silvestro that has been published by Paul Kalkoff,[98] he at first refused the appointment but, probably at Silvestro's insistence, eventually accepted it. Kalkoff argued that Silvestro's choice of Aleandro was no more than the obvious one in the light of Aleandro's renowned superiority as a rhetorician over other members of the papal court at the time. Yet, Silvestro's choice of Aleandro might also indicate that he knew him well and that their relationship might have been long-standing. Silvestro and Aleandro had, after all, shared at different times common patrons in the persons of both the bishop of Paris, Etienne Ponchier, and Cardinal Domenico Grimani.

Aleandro was subsequently appointed by Leo X on 17 July 1520 as papal nuncio, with the task of promulgating *Exsurge Domine* in Germany. He was to be accompanied by Johannes Eck, who was appointed protonotary apostolic and who, as recently as 1518, had listed Silvestro in one of his works in a series of "sancti et boni theologi." There is no evidence that Silvestro played any role in these appointments. Yet it is perhaps instructive that Leo X would appoint Silvestro himself to a similar task in Italy during 1521. Whatever the case, Silvestro's initial choice of Aleandro would certainly prove, from his point of view, to have been correct. Aleandro would be uncompromising with Luther and, albeit with no success, did his uttermost to have him delivered to Rome.

Silvestro's personal involvement in the Luther case seems to have ended after his nunciature and return to Rome a few months after Adrian VI's own arrival there. His literary involvement in it had ended some three years earlier. Although Silvestro's last work against Luther, the *Errata et argumenta,* was printed only at the end of March 1520, it had been completed by August 1519. Since the *Dialogus* was written at the end of May or the beginning of June 1518, all of Silvestro's literary efforts against Luther were concentrated in a period of fourteen months and ended abruptly. I shall return later in this chapter to the most likely reason for his surprising, sudden loss of interest in the matter during the second half of 1519.

Records of Luther's opinion of Silvestro are numerous and appear even in works composed after their clash and, indeed, long after Silvestro's death.[99] On the other hand, there are no records of Silvestro's opinion of Luther other than those which appear in his four polemical works against him and two, not particularly informative, asides in the *Conflatum.*[100]

One of Luther's most unpleasant remarks made against Silvestro in his *Responsio* to the *Dialogus* is of interest not because of its content but because of the reply that it elicited from Silvestro in the *Replica.* Luther had asserted that Silvestro was a flatterer who was only defending the Holy See so as to ingratiate himself with the pope in order to enhance his career. Silvestro responded by pointing out that at his age (he was then sixty-two) a career was the least of his preoccupations and that as a young man he had refused a bishopric with an annual income of six hundred gold ducats[101]—an event in Silvestro's life about which it has not been possible to discover any further information. It is certainly not difficult to believe that Silvestro's greatest desire at this time was simply to have the time and the peace of mind to be able to continue working on the *Conflatum.* Indeed, when that work's first volume appeared in 1519, Silvestro explicitly complained about the distraction that Luther had represented in this regard and even expressed his willingness to be released by the pope from the post of Master of the Sacred Palace in order to be able to complete his great project.[102]

Silvestro has often been criticized on account of his handling of the Luther case. Generally, Protestant authors, in their usually merely perfunctory references, have simply repeated Luther's gross invectives against Silvestro, which, it must be admitted, were not entirely unjustified as responses to Silvestro's initial invectives against Luther. But to remain at invectives is hardly to do justice to the issue, no matter how consonant it might be with the customs of the early sixteenth century. Even Roman Catholic authors have not been particularly lenient with Silvestro and have often accused him of theological incompetence or, at least, of a lack of tactical prudence. This seems to have begun with Erasmus, but the matter of Erasmus's attitude to Silvestro will be considered at a later point. It would be tedious to cite examples of Silvestro's poor reputation with modern Roman Catholic scholars. In general they have tended to accept what, at least for the sake of convenience, might be called the "Lortz-Iserloh thesis": Silvestro was simply the worst of a rather poor lot, inasmuch as theologians immediately before the Reformation were all guilty of theological vagueness and confusion and, therefore, were totally unprepared to grasp the significance of the Luther phenomenon.[103] It will suffice to mention that as recently as 1983 the standard attitude was summed up by Jared Wicks in these words: "In the summer of 1518 Sylvester Prierias made his hostile march through Luther's Ninety-Five Theses, in a response not showing Roman theology at the top of its form."[104]

There has been, nonetheless, also a certain tendency to be kinder to Silvestro. The first step was taken by Franz Lauchert (1912), who although like all subsequent writers relied exclusively on Michalski's unreliable account for biobibliographical data, presented a brief but objective account of Silvestro's four polemical works.[105] Following Quétif and Échard,[106] Lauchert also clearly indicated as spurious some defamatory works which intentionally had been falsely attributed to Silvestro during the middle of the sixteenth century and which, amazingly, are once again ascribed to him in a recent inventory (1978) of his works.[107] Heiko A. Obermann (1969) argued that Silvestro does not deserve his poor reputation since he demonstrated his theological acumen by correctly perceiving the ecclesiological implications of the Ninety-five Theses and because the essential elements of his ecclesiology have become an integral part of Catholic doctrine and anticipated the teachings of Vatican I and II.[108] Carter Lindberg (1972) pleaded for the recognition of Silvestro's competence as a theologian and canonist and stressed the important role played by his intervention as a catalyst in Luther's self-understanding and development.[109] Remigius Bäumer (1975) outlined Silvestro's theology of ecumenical councils and concluded that it accurately expresses the doctrine of the Fifth Lateran Council and has exercised an important influence on subsequent theologians.[110]

Nevertheless, other recent studies have not endorsed this tendency toward a measure of rehabilitation. Peter Fabisch (1984) questioned the accuracy of Obermann's evaluation of Silvestro's ecclesiology and characterized Silvestro's intervention in the Luther case as tragic, at least insofar as his most important contribution, the *Errata et argumenta,* arrived too late to receive the attention that it deserved.[111] Ulrich Horst (1985) closely examined Silvestro's ecclesiology and, while in no way accusing him of theological incompetence, suggested that his fundamental failure was the attempt to respond to Luther with, in effect, a series of anticonciliarist tracts, thereby revealing a profound misunderstanding of the entire affair.[112]

In this biography it is not possible to enter into the details of Silvestro's ecclesiology, let alone the question of its objective merits or lack thereof. Silvestro's ecclesiology, as we have just seen, has already received a considerable amount of attention and has been the subject of different evaluations. Nonetheless, it is clear from these discussions that his very adhesion to a Thomist, papalist and anticonciliarist ecclesiology cannot be automatically adduced as a proof of any supposed theological incompetence. Yet the fact remains that Silvestro's *Dialogus* was generally received very negatively when it first appeared and that it is largely on its account that he acquired his poor reputation. It is necessary, then, to examine the *Dialogus,* and to a certain extent the ecclesiology that it proposes, and attempt to see just which of its features were probably responsible for this.

Silvestro's *In presumptuosas Martini Luther conclusiones de potestate pape dialogus* is a very short work. Its first edition, published in Rome by Iacopo Mazzochio in mid 1518, consists of only twenty-seven pages. After its ornamental title page, it contains a dedicatory letter to Pope Leo X, where Silvestro tells us that he had completed the work in three days, and a letter to Luther, where he complains that Luther had failed to furnish in the Ninety-five Theses the *fundamenta* from which he had deduced his contentions. These introductory pieces are followed by Silvestro's "Responsio" to Luther, which is best divided into two parts. The first presents four *fundamenta* accompanied by a corollary. The second part is structured in the form of a dialogue: it reproduces eighty-five excerpts from Luther's Ninety-five Theses, each of which is accompanied by a critical response from Silvestro.

Silvestro's strategy in the *Dialogus* consists of four basic moves. It is important to dwell on the full title of the *Dialogus,* for it immediately reveals the first two of these. Although the task entrusted to Silvestro by the Holy See had envisaged the preparation of a theological evaluation of the Ninety-five Theses which had been submitted by Luther as a series of arguable opinions (*disputabilia*) on the limited topic of indulgences, Silvestro (1) takes the Theses to be definitive positions (*conclusiones, determinationes*), and (2) makes the real issue at stake to be that of papal power. By the first move the potentially objectionable elements in Luther's Theses become automatically not only erroneous but heretical and his person is rendered a possible subject not merely of correction but of condemnation. By the second move the focus is shifted away from a comparatively minor issue to an extremely sensitive, major issue and, indeed, an issue fraught with dangers for those who had the temerity to address it.

On the basis of these first two moves alone it is easy to see why so many of Silvestro's contemporaries, such as Erasmus, felt that the entire series of events which eventually became the Protestant Reformation was at least partially due to Silvestro's initial mishandling of Luther. Now, it could well be argued, in fairness to Silvestro, that his second move, the shift of focus from indulgences to papal power, really witnesses to his theological sophistication. It shows that he immediately discerned the ecclesiological implications of the Ninety-five Theses, in the first place the issue of the identity of the bearer of the church's *regula fidei,* while it might even be the case, as has been argued by several authors, that Luther himself only came to do so as the result of Silvestro's intervention.

But it is well nigh impossible to provide any kind of excuse for Silvestro's first move, the transformation of Luther's *disputabilia* into *conclusiones.* Yet, it is extremely difficult to see just how as competent and experienced a theologian and canonist as Silvestro could commit such a glaring technical howler. It must be remembered, though, that we have no record whatsoever of the text of the Ninety-five Theses that was actually submitted to Silvestro. Could it be at all possible that, because of various modifications due to repeated recopying along the way, the text of the Theses received by Silvestro did indeed give the impression that it consisted of a series of *conclusiones?*

Silvestro's four *fundamenta* are a pithy summary of his ecclesiology, and the accompanying corollary represents the application of that ecclesiology to the issue of indulgences. Silvestro did not invent the ecclesiology proposed by his *fundamenta* in order to rebut Luther. He had previously already outlined it in the apposite sections of the *Summa silvestrina* (compl.1506) and, far from being of his own making, it represents an early-sixteenth-century reformulation of a strongly papalist and anticonciliarist ecclesiological tradition that had been gradually elaborated during the two preceding centuries, especially by Dominican theologians such as Hervaeus Natalis (d. 1323), Pierre de la Palu (d. 1342), St. Antoninus of Florence (d. 1459), and Juan de Torquemada (d. 1468). Silvestro would continue to uphold and refine this ecclesiology throughout his conflict with Luther. He composed a further summary of it in the *Epithoma* (1519) and finally presented a detailed exposition of it, refurbished with copious biblical, canonical, and patristic material, in the lengthy *Errata et argumenta* (1520).

It will be best to allow these five statements, which are of considerable importance insofar as they undoubtedly set the central focus of the opening phase of Reformation controversy, to speak for themselves by citing them in full:

1. Essentially the universal church is the assembly in divine worship of all who believe in Christ. The true universal church virtually is the Roman Church, the head of all churches, and the sovereign pontiff. The Roman Church is represented by the College of Cardinals; however, virtually it is the pope who is the head of the Church, though in another manner than Christ.

2. As the universal church cannot err when it decides on faith and morals, so also a true council cannot err if it does its best to know the truth, at least not in the end result—and that I understand under the inclusion of the head. For even a council can initially be mistaken so long as the investigation of the truth is still in process; indeed a council has sometimes erred: nevertheless it finally knows the truth through the Holy Spirit. Accordingly, the Roman Church and the pope cannot err when he in his capacity as pope comes to a decision, i.e., when he comes to a decision in consequence of his office and thereby does his best to know the truth.

3. He who does not hold the teaching of the Roman Church and the Pope as an infallible rule of faith, from which even Holy Scripture draws its power and authority, he is a heretic.

4. The Roman Church can establish something with regard to faith and ethics not only through word but also through act. And there is no difference therein, except that the word is more suitable for this than the act. In this same sense custom acquires the power of law, for the will of a prince expresses itself in acts which he allows or puts into effect. And it follows that as he is a heretic who wrongly interprets Scripture, so also is he a heretic who wrongly interprets the teaching and acts of the Church in so far as they relate to faith and ethics.

Corollary: He who says in regard to indulgences that the Roman Church cannot do what she has actually done is a heretic.[113]

Silvestro's espousal of the ecclesiology encapsulated by these five statements may be considered his third move in the *Dialogus*. It represented a
serious blunder in the opinion of many of his contemporaries, for this
ecclesiology, with its arguably excessive emphasis on papal primacy and
prerogatives and its apparent downgrading of Sacred Scripture, was generally considered to be an extremist one. Its corollary that the very question-
ing of current practices in the matter of indulgences implied a heretical
diminution of the supreme pontiff's role as the infallible custodian of the
rule of faith would, in particular, have had few totally convinced exponents
outside narrowly Dominican theological circles. It must be added, though,
that this ecclesiology would, surely, have been highly appreciated by the
Roman curial officials among whom Silvestro moved as Master of the
Sacred Palace. Moreover, his unhesitant propagation of it may also be
looked upon as reflecting the constantly increasing influence of Thomism
in Renaissance Rome.

Silvestro's fourth and final move in the *Dialogus* was his critical evaluation of Luther's supposed *conclusiones* in the Ninety-five Theses almost
exclusively in terms of his extremist ecclesiology, its corollary concerning
the practice of indulgences and occasional appeals to the teachings of Aquinas. Consequently, as Luther himself repeatedly pointed out in his *Responsio* (August 1518) to the *Dialogus,* Silvestro failed to present against what
were really mere *disputabilia* any arguments drawn from Scripture, the
fathers of the church, traditional canonical teaching, and scholastic authorities other than Aquinas. The result was that, in the second part of the
"Resolutio" in the *Dialogus,* Silvestro presented "(i) three assertions that
Luther 'thought wrongly' about the practice of the church, (ii) six charges
that Luther was derogating from papal authority, and (iii) five outright
accusations that Luther was teaching heresy"[114]—which probably appeared
to most readers of the *Dialogus* to be precipitous, unwarranted, and unjust.

It is very likely, then, that the poor reception accorded to the *Dialogus*
and Silvestro's consequent notoriety are largely to be explained in terms of
what I have indicated as being his four rather clumsy basic moves in that
work. While it would be difficult to argue that they can justify the accusation of theological incompetence in a narrowly technical, professional
sense, there can be little doubt that, taken together, they did constitute a
serious mishandling of the Luther affair at its very beginning.

The real issue, if we focus precisely on Silvestro rather than on Luther, is
that, if not of excusing, at least of accounting for such blundering. It is
precisely at this point that the previous course of Silvestro's life, which has
been traced in this biography, becomes relevant. Silvestro brought to the
Luther case many years of experience as a superior in the Congregation of

Lombardy. If there was one phenomenon with which he would have been intimately, tediously familiar, it was that of the peculiarly obstreperous species who were the friars of the time. Indeed, in his dedication to Leo X of the *Conflatum* Silvestro expressly thanked the pontiff for finally having freed him of the burden of having to serve as a religious superior by naming him Master of the Sacred Palace.

On the basis of the very limited material that Silvestro had to go on during the first half of 1518, Luther might well have appeared to him as, in the first place, only yet another truculent, insubordinate friar. Perhaps, then, Silvestro impatiently judged that the matter would be best and rapidly resolved by immediate and stern disciplinary measures—a judgment that he then expressed through his authoritative, pugnacious, and theologically rash approach. One need not, of course, condone Silvestro's attitude, but one could hardly fail to understand it. Certainly one would need to ponder before describing Silvestro as *streitlustig*, as Kalkoff did while knowing remarkably little about him: Silvestro's brusque tactics were, quite possibly, not meant to provoke strife but to nip it in the bud. Perhaps Silvestro's basic failure was simply that he tactlessly treated Luther as he would have treated some miscreant member of the Congregation of Lombardy, rather than as the sincerely concerned, learned professor of Sacred Scripture of the University of Wittenberg that he was.

There is another factor that should be considered when evaluating Silvestro's handling of the Luther case. It is a factor which, surprisingly, has not been noticed by previous authors. It is possible that, when he was first confronted by the case of Luther, Silvestro recalled that of Savonarola, whom he is likely to have known very well some thirty years earlier and who was still very much alive in the collective memory of the Congregation of Lombardy. The two cases might have seemed to Silvestro as analogous, for Savonarola too had commenced with an outburst of religious fervor which eventually resulted in rebellion against the Holy See and an appeal to the supremacy of general councils over the pope. Perhaps Silvestro believed that if his erstwhile confrere had been disciplined more promptly to begin with, his case might not have ended in the tragic way it did.

Furthermore, Silvestro might well also have believed that the real problem with the Savonarola affair had been that Savonarola benefited too long from the support of Cajetan's eventual great patron, Cardinal Oliviero Carafa, and the hesitations of Alexander VI. Perhaps he hoped that a harsh, resolute intervention in the Luther case might just avoid the repetition of similar circumstances. Be that as it may, Silvestro had no power to overrule Leo X's own hesitations and Luther managed to acquire patrons of greater independence from Rome than any curial cardinal. Moreover, if Silvestro did indeed look upon the case of Luther as analogous to that of Savonarola, we have a ready explanation of why, as U. Horst observed, he attempted to rebut Luther by means of, in effect, a series of anticonciliarist tracts.

Silvestro's approach was also not entirely without impact. Luther himself would still recall many years later that the only time that he had felt seriously shaken was on the occasion of Silvestro's first attack.[115] What enabled Luther to gather his strength and resist on that occasion might well have been the intuition that Silvestro, and every other representative of the Holy See thereafter, did not necessarily have the unqualified backing from higher quarters that he required to be effective. Luther's initial intuition would then have been confirmed with the arrival on the scene of Karl von Miltitz in December 1518.

It has often been claimed that Silvestro lost favor with Leo X because of the way he handled the Luther case.[116] Erasmus even asserted that the pope harshly reprimanded Silvestro and imposed silence upon him.[117] But, as both Paulus and Lauchert have pointed out, there is no reliable evidence for this whatsoever, and such claims seem to originate solely in the intrigue-fostering gossip of Karl von Miltitz.[118] Whatever substance there might have been to the content of Miltitz's chatter probably corresponded to no more than Leo's possible, initial impatience with Silvestro's insistence on the heterodoxy of the Ninety-five Theses. This was then perhaps exaggerated by Erasmus as the result of his own antischolastic stance. Be that as it may, it is certainly unlikely that if Leo X had indeed reacted in such a radical manner that Silvestro would have continued to play the prominent role at his court that he did. Bartolomeo Spina, writing in 1523, mentions that Silvestro had been singularly honored by Leo X.[119]

Furthermore, at least in certain circles it was felt that the responsibility for the Roman failure to settle the Luther affair quickly and successfully was to be imputed to Leo X's unwillingness to pay prompt heed to Silvestro's warnings, rather than to Silvestro himself. Matteo Bandello, who along with his proficiency as a raconteur knew so many of his contemporaries well and invariably reported their doings and sayings accurately in the prefaces to the *Novelle*,[120] presents this as a common opinion on several occasions.[121] Certainly Leo X himself did not hesitate, a little later, to acknowledge that Silvestro had acted in accordance with the "job description" of the office of Master of the Sacred Palace at the beginning of the affair.[122]

Leo X's successor, Adrian VI, is likely to have been sympathetic to Silvestro, since Adrian Florensz had himself been one of Luther's earliest and most intransigent antagonists. In 1519 he had instigated the condemnation of the Ninety-five Theses by the theological faculty of the University of

Louvain (a move severely criticized by Cajetan) and in 1521 he had urged Charles V to deliver Luther to Leo X so that he could be punished as he deserved. Throughout his brief pontificate he constantly insisted on the importance of extirpating the Lutheran heresy, if need be by force.[123] By the time that Cardinal Giulio de' Medici became Pope Clement VII at the end of 1523, the time was probably past for any possible recriminations about the beginnings of the affair.

The Consilium super reformatione ecclesiae

The twelfth volume of the monumental edition of materials concerning the Council of Trent published by the Görres-Gesellschafft reproduces a *Consilium datum Summo Pontifici super reformatione ecclesiae christianae.*[124] This tract belongs with several other such works presented to Adrian VI and has been dated about 1522. The "original" of this tract is a copy contained in a codex which belonged to Girolamo Aleandro and is now preserved in the Vatican Library. This brief tract deals with the practical steps that should be taken by the pontiff in order to reform the church. It limits itself to five key points: (1) bishops ought to reside in their dioceses; (2) the college of cardinals ought to be reduced in size and the income of cardinals limited; (3) provisions ought to be made for the proper training of the clergy and the establishment of theological colleges in principal cities; (4) bishops ought to be canonically elected by the clergy of the local churches; (5) the religious orders must be reformed.

This tract has been much admired by historians of the Reformation. They have generally evaluated it very highly as a piece of superlatively incisive advice that could have had a significant impact if only Adrian VI's pontificate had lasted long enough for its suggestions to have been implemented. They have also seen it as anticipating, by some fifteen years, the recommendations of the commission of cardinals that presented to Paul III the famous *Consilium de emendenda ecclesia* in 1537.[125]

The existence of this tract was first mentioned by J. Paquier in his inventory of the contents of the codices of Girolamo Aleandro.[126] Its contents were then briefly summarized by Ludwig Pastor, and in 1919 Kalkoff affirmed that the work was "undoubtedly" the work of Cajetan.[127] Kalkoff has been followed in this attribution by the editors of the *Concilii Tridenti Tractatuum* and all subsequent historians who have discussed it. I shall argue, instead, that Kalkoff's attribution of this tract to Cajetan, for which he provides no substantial argument, is mistaken. Its attribution to Silvestro, while not absolutely certain, is far more plausible.

There are several initial, external factors which make the hypothesis of

Silvestro's authorship of the tract at least worthy of consideration. The tract dates from late 1522. At this time, a few months after Adrian VI's arrival in Rome, Silvestro himself had returned there. As we have seen, Silvestro was well received by Adrian VI, who left him undisturbed in the office of Master of the Sacred Palace and who was substantially in agreement with his attitude to Luther and is likely to have been sympathetic to his handling of the case. It would have been entirely appropriate for Adrian VI to solicit from his Master of the Sacred Palace, as well as others, advice on such matters as those dealt with by the tract.

Furthermore, the only extant copy of the tract is to be found in a codex of Girolamo Aleandro, where it is included with no indication as to its author. The very fact that the tract's author is not mentioned might indicate that he was so well known to Aleandro as to render the recording of such information superfluous from Aleandro's point of view. I have already suggested the close relationship that might have existed between Silvestro and Aleandro.

Finally, it is certain that during 1522–23 Silvestro gave some thought to the issue at hand, the practical steps required for an internal reform of the church. This is evident from his *Brevissima practica*, dedicated to Clement VII and avowedly composed "gratia reformationis." The matter-of-fact tone of this brief work, with its emphasis on the need to properly prepare the clergy for the administration of the sacrament of penance, is remarkably similar to that of the tract in question.

But it is elements internal to the tract which make its attribution to Silvestro rather than Cajetan plausible. Kalkoff undoubtedly noticed that within the course of the tract's fifth section, dealing with the reform of religious orders, its author identifies himself as a Dominican and it is probably on account of this that he hurriedly attributed it to Cajetan. This factor, of course, applies equally well to Silvestro. One important point missed by Kalkoff is that the tract's author expresses his reticence at dealing with the first point considered, the residential obligation of bishops, because, he tells us, being a bishop was no part of his experience.[128] The author was a Dominican but not a bishop; Cajetan, on the other hand, had been initially the nonresidential bishop of Palermo from 1518 and, after being forced to relinquish that see, of Gaeta from 1519.

The second, the third, and the fourth sections give no autobiographical clue as to the identity of the tract's author. But they do make passing remarks worthy of comment. The third section, advocating the establishment of diocesan theological schools, pleads at a certain point for the promulgation by the pope of a universal decree making conformity with the teaching of the principal doctors of the church obligatory to all. The argument for this is that it would impede the proliferation of heresies and has clearly the case of Luther in mind. The tone and vocabulary of this passage, as well as its proposal, closely resonates those of Silvestro's works against Luther.

The fourth section, suggesting the canonical election of bishops by the local clergy, has been described often as a daring innovation by Cajetan. Yet, it was a notion familiar to Silvestro, who believed it to have been customary in the primitive church and mentioned it as early as in the *Vita da Sancta Maria Magdalena* (1500).[129]

In the third section, while discussing the obligations of the parochial clergy, the author stresses that this includes preaching on important feasts. When a pastor cannot fulfill this duty himself, he should procure the services of members of religious orders. The author stresses that such preachers should be obtained from reformed communities, for only such as these are truly interested in the salvation of souls while preachers belonging to conventual communities are only interested in material gain—a point made repeatedly in Silvestro's vernacular tracts. The author's antagonism against conventual religious communities is continued and is indeed at the center of the tract's fifth section dealing with the reform of the religious orders.

It is this part of the tract, completely overlooked by Kalkoff, that renders its attribution to Silvestro, rather than Cajetan, extremely plausible. Its severe, intransigent character as well as the peculiarities of its proposals are such that it is evidently the product of a doctrinaire, polemically disposed member of the Observant Congregation of Lombardy. It corresponds, in effect, to a programmatic summary of both the policies and the practices of the Congregation and includes characteristic elements that are entirely incompatible with Cajetan's own stand on the matter. Let us consider some of its salient points in detail.

The author commences by affirming that the conventuals should be completely extirpated and their convents summarily handed over to the observants. The uncompromising harshness of this suggestion conforms perfectly to the reform tactics of the vicars general of the Congregation of Lombardy. It clashes completely, however, with Cajetan's own, milder approach evidenced by his immediate revocation of the severe prescriptions of Master General Vincenzo Bandello, a former member of the Congregation, at the time of his own election as master general in 1508.[130] On the rare occasions when Cajetan became inflexible with conventuals unwilling to be reformed, as in the affair of Sant'Eustorgio, it was not because he intended to extirpate them but because he felt that his prestige as master general had been injured by their disobedience.

It might be objected, at this point and on the basis of an aside made by Cajetan in his commentary on Aquinas's *Summa Theologiae,* II–IIae, q. 189, a. 5, that Cajetan himself advocated the extirpation of conventual communities. But this would not be correct, for Cajetan in this text goes no further than to suggest that scandalously dissolute, unreformable conventual communities could simply be allowed to die out (*exstinguerentur*) by being impeded from accepting any further new, young recruits. This, of course, is an entirely different, far more charitable procedure than that advocated by the author of the *Consilium* and of which no echo whatsoever is to be found in any of Cajetan's works.

The author of the *Consilium* then proposes that the task of extirpating the conventuals and handing over their houses to the observants should be committed to a vicar appointed directly by the pontiff so that the superiors of the conventuals *or any other superior* would in no way be able to impede the progress of the reform. This proposal encapsulates the entire history of the Congregation of Lombardy and its constant attempts to secure papal favor and intervention in order to render its actions as independent as possible even of the order's master general. But such diminution of the master general's authority was constantly resisted by Cajetan, who looked upon it not only as detrimental to his own prerogatives but also as destructive of the order's unity and, hence, as an even greater evil than the peccadillos of the conventuals.

Finally, the author suggests that the terms of office of the superiors of the observant friars themselves should be strictly regulated. Priors should hold their office for no longer than a biennium and provincials for no longer than a triennium. No superior of any rank should hold the same office twice. The appointment of superiors of all ranks should take place as the result of elections by means of secret ballots. The terms of office of even the masters general should be circumscribed by the general chapters. The author of the tract is generally repeating here the provisions of the internal legislation of the Congregation of Lombardy. The single exception is the last point, which might have represented the most daring hope of the Congregation and would certainly have been completely inimical to Cajetan.

Indeed, the author's insistence that the election of major superiors should be secret, according to conscience and without consideration of friendship or fear, might even be a reference to Cajetan's election in 1508 as the result of the unabashed pressures exercised on that general chapter by Cardinal Oliviero Carafa. If the author is in fact Silvestro, this insistence might also be a last, disgruntled reference to his own failure to be elected master general in late May 1518 as the result, if we are to believe Borzino, of Cardinal Cajetan's interference.

It is reasonable, then, to attribute this tract to Silvestro and, whatever the case, not to Cajetan. Though historians have hitherto probably erred in the matter of the tract's authorship, they have nonetheless certainly been correct in their high estimation of its proposals: "The *Consilium* . . . handles the question of reform with fine insight and prudence . . . Cajetan's proposal on the election of bishops was not in keeping with the mentality of the curial circles with which he was affiliated; for his plan that bishops be elected by the local clergy, while respecting the prerogatives of the Holy See in such matters, would have eliminated the preponderant influence of the Curia over the episcopacy and would, thereby, have undercut severely the benefice system so ruinous to the Church. Had the recommendations of Cajetan been followed here, within a generation a wholly new Catholic hierarchy might have emerged in the Church."[131] There is surely no need to modify such an evaluation just because the tract's author is not Cajetan but, probably, Silvestro.

Erasmus

Erasmus makes several unfavorable remarks about Silvestro in the *Opus Epistolarum* and other works as well. These references, in letters and various tracts addressed to third parties, commenced in 1518 and continued for well over a decade. They are invariably critical of Silvestro's manner of handling the Luther case. More than once Erasmus expresses the conviction that the Luther affair had developed the way that it did, "a small spark which turned into a great fire," primarily because of Silvestro's initial bungling.[132] Erasmus had been familiar with Silvestro's *Dialogus* from the middle of October 1518 at the latest and from the first his reaction to it had been completely negative.[133]

Yet, no matter how poorly Erasmus thought of Silvestro's approach and of the *Dialogus* in particular, on no occasion does he criticize him personally, nor does he ever accuse him of professional, theological incompetence. Indeed, when in late October 1518 Erasmus discovered on a journey that someone had stolen his copy of the *Dialogus* from his baggage, he immediately took steps to acquire another copy.[134] He stressed on several occasions that his criticisms of Silvestro concerned pragmatics and not Silvestro's theological acumen and erudition.[135] Furthermore, at least as far as practical results were concerned, Erasmus rated Cajetan's efforts no higher than Silvestro's.[136] But at no time did he conceal his lack of sympathy for what he considered to be the excessively scholastic, papalist ecclesiology defended by Silvestro, Cajetan, and Dominicans in general.[137] At times, though, when importuned by some correspondent for his opinion on the substance of the conflict between Luther and Rome, he had no hesitation about directing him to Silvestro as the proper authority on the matter[138]— though this could have been no more than a way of avoiding the issue and, perhaps, even somewhat sarcastic.

The relationship between Silvestro and Erasmus might well have been closer than one might be led to surmise on the sole basis of a cursory glance at the latter's references to the former's dealings with Luther. It seems to have been a long-standing one and, perhaps, was due to the fact that, at one point, Silvestro and Erasmus had shared a common patron in the person of Cardinal Domenico Grimani. There is not, however, any reference to Erasmus in Silvestro's works.

It is evident, though, that Silvestro always treated Erasmus with great courtesy and kindness and that Erasmus openly acknowledged this. In a letter to Marcus Laurinus, dated 1 February 1523, Erasmus mentioned, along with several anti-Luther remarks and expressions of sympathy for the Roman cause, that Silvestro very benignly wrote to him after Cardinal Mattias Shinner had invited him to settle in Rome and that he had seriously considered doing so.[139] Ulrich von Hutten immediately attacked Erasmus over this letter with his *Expostulatio,* accusing him, among other things, of having written so well of Silvestro in order to gain his favor and, especially, out of envy of Luther.[140] Erasmus responded to Hutten with the *Spongia.* He rejected the accusations of flattery and envy and, far from withdrawing his favorable representation of Silvestro, pointed to it, once again, as one of the reasons why he had entertained the plan of visiting Rome.[141]

Adrian VI himself, after the death of Cardinal Shinner in September 1522, invited Erasmus to visit Rome in December 1522 and, again, in January 1523. Soon after his election in late November 1523, Clement VII repeated the invitation. At that time Silvestro wrote again to Erasmus. Although Silvestro's letter is not extant, the substance of its content can be reconstructed from Erasmus's reply, which was probably written in late January 1524.[142] It must be mentioned that this letter of Erasmus has often been incorrectly dated, especially in recent editions of the *Opus Epistolarum.*[143] This has happened because the various editors have taken for granted the often repeated, but erroneous, claim that Silvestro died of the plague in 1523. I shall return to the issue of the date of Silvestro's death in the final section of this biography.

Erasmus had been the object of the hostile critiques of the Spanish theologian Diego López Zúñiga (Stunica) for several years. While still at the University of Alcalá, where he had been one of the editor's of the famous polyglot Bible, Zúñiga had published in 1520 a tract against Erasmus's edition of the New Testament. Zúñiga moved to Rome in February 1521 and thereafter intensified his attacks on Erasmus. Erasmus published a reply to Zúñiga in September 1521, to which Zúñiga responded with two further tracts early in 1522. Erasmus then published two further apologies against Zúñiga in August 1522. There is little need to enter into this controversy, which continued for quite some time and only ended with the Sack of Rome in 1527, by which time relations between Erasmus and Zúñiga had improved considerably.[144]

It is important to note, though, that this controversy provided the occasion for Silvestro's letter to Erasmus. There is an instructive letter by Zúñiga to Juan de Vergara dated 9 January 1522 in which he mentions that "a learned Italian" had read all of Erasmus's works, from which he had culled more than a hundred questionable passages and of which he had informed the pope. The pope, still according to Zúñiga, passed on these animadversions to "a certain scholar at [the papal] court" for further examination and the preparation of a response.[145] It is quite likely that this scholar was Silvestro himself, for the task at hand was precisely of the kind that fell to the Master of the Sacred Palace.

Even if Silvestro was not the scholar in question, he would surely have known about the matter and understood that it represented an attempt to initiate a juridical process against Erasmus. In his letter, Silvestro must have advised Erasmus as to how he ought to behave in order to prevent the matter from going any further: by providing suitable clarifications of the controversial passages. It is also probable that he pleaded with Erasmus to come out openly against Luther. Finally, Silvestro must also have asked Erasmus just what he thought of his literary works.

Erasmus's reply expressed his gratitude to Silvestro for taking such interest in his case and asked him to be more precise about the passages in question. Erasmus then referred to the attack on him by Zúñiga, emphasized his own unfavorable attitude to Luther, and stressed his fidelity to the Roman Church. He protested that it would be best if people such as Zúñiga left him to continue in his orthodoxy in peace. Erasmus then claimed that he had never had any misgivings about Silvestro's own attitude to him. He mentioned that he had only on one occasion referred to Silvestro's works, along with those of Cajetan, in an earlier letter to Jacob Hochstraten: their tracts aimed at the anticouncil of Pisa-Milan which had been unfavorably received by the theologians of the University of Paris. Finally, Erasmus concluded very tactfully by observing that it was not up to him to express a judgment on Silvestro's writings.

Silvestro does not seem to have responded to Erasmus's request for more detailed indications on the passages drawn from his works that were being used against him in Rome. In a letter of 15 June 1525 Erasmus complained to Natalis Beda about Silvestro's silence. He added, though, a few more words in favor of Silvestro's character.[146] It is possible that Silvestro lost interest in Erasmus's difficulties with Zúñiga once he fully realized that Erasmus had no intention of allowing himself to be enlisted as a Rome-guided, public antagonist of Luther.[147] Be that as it may, Erasmus was evidently well aware that at this time Silvestro was still very much alive.

The Sect of the Witches

Silvestro completed his last, longest work against Luther, the *Errata et Argumenta*, by August 1519. Thereafter, the Luther case seems to have held no interest for him as a subject of literary polemics. Nor did he at this time return definitively to his *Conflatum*, even though he must have done so in passing, perhaps just a short while before completing the *Errata et argumenta*, since the inventory of his works appended to its first volume contains a brief mention of some of his previous tracts against Luther. It is possible that neither Luther's rebellion against the Holy See nor Cajetan's Thomistic deviations appeared to him, at that time, to be as seriously menacing threats as that which he believed to be posed by the supposed sect of the witches. It is to this issue, then, that he dedicated his last major literary effort, the *De strigimagarum daemonumque mirandis, libri tres*, which he completed by November 1520 and published in 1521.

We have seen in previous sections the lifelong character of Silvestro's preoccupation with the issues of demonology and witchcraft. The first instructions that he is likely to have received from Domenico da Gargnano as a young student in Bologna had been supplemented by his own experiences as an exorcist, and as a probable collaborator of the inquisitor Giovanni Cagnazzo da Taggia, during his time as regent master in Bologna. The final touches to his continuing education in the matter were undoubtedly provided by his activities as inquisitor in Brescia and Crema during 1508–11 and in Milan, Piacenza, and Lodi during 1511–12.

That his final burst of energy should be dedicated to precisely this matter finds its probable explanation in the fact that in northern Italy the persecution of witches attained its greatest intensity ever around 1520.[148] This was the case especially in those regions which fell within the inquisitorial districts controlled by the Congregation of Lombardy, such as Emilia and the Valtellina.[149] Silvestro even made the alarming assertion that in the Apenines, at this time, the adherents to the sect of the witches were themselves claiming that they were rapidly becoming more numerous than the Christians.[150]

It was remarked earlier that there is only very limited, purely circumstantial evidence, that Silvestro himself actively participated in the prosecution of witches while he was inquisitor for Brescia and Crema, and none at all for his having done so while he was such for Milan, Piacenza, and Lodi. There is, moreover, only a single piece of evidence for his doing so while he served as Master of the Sacred Palace and, contemporaneously, held the post of Roman Inquisitor during 1515–27.

Silvestro himself informs us, in the *De strigimagarum daemonumque mirandis,* that at least on one occasion he served as one of the judges in the Roman trial of a wizard who had been delated by a renowned Dominican inquisitor, Agostino da Pavia. He laments, though, that at first the other judges refused to prosecute the accused because they could not bring themselves to take the matter seriously on account of their persisting attachment to the traditional interpretation of the *Canon Episcopi.* Silvestro adds that it was this experience of the then general Roman skepticism about witchcraft that first induced him to begin the composition of the *De strigimagarum daemonumque mirandis.*[151] (It is instructive that Cajetan, in his commentary on Aquinas's *Secunda Secundae* completed in Rome in 1517, had taken an extremely cautious stand on the issue.[152]) In the *De strigimagarum daemonumque mirandis* Silvestro also proposed the bringing to Rome from the region around Como and Brescia of a number of children who could perform the diabolically inspired dances that they had been taught while supposedly participating at the sabbath. Silvestro argued that, thereby, the Roman populace would not only be provided with an exceptional piece of entertainment but, and more importantly, might also be induced to overcome its engrained disbelief about such matters.[153]

That there were, nonetheless, other occasional trials and burnings of sorcerers in Rome up to the middle of the 1520s is reported by Paolo Grillando da Castiglione in his *Tractatus de hereticis et sortilegiis . . .* (ca. 1525, first published 1536).[154] Grillando, a civil lawyer who took part in several such trials in Rome and its surroundings at this time, was well acquainted with Silvestro's *De strigimagarum daemonumque mirandis,* which he cites often, and he is very likely to have known Silvestro personally. But Silvestro never appears as a participant in Grillando's reports of these trials, which seem to have been entirely the responsibility of the civil courts under the jurisdiction of the lay Governor of Rome. These civil courts, moreover, seem to have prosecuted sorcerers solely on account of their supposed performance of *maleficia* and not at all on that of any putative membership of the heretical sect of the witches.

Nevertheless, even though Silvestro's personal involvement in the matter seems to have been only slight, a very active role in the prosecution of witches was certainly played by many of his former teachers and colleagues in the Bolognese studium: Domenico da Gargnano, Giovanni da Taggia, Giorgio da Casale. It was especially the case with many of his former students: Girolamo da Lodi, Francesco Silvestri, Gerolamo Armellini da Faenza, Leandro Alberti, Bartolomeo Spina da Pisa. The intense participation of all these men in bouts of witch-hunting is well documented and has been the subject of important recent studies.[155]

It is probable that at least some of these fellow members of the Congregation of Lombardy, almost all of whom held inquisitorial posts at the time, kept Silvestro informed and presented the situation to him in such an emphatic manner as to distract him definitively from his preoccupations with his two other antagonists, Cajetan and Luther. It is also quite likely that it was at Silvestro's insistence, or at least through his mediation, that Leo X, Adrian VI, and Clement VII conceded their briefs *Honestis petentium votis* (15 February 1521), *Dudum, uti nobis* (10 July 1523), and *Accepimus non sine animi* (18 January 1524), encouraging and facilitating the prosecution of witches by the inquisitors of the Congregation of Lombardy.

The *De strigimagarum daemonumque mirandis* has already received some, at least passing attention from scholars.[156] First published in Rome by Antonio Blado in September 1521 and dedicated to Cardinal Agostino Trivulzio, it is divided into three books. The first comprises fourteen chapters and deals with the author's intentions; it sets out to distinguish clearly the adherents to the modern sect of the witches from the sorcerers spoken of by the *Canon Episcopi* and delineates an elaborate theory of spiritual, immaterial substances. The chapters dealing with this last theme (3–14) consider the immateriality and immortality of the human soul and the existence of spiritual substances superior to man and identifies demons as fallen instances of these. These chapters thus go well beyond Silvestro's preoccupation with the witches and seem to aim as well at those radical Aristotelians, such as Pomponazzi, who were arguing not only for the rational indemonstrability of the immortality of the soul but also against the existence of angels and demons.

The second book comprises twelve chapters. It commences with an exegesis of the *Canon Episcopi* and presents a phenomenology of the witches illustrated with many examples. These examples are only very rarely firsthand, for they are usually derived from Silvestro's principal written sources: Eymerich's *Directorium*, Nider's *Formicarium* and *Praeceptorium* and, especially, Kramer and Sprenger's *Malleus Maleficarum*. Some examples are based on oral reports to Silvestro from other inquisitors.

The third book is concerned with juridical procedure. It comprises four chapters which raise the issues whether the witches are to be treated as a heretical sect and how to initiate, follow through, and conclude a trial for witchcraft. At the very end of the work, Silvestro informs us that he had completed it on 24 November 1520.

The *De strigimagarum daemonumque mirandis* has often been considered, quite correctly, one of the most intransigent works ever written against the witches. Its fundamental argument is that the modern sect of the witches began a little before the publication of Innocent VIII's *Summis desiderantes affectibus* (1484) and is quite different from the sorcerers mentioned by the *Canon Episcopi*. Silvestro stresses the reality of the supposed characteristics of the sect: the repudiation of baptismal vows and the pact with the devil; the participation at the sabbath, where the witches arrive by nocturnal flight and which culminates with worship of the devil followed by an orgy; the performance of *maleficia* such as infanticide and the destruction of animals and harvests. The witches constitute, accordingly, a dangerous heretical sect and, as such, should be prosecuted by the Inquisition.

Silvestro's work shows, all in all, little originality and adds little of substance even with regard to his previous, much briefer treatment in the *Summa silvestrina*. There is, however, one noteworthy innovation in his employment of the neologism "strigimagus." It has been argued that, by doing so, it is likely that Silvestro was concerned to assimilate to the sect of the witches the adepts and advocates of the refined, cultured conception of "natural magic."[157] Ultimately Hermetic and Neoplatonic in inspiration, this conception saw in astrology the theoretical foundation for magical, ritual practices supposedly productive of occult, prodigious phenomena. Such practices relied on the presumed correspondences or "sympathies" between the natural elements constituting the sublunary sphere and the intelligences which regulated the planets and stars embedded in the higher spheres of the cosmos.

Although it had significant medieval antecedents, the notion of natural magic had flowered particularly during the second half of the fifteenth century and had among its proponents Marsilio Ficino and, for a while at least and with an added dash of Cabbala, Giovanni Pico della Mirandola. It even encroached, although it was often subjected to an avowedly de-demonizing interpretation, among such radical Aristotelians as Agostino Nifo, Alessandro Achillini, and Pomponazzi. It would continue to have a significant following throughout the sixteenth century and be advocated by such figures as Cornelius Agrippa, Girolamo Cardano, and Giambattista Della Porta.

It would be wrong, though, to interpret Silvestro's lumping together of the *striges* and the *magi* in the *De strigimagarum daemonumque mirandis* as some kind of final attempt to strike at Pomponazzi, for Silvestro had, de facto and without the benefit of his neologism, achieved the assimilation many years before his polemics with Pomponazzi. This is evident from the entry "Superstitio" in the *Summa silvestrina* (completed by 1506) and, as well, the corresponding sermon "De superstitionibus" in the *Quadragesimale aureum* (first composed 1507).

In these works Silvestro had considered the phenomenon of superstition and the catalog that he provides of superstitious practices is exhaustive. He divides superstition into four species. The first two are of little interest in the present context and are indeed barely mentioned by Silvestro: the superstitious practices which represent improper manners of worshipping the true God (*superstitio indebiti cultus*) and those which are idolatrous (*superstitio idolatriae*). The third species of superstition is constituted by divinatory practices (*superstitio divinatoria*). These are of two kinds.

The first kind relies on a manifest, explicit invocation of demons and, accordingly, corresponds to "necromancy" in its broad sense. It comprises nine types: (1) *praestigium*—divination by illusory apparitions, (2) oneiromancy—divination by dreams, (3) necromancy in its narrow sense—divination by contact with dead persons, (4) pythomancy—divination by living persons or oracles in the manner of Python Apollo, (5) geomancy, (6) hydromancy, (7) aeromancy, (8) pyromancy, (9) *aruspicium*—divination by the remains of animals sacrificed on altars. The second relies on an implicit, tacit invocation of demons and comprises six types: (1) astrology, (2) auguries, (3) omens, (4) chiromancy, (5) the examination of animal entrails, (6) sortilege or the casting of lots.

The fourth species of superstition (*superstitio observantiae*) is concerned with producing effects such as health and illness and, accordingly, corresponds to the *ars notoria*. It also relies on an implicit, tacit invocation of demons and comprises four types: (1) images and amulets, (2) spoken charms or incantations, (3) written charms or talismans, (4) the selection of auspicious days and times.

Silvestro's thesis is, then, that all the practices indulged in by the adepts of natural magic to produce occult phenomena fall within one or another of his classifications of superstitions. Silvestro insists that all these practices are inefficacious in their own right. When they do procure some result, it is not because of any intrinsic power but solely because of diabolical interference. Silvestro argues that they all involve either the explicit or the implicit invocation of demons and that their practitioners either expressly or tacitly enter into a pact with the devil. There is no radical difference, for Silvestro, between the *strix* confecting a *maleficium* while openly invoking the devil and the *magus* indulging in natural magic who, at the same time, might even be theoretically convinced of the nonexistence of demons. It is instructive that in the entry "Maleficium" in the *Summa silvestrina* the term "strix" never appears and the confector of *maleficia* is invariably called "magús."

In his opposition to natural magic Silvestro was, accordingly, ideologically very close to Giovanfrancesco Pico della Mirandola, who also argued for its ultimately diabolical character. In the fourth book of the *De rerum praenotione* (1507) Giovanfrancesco presents a division of superstition into its species which he admits he copied from other works and which is remarkably similar to that of the *Summa silvestrina*.[158] The parallels between the two expositions are, in fact, too close to be merely coincidental. Furthermore, Giovanfrancesco's relations with members of the Congregation of Lombardy are well known, as is his cooperation with some of its inquisitors, who were invariably Silvestro's former students, in the prosecution of witches.

One must be careful here, though, not to conclude that this interpretation of natural magic as ultimately presupposing an implicit pact with the devil is a peculiarly late, Renaissance phenomenon. For Silvestro's catalog of superstitions, as well as the fundamentally demonic interpretation of them that he proposes, are simply and quite literally borrowed from Aquinas's discussion of superstition in *Summa Theologiae*, II–IIae, qq. 92–96. Aquinas, in turn, does little more than systematize the opinions of St. Augustine and St. Isidore of Seville. Furthermore, the entire issue is somewhat defused by Silvestro's insistence that those who are guilty of comparatively slight superstitious practices, and are in no way proponents of formal heresies, should not be excessively harassed by inquisitors.[159]

The *De strigimagarum daemonumque mirandis* was reprinted in Rome in 1575 along with Bartolomeo Spina's *Quaestio de strigibus et lamiis*. Spina's work had been first published in 1523 and generally follows the lines proposed by his teacher and mentor. Both works would be considered quite dated by the end of the sixteenth century, for by then the Roman Inquisition, long before all other European courts of law, had come to take a lenient attitude to the witches' malpractices and largely dismissed their supposed effects as delusions.[160]

Death during the Sack of Rome

It has been remarked already that, although Silvestro lived well into the pontificate of Clement VII, there are no traces of his activities after 1524. We have also seen, however, that Erasmus was still expecting some response from Silvestro to his letters in mid-1525.

It is likely that although Silvestro continued to hold the office of Master of the Sacred Palace, which was customarily a life appointment, he lived his last few years in retirement. The burdens of the office, especially such routine chores as the choosing of preachers and the vetting of their sermons for papal functions as well as the censoring of books, would have been assumed by the Master of the Sacred Palace *supernumerarius,* Tommaso Radini Tedeschi. In line with this, the record of a letter in the register of Master General Francesco Silvestri, dated 14 October 1524, refers to Radini Tedeschi as the Master of the Sacred Palace without further ado.[161]

Giovanni Maria Borzino claims that Silvestro led, during his last few years, a hermitlike existence entirely dedicated to prayer, living in a kind of grotto in the garden of the convent of Santa Sabina.[162] If there is any truth in this, such a situation is likely to have been due not only to his advanced age but also to some kind of debilitating infirmity. There is, in fact, a mention of Silvestro's poor health as early as in the *Conflatum* (1519).[163] This might also be indicated by the early appointment, around 1519 at the very latest, of Radini Tedeschi as his vicar as Master of the Sacred Palace and his assistant at the Sapienza. Further evidence is the letter (1521) of the Dominican procurator general, Jeronimo Peñafiel, that was first discussed as part of the attempt to determine the matter of Silvestro's original conventual affiliation.[164] Its provisions for the distribution of Silvestro's monies and literary remains in the case of his demise has the character of a last will and testament and is likely to have been motivated by some grounded concern about his life expectancy.

What has always been extremely problematic for historians is the determination of the date and circumstances of Silvestro's death. Fontana (1666) was the first to claim that during the plague epidemic which ravaged Rome in 1522–23, Silvestro volunteered to minister spiritually to the infected, contracted the plague himself, and died of it in 1523.[165] Fontana has been followed on this by Quétif and Échard (1721)[166] and all subsequent writers with, as we shall see, an important exception. The uncritical following of Fontana and Quétif and Échard has resulted in the greatest possible confusion on the part of later historians. J.-J. Berthier, for example, in his history of the convent of Santa Sabina (1912), does not hesitate to assert that Silvestro died of the plague in 1523 and, within a few pages and on the basis of Silvestro's lease of a vegetable garden from that convent, lists Silvestro as the prior of Santa Sabina in 1524![167]

Fontana did not invent the plague as the cause of Silvestro's death. The earliest mention of it is in Sebastian Olmeda's *Chronica Ordinis Praedicatorum* composed between 1530 and 1558, and Fontana explicitly acknowledges Olmeda as his source. The sources used by Olmeda himself in his treatment of Silvestro are obvious: he collated the reference to Silvestro in the *Acta* of the general chapter of 1505 with the entries on him in Alberto da Castello's *Chronica brevissima* (1516) and Leandro Alberti's *De viris illustribus* (1517). The only additional element is the assertion that Silvestro died of the plague.[168] It should be noticed, though, that Olmeda attaches no particular date to this. The fixing of 1523 as the year of Silvestro's death is Fontana's own contribution. But Fontana is mistaken, for we have seen that Silvestro lived into the pontificate of Clement VII (elected 19 November 1523), and there are traces of him in 1524.

Borzino is equally mistaken in claiming that Silvestro lived to the ripe old age of ninety-seven, died in 1533, and was buried in the convent of Santa Sabina.[169] Olmeda, who gathered his data while staying in Santa Sabina around 1530, had no doubt that by then Silvestro was dead and had been interred in the church of Santa Maria sopra Minerva. As we shall see, while he might have been wrong about Silvestro's burial place, it is hardly likely that he could have been mistaken about whether Silvestro was dead or alive at the time when he was himself in Rome. The documentation that Borzino invokes to confirm his claim, consisting of references to a Silvestro da Prierio in the archive of the Archdiocese of Genoa and in the *Libro delle Compere* of the Genoese Banco di San Giorgio, undoubtedly refer, then, to our Silvestro's homonymous nephew.

That Silvestro lived up to the middle of 1527 is certain, however, in the light of the evidence first discovered and published by Innocenzo Taurisano (1916).[170] Taurisano, whose work has been neglected by almost all subsequent writers, discovered that payments of Silvestro's stipend as Master of the Sacred Palace of ten *ducati aurei* each month were made by the Apostolic Camera at least as late as 21 January 1527. Taurisano also reasoned that Silvestro must obviously have died before the appointment of his successor as Master of the Sacred Palace. Silvestro's successor, Nicola Columbi da Perugia, died himself, on 1 October 1527 in Florence, before he could take over the office.[171] He was eventually succeeded by Tommaso Badìa da Modena on 17 February 1529.[172] If we assume that Columbi was appointed Master of the Sacred Palace at least a month or so before his death and that Silvestro died at least a month or so before Columbi's appointment, Silvestro's death is to be seen as taking place around the middle of 1527.

A further confirmation of Silvestro's death as occurring roughly at this time is in the *Acta* of the provincial chapter of the Dominican Province of Lower Germany (*Germaniae Inferioris*) held in Antwerp in May 1528. Silvestro is listed in these *Acta* among those who are to be prayed for insofar as their deaths had taken place since the previous provincial chapter which had been held in May 1526.[173]

Nothing is known of the manner of Silvestro's death in mid 1527. Taurisano suggested that Silvestro probably died during the Sack of Rome. This conjecture is extremely plausible, for it is only the chaotic conditions of Rome during that event which can explain why the death of the *Magister Magistrorum*[174] passed unnoticed and without leaving any precise record.

Furthermore, it is instructive that Silvestro's assistant and Master of the Sacred Palace *supernumerarius,* Radini Tedeschi, died as well in 1527 and, in his case, Leandro Alberti tells us in the *Descrittione di tutta Italia* (1550) that he died during the Sack.[175] When we bear in mind that Radini Tedeschi died at the young age of thirty-nine, it is reasonable to suspect that he died violently and that Silvestro did so at the same time and in the same circumstances. It is known that during the Sack the convent of Santa Sabina, where both Radini Tedeschi and Silvestro resided, was stormed and partially destroyed.[176] But then, it is also possible that Olmeda was correct and that Silvestro died of the plague. But this would not have been the plague of 1522–23, as conjectured by Fontana, but the plague that broke out in 1527, in the immediate aftermath of the Sack.

According to Olmeda, as we have seen, Silvestro was buried in the church of Santa Maria sopra Minerva; according to Borzino, it was the church of Santa Sabina. But in neither church is there any trace of a tombstone. Certainly, there is no reason why Silvestro should have been buried in Santa Maria sopra Minerva when he had chosen to live and had died in Santa Sabina. Undoubtedly, if he had had any say in the matter, he would have chosen to be buried among the brethren of the Congregation of Lombardy, rather than the unreformable conventuals. The discrepancy about his burial place makes one suspect that there might have been no formal, final obsequies at all and lends further credence to the hypothesis of a violent death.

There is something persistently mysterious about Silvestro's death. It is remarkable that Leandro Alberti, who, in the *Descrittione* (1550), informs us about the demise of Radini Tedeschi and, indeed, about the deaths of so many of the Dominicans whom he had previously praised in the *De viris illustribus* (1517), passes over Silvestro in absolute silence. Alberti's reticence is emblematic of the unanimous silence of all other contemporary sources.

A possible, final scenario is at least imaginable: Silvestro's end was so appalling and would have provided such a propaganda scoop, such a supposed sign of divine vindication, to the ultramontane heretics, if they were to come to know about it, that the friars of the Congregation of Lombardy thought it best to hush up the entire matter and encouraged innocuous, pious confabulations, such as Olmeda's, as a suitable smoke screen. The Sackers themselves had undoubtedly never suspected that the infirm, perhaps senile, geriatric whom they summarily despatched to his God was the former *contubernalis* of Savonarola who had made Martin Luther realize that there was no place for him in the Roman Catholic Church.

Cajetan's own fate during the Sack deserves a mention. Though the different accounts of it vary significantly, it seems certain that he was taken hostage by the Sackers.[177] The most vivid of these accounts would have him paraded around Rome mounted backwards on an ass and, but for a day laborer's cap on his head, completely naked. He was, nonetheless, eventually set free upon the payment of a ransom of five thousand gold ducats. One wonders if, during the humiliating cavalcade, his thoughts ever went back to the beginnings of the Luther affair, Silvestro's part in it, and his strained relations with him at the time.

Silvestro's final thoughts, if he was indeed capable of such at the time, might well have echoed the statement with which he concluded the first volume of the *Conflatum:* "Porro quae hactenus scripsi . . . sanctae Romanae ecclesiae Romanique pontificis iudicio, quod contra Martinum caeleste oraculum fore demonstravi, ac si Dei ipsius iudicio submitto. Vale lector charissime, et Deo pro me preces effundas oro."[178]

Appendix: Works by Silvestro da Prierio

1. *Compendium dialectice fratris Silvestri de prierio sacri ordinis praedicatorum.* Venice: Otto da Pavia, 1496.

2. *Egregius vel potius divinum opus in Johannem Capreolum tholosanum sacri predicatorum ordinis.* Cremona: Carlo de' Darlieri, 1497.

3. *Additiones in Johannem capreolum.* Cremona: Carlo de' Darlieri, 1497.

4. *Apologia magistri silvestri de prierio or. predic. in diale[c]ticam suam cum explanatione clarissima totius materiae intentionalis.* Bologna: Ugo Ruggeri, 1499.

5. *Vita de la seraphina e ferventissima amatrice de Jesu Christo salvatore sancta Maria Magdalena.* Bologna: Giovanantonio de' Benedetti, 1500. Further editions: Bologna, 1501; Florence, 1592.

6. *Exortatione del coniugio spirituale e celeste sposo: e come ogni Anima etiam posta in matrimonio po e debbe pigliare lo incarnato verbo di Dio per suo sposo: per il reverendo padre e maistro frate Silvestro da prierio, prima recitata, e poi anchora scripta.* Bologna: Giovanantonio de' Benedetti, 1500.

7. *Il modo di contemplare Dio e Li Gradi de la Vita Spirituale.* Bologna: Giovanantonio de' Benedetti, 1500.

8. *Trialogo chiamato Philamore, cioe Parlare de tre persone, Christo, Gesu e S. Maria Maddalena.* Bologna: Giovanantonio de' Benedetti, 1500. Further edition: Florence, 1592.

9. *Refugio di sconsolati.* Bologna: Giovanantonio de' Benedetti, 1500.

10. *Devota meditatione in tutto il peregrinagio di Salvatore Jesu Christo.* Bologna: Giovanantonio de' Benedetti, 1500.

11. *Scala del sancto amore.* Bologna: Giovanantonio de' Benedetti, 1501.

12. *Summario per confessarsi.* Bologna: Giovanantonio de' Benedetti, 1501. Further edition: Rimini, after 1515.

13. *Vita e conversione sancta: del beato Iacobo converso de lordine de predicatori novamente morto a Bologna.* Bologna: Giovanantonio de' Benedetti, 1501.

14. *Opere vulgare di Maestro Silvestro da Prierio. Ordinis predicatorum. Scala del sancto amore divotissima e scientifica: utile a docti e simplici, chi cerchano havere il divino e sancto amore: quantumche alquanto scuro sia el capitulo secundo e quinto. Cento breve meditatione della passione del signore cum cento petitione proportionate aquelle revelate da Jesu Christo. Philamore idest trialogo de le tre querelle: che a christo sa ogni anima sancta e fece la seraphina Magdalena: in la speluncha de la soa penitentia. Summario da confesarsi per docti e simplici nel quale si distingue cum gran doctrina: li peccati mortali da li veniali. Vita de sancta Maria Magdalena: cum molte dolce historie, incognite nele parte italice. Tractado del Nascere Vivere et Morire. De la Regina del Cielo: et de tute le cose pertinente a quella, secondo la doctrina di Alberto magno: et del sancto Doctore come appare in la Tavola infra posita.* Bologna: Benedetto di Ettore, 1501. Note: Despite the indications on the title page, this edition does not contain the *Vita* and

the last two titles (*Tractado del Nascere, De la Regina del Cielo*) do not refer to separate tracts but to parts of the *Scala del sancto amore*. Further edition: Milan, 1519.

15. *Silvestri Prieratis. Tractatulus, quid a diabolo sciscitari et qualiter, maligno spiritus, possit quisque expellere de obsessis*. Bologna: Caligula de' Bazalieri, 1502. Further edition: Bologna, 1573.

16. *Aurea Rosa Idest preclarissima expositio super evangelia totius anni de tempore et de sanctis tum secundum Ordinem predicatorum quam secundum Curia continens Flores et Rosas omnium expositionum Sanctorum doctorum Antiq. Preclarissimi et excellentissimi Sacre Theologie Doctoris Magistri Silvestri de Prierio pedemontani Sacri Ordinis Fratrum predicatorum de observantia*. Bologna: Benedetto di Ettore, 1503. Further editions: Hagenau, 1508; Bologna, 1510; Hagenau, 1510, 1516; Lyon, 1516; Milan, 1519; Lyon, 1521; Bologna, 1524; Venice, 1524; Lyon, 1524, 1528; Bologna, 1534; Lyon, 1535, 1551; Venice, 1569, 1573, 1582, 1599.

17. *Libellus de sublevatione morentium: in quo multa continentur persuasoria et exhortatoria de fide ac spe nec non passio Domini sm Matheum et Iohannem: insuper et multe orationes valde pulchre super infirmis ac morientibus recitande: maxime quibus anima deo commendatur*. Brescia: Angelo Britannico, 1509.

18. *Reverendi Patris Silvestri de prierio Sacre Theologie Doctoris eximii: Vicarii generalis congregationis utriusque Lombardie ordinis predicatorum de observantia: Tractatus de expositione misse: seu de Immolatione spiritalis agni et sacrificio nove legis ad Reverendissimum Dominum Ludovicum de Ambasia Cardinalem Albiensem*. Milan: Gotardo da Ponte, 1509.

19. *La sacra hystoria de sancta Agnese de Montepoliciano*. Bologna: Girolamo Pelati, 1514.

20. *Clarissimi sacre Theologie omniumque bonarum artium professoris Reverendi patris fratris Silvestri De Prierio, congregationis Lombardie Sacri ordinis predicatorum in spheram ac Theoricas preclarissima Commentaria*. Milan: Gotardo da Ponte, 1514. Further editions: Paris 1515, 1525 (only *In Theoricas*).

21. *Reverendi P. fratris Silvestri de Prierio almi predicatorum ordi. ac sacrae theologiae professoris. Malleus in falsas assumptiones Scoti c. divum Thomam in primo sententiarum*. Bologna: Benedetto di Ettore, 1514.

22. *Summa summarum: que Silvestrina dicitur*. Bologna: Benedetto di Ettore, 1514–15. Further editions: Strasbourg, 1518; Hagenau, 1519; Lyon, 1519, 1520, 1524, 1528, 1533, 1544, 1546, 1551, 1553, 1554, 1555, 1562; Venice, 1569; Antwerp, 1569; Lyon, 1572; Antwerp, 1578, 1579, 1581; Venice, 1581; Lyon, 1585; Venice, 1587, 1593; Lyon, 1593, 1594; Venice, 1598, 1601.

23. *Eximii sacrae Theologiae doctoris R.P.F. Silvestri de Prierio Ordi. Praedicato. Quadragesimale aureum*. Venice: Lazaro dei Soardi, 1515.

24. *R. p. fratris Silvestri Prieratis ordinis predicatorum: et sacre Theologie professoris celeberrimi: sacrique palatii apostolici magistri: in presumptuosas Martini Luther conclusiones de potestate pape dialogus*. Note: This first edition gives no indication as to place, typographer and date. But it is evident that it should be Rome: Iacopo Mazzochio, 1518, since the ornamental design of its title page is identical with that of other works published by Mazzochio at this time. For further editions see Fabisch and Iserloh, *Dokumente*, 1:45–46, who also supply a modern edition, 52–107.

25. *Replica fratris Silvestri prieriatis: Magistri sacri Palatii apostolici: ad Fratrem Martinum*

luther: ordinis heremitarum. Note: This first edition gives no indication as to place, typographer, and date. The highly decorated title page suggests Rome. For further editions see Fabisch and Iserloh, *Dokumente,* 1:109–10, who also supply a modern edition, 116–28.

26. *Conflati ex angelico doctore S. Thoma. Primum volumen.* Perugia: Girolamo di Francesco Cartolario, 1519.

27. *Silvestri Prieratis Epithoma responsionis ad Lutherum.* Perugia: Girolamo di Francesco Cartolario, 1519. For further editions see Fabisch and Iserloh, *Dokumente,* 1:135–36, who also supply a modern edition, 138–87.

28. *Errata et argumenta Martini Luteris recitata, detecta, repulsa et copiosissime trita: per fratrem Silvestrum Prieriatem Magistrum Sacri Palatii.* Rome: Antonio Blado, 1520. For further editions see Fabisch and Iserloh, *Dokumente,* 1:136–37.

29. *Reveren. Patris Fratris Silvestri prieratis Or. Pre. ac Theologiae Professoris celeberrimi sacrique Palatii Apostolici Magistri, dignissimi de strigimagarum, demonumque mirandis libri tres.* Rome: Antonio Blado, 1521. Further edition: Rome, 1575.

30. *Brevissima practica: qua et sacerdotes audire et peccatores confiteri docentur: gratia reformationis, latine et vulgariter per magistrum sacri palatii edita.* Note: This edition gives no indication as to place, date, and typographer. Silvestro's dedication to Clement VII makes it likely that it is to be dated late 1523 or early 1524.

NOTES

Abbreviations

AFP	*Archivum Fratrum Praedicatorum* (Rome, 1930–)
AGOP	Archivio Generale Domenicano, Rome
AHP	*Archivum Historiae Pontificiae* (Rome, 1963–)
AOP	*Analecta Sacri Ordinis Praedicatorum* (Rome, 1893–)
ASDB	Archivio San Domenico, Bologna
ASM	Archivio di Stato, Mantua
ASMCG	Archivio Santa Maria di Castello, Genoa
ASV	Archivio di Stato, Venice
BAV	Biblioteca Apostolica Vaticana, Vatican City
BOP	*Bullarium Ordinis Praedicatorum*, 1–8 (Rome, 1729–40)
CC	*Corpus Catholicorum* (Münster, 1919–)
MOPH	*Monumenta Ordinis Fratrum Praedicatorum Historica* (Rome, 1896–)
ZKG	*Zeitschrift für Kirchengeschichte* (Stuttgart, 1877–)

I. Friar Preacher

1. "Annum agens in mundo quidem sexagesimum. In vita autem regulari sancte congregationis Lombardie quadragesimum quintum." *Conflatum*, f. VI*v.* All references are to the first editions of Silvestro's works unless otherwise noted. For full titles and editions of his works see Appendix: Works by Silvestro da Prierio.

2. "Ego autem qui minimus sum inter scriptores ordinis mei, non modo quando iam annum 60m ago." *Conflatum*, f. 171*r.*

3. "Ille primus gravi passu gradiens cogitabundus SILVESTER ex oppido Prierio Italiae est, vir praeclarissimis dotibus ornatus. Qui patriam veluti Aristoteles Stagiram illustravit sua doctrina, et virtutum praeeminentia." Leandro Alberti, *De viris illustribus Ordinis Praedicatorum* (Bologna, 1517), f. 140*r.*

4. "Ad beatissimum, item et vere optimum Dominum nostrum D. Leonem X pontificem max. Fratris Silvestri Mazolini Prieriatis ordi. predicatorum, sacri palatii apostolici magistri." *Conflatum*, f. II*r.*

5. "De iuridica et irrefragabili veritate Romane ecclesie, Romanique pontificis, per eximium sacrarum litterarum professorem, fratrem Silvestrum Mazolinum Prieriatem or. pred. vite regularis, magistrum sacri palatii apostolici." *Errata et argumenta*, f. I*r.*

6. See F. Michalski, *De Silvestri Prieriatis Ord. Praed. Magistri Sacri Palatii (MCCCCLVI–MDXXIII) Vita et Scriptis* (Münster, 1892), 8.

7. G. B. Melloni, *Atti, o memorie degli uomini illustri in santità nati, o morti in Bologna. Della classe di quei, che da tempo immemorabile sembrano aver culto pubblico e titolo di beati, o di santi con tolleranza della chiesa* (Bologna, 1780), 3:226–27.

See also G. Zarri, *Le sante vive: profezie di corte e devozione femminile tra '400 e '500* (Turin, 1990), 154, 166, 183.

8. On Aurelio Mazzolini see: AOP 1 (1883–84): 141; *Acta Capitulorum Generalium O.P., IV, ab anno 1501 usque ad annum 1553,* MOPH, vol. 9, ed. B. M. Reichert (Rome, 1900), 235, 279, 285; A. Vigna, *I Domenicani illustri del convento di Santa Maria di Castello in Genova* (Genoa, 1886), 115, 175, 187; A. Vigna, *Monumenti storici del convento di Santa Maria di Castello in Genova* (Genoa, 1888), 1:166; C. Piana, "La Facoltà teologica dell'Università di Bologna nella prima metà del Cinquecento," *Archivum Franciscanum Historicum* 62 (1969): 243–45; C. Piana and C. Cenci, *Promozioni agli ordini sacri a Bologna e alle dignità ecclesiastiche nel Veneto nei secoli XIV–XV* (Florence and Quaracchi, 1968), 245.

9. Vigna, *Monumenti,* 1:166; Piana, "La Facoltà," 210.

10. "Ad Asti nel 1532, durante una predica che il Mainardi sosteneva in disputa con il P. Domenicano Silvestro da Priero, il Vescovo riconobbe ambedue caduti in proposizioni ereticali." M. F. Mellano, *La Controriforma nella Diocesi di Mondovì* (Turin, 1955), 39.

11. "Is enim in adolescentia togam praedicatorum sumpsit." Alberti, *De viris,* f. 140r.

12. "Annum agens in mundo quidem sexagesimum. In vita autem regulari sancte congregationis Lombardie quadragesimum quintum." *Conflatum,* f. VIv. "annos iam sex supra XL religione sancta percurrens." *Conflatum,* f. IIr.

13. "quadragintaseptem annos et eo amplius in vita regulari virilitate tenui." *Replica,* 126. I cite the edition in P. Fabisch and E. Iserloh, *Dokumente zur Causa Lutheri (1517–1521). 1 Teil: Das Gutachten des Prierias und weitere Schriften gegen Luthers Ablassthesen (1517–1518)* (Münster, 1988), 116–28 (CC, 41).

14. For an outline of the history of the Congregation of Lombardy see: R. Creytens and A. D'Amato, "Les Actes Capitulaires de la Congrégation de Lombardie (1482–1531)," AFP 31 (1961): 213–306; R. Creytens, "Les Vicaires Généraux de la Congrégation Dominicaine de Lombardie," AFP 32 (1962): 211–84.

15. "Item monentur iidem presidentes quod in conventibus suis cum effectu provideant quod in ipsis conventibus sint carceres et compedes ad emendandos qui postposito Dei timore et honore religionis graviora committunt scandala, et si nullatenus haberi possunt carceres, fiat omnino cippus, qui in aliquo honesto loco teneri possit, et compedes simul habeantur." Creytens and D'Amato, "Les Actes," 254–55; "Item quod presidentes conventuum provideant quod in suis conventibus habeantur carceres cum bonis clavibus et seris cum rebus aliis necessariis ad coherendos delinquentes, pertinaces, rebelles et inobedientes." Ibid., 268.

16. A. Mortier, *Histoire des maîtres généraux de l'ordre des frères prêcheurs,* vols. 1–8 (Paris, 1907–11).

17. *B. Raymundi Capuani XXIII magistri generalis ordinis Praedicatorum opuscula et litterae* (Rome, 1899), 55.

18. See the discussion of this issue in S. Tugwell, "La Spiritualità Domenicana," *Compendio di Teologia Spirituale* (Rome, 1992), 334–67.

19. See: R. Creytens, "Raphaël de Pornassio (+1467). Vie et oeuvres," AFP 49 (1979): 145–92; "Raphaël de Pornassio (+1467). Vie et oeuvres. II. Les écrits relatifs à l'histoire dominicaine," AFP 50 (1980): 117–66.

20. J. Quétif and J. Échard, *Scriptores Ordinis Praedicatorum*, 2 vols. (Paris, 1719–21), 2:14.

21. Mortier, *Histoire*, 5:163.

22. "Thomas de Vio Cajetanus, de Provincia Regni . . . Qui et majorum operam in reformando Ordine nonnunquam risit . . . " S. Olmeda, *Chronica Ordinis Praedicatorum* (Rome, 1936), 188.

23. "Fratri Thome de Gaeta magistro sub excommunicationis pena mandatur ut fratri Bernardo de Gaeta solvat ducatos 7 vel cum eo componat in termino 3 menssium etc. Die 19 Dec. [1495] Bononie." AGOP IV, 11, MS *Registrum litterarum et actorum fr. Joachini Turriani mag. O.P. pro annis 1494–96*, f. 82v.

24. "Fratri Johanni de Vio, Caietano, conceditur camera constructa per Reverendissimum Magistrum Ordinis in Conventu S. Dominici de Caieta. 20 Jun. [1508] Romae." *Registrum Litterarum Fr. Thomae de Vio Caietani O.P. Magistri Ordinis 1508–1513*, MOPH, vol. 17, ed. A. De Meyer (Rome, 1935), 153.

25. R. Ridolfi, *Vita di Girolamo Savonarola* (Rome, 1981), 12.

26. "adolescens XV annorum facto Praedicatorum ordini nomen dedit Genuae in conventu S. Mariae de Castello, si Rovetta fides." Quétif and Échard, *Scriptores*, 2:55.

27. "anno a reparatione orbis millesimo quingentesimo vigesimo tertio floruit in Provincia Lombardiae Fr. Silvester de Prierio Pedemontanus Conventus Sancta Mariae de Castello Ianuensis alumnus." A. Rovetta da Brescia, *Bibliotheca Chronologica Provinciae Lombardiae Ordinis Praedicatorum* (Bologna, 1691), 105.

28. "Fr. Silvester Mazzolinus de Prierio. Receptus fuit Bononiae, et postea receptus in filium huius conventus, de consensu filiorum conventus et auctoritate rev.mi magistri ordinis, patris fratris Thomae de Vio, Caietani. Iste fuit magister in theologia valde doctus, et regens Bononiae, et prior in multis conventibus, nec non vicarius generalis, et multa scripsit. Obiit Romae, existens magister sacri palatii." Vigna, *Monumenti*, 1:111.

29. "In Dei filio sibi carissimis, reverendo sac. theol. professori fr. Silvestri de Prierio, sacri palatii apostolici magistro, et fratribus Aurelio et Silvestro de Prierio, conventus s. Dominici de Bononia, Ordinis pred., fr. Thomas de Vio, Caietanus, s. theol. professor ac totius Ord. prefati Generalis magister et servus salutem . . . Quoniam conventus S. Marie de Castello de Genua petivit vos in filios nativos, ex vestris conventibus nativis, ad eum transferri, ed id ipsum vos desideratis, volens illius conventus petitioni et vestro desiderio facere satis, per presentes ex vestris conventibus nativis transfero ad dictum conventum genuensem S. Marie de Castello, et illius vos filios efficio, ac si in et pro eo professionem emisissetis. In cuius fidem et robur, presentes sigillo officii mei feci muniri. Romae, die quinta martii MDXVI assumptionis mee anno VIII." ASMCG, MS *MCCCCLIX Liber conciliorum conventus Januensis Sancte videlicet Marie de Castillo*, f. 26r.

30. "Sunt iam anni 30 vel circa, quo tempore Ferraria acriter impugnabatur a Venetis, quod infirmatus apud Mantuam tam graviter, ut mors mea nunciaretur, deinde remansi cum febricula quam credo per 15 menses portavi tandem tisi adiudicatus, Saonam missus sum, ubi religionis sancte habitum quasi in regione vicina propriae suscepi, pro aeris proprii remedio." *Quadragesimale aureum*, f. 15r.

31. "In civitate Albiganensi temporibus meis forte circa annos domini 1470 res famosa accidit, cuius tota civitas testis fuit, et cuius substantia est licet non plene particulariter omnia recolam. Quidam Nicolaus Capellus usurarius famosus se diabolo dederat . . . Haec est rei substantia, quam quum novitius essem praedicavit Saone frater Bartholomeus Cremorinus et mihi narravit frater Hieronymus de Albingana connovitius meus qui adhuc vivit, et tunc fuit presens Albinganae." *Quadragesimale aureum*, ff. 41*v*–42*r*.

32. "Magister Silvester de Prierio transfertur a conventu Saonensi ad conventum S. Eustorgii de Mediolano et illius fit filius nativus ad suam petitionem. Litterae non valeant aliquid, nisi quando ipse voluerit. 5 Dec. [1510] Romae." MOPH, 17:267.

33. "Rev. P. Mag. Sacri Palatii fr. Silvestro de Prierio quantum ex Ordinis pendet auctoritate conceditur quod pecuniae suae, quae in S. Giorgio Ianuae positae sunt aut ponentur, ibi sint et inde non removeantur sine assensu vicarii congregationis pro tempore et dicti magistri; proventus est plena dispositio capitalis, dum exemptus ab Ordine fuerit, sibi attineat; si in ordine residebit, illi conventui attineat in quo morabitur; post mortem vero medietatem capitalis conventus S. Mariae de Castello Ianuensis habeat, quartam partem Conventus Saonensis et aliam quartam conventus in quo decesserit; si vero in conventu eodem Ianuensi vel extra omnem conventum Ordinis decesserit, conventus praedictus Ianuensis dictam quartam etiam habebit. Item sibi conceditur facultas disponendi in vita donando et in morte relinquendo quibus placuerit quaedam opera sua non impressa manu sua conscripta." *Magistrorum ac Procuratorum Generalium O.P. Registra Litterarum Minora (1469–1523)*, MOPH, vol. 21, ed. G. Meersseman–D. Planzer (Rome, 1947), 70.

34. AOP 1 (1893): 140–45.

35. "Silvester de Prierio receptus fuit Bononie et postea receptus in filium huius conventus, de consensu filiorum conventus et auctoritate Rmi. M. ordinis p. f. Thomae de Vio Gaietani." ASMCG, Cassetta 8 Codici: MS *Codice Carbone*, n. 376.

36. "F. Silvester de Prierio r[eceptus] f[uit] Bononie postea factus est filius huius conventus de licentia supra dicti generalis et consensu f. Mathio de Pontecurono vicarius generalis." ASMCG, Cassetta 8 Codici: MS *Codice Bottaro*, n. 209.

37. S. L. Forte, "Le Province Domenicane in Italia nel 1650. Conventi e religiosi. V. La *Provincia utriusque Lombardiae*." AFP 41 (1971): 440–41.

38. "Nam cum ex studiorum matre Bononia quo me disciplinarum gratia contuleram, Vincentiam remeassem, preter, quinimmo et contra omnem meum cogitatum, agrum non modo amenissimum quippe qui campester ac montuosus est, et vivacibus aquis irriguus, sed et omni pomorum ac frugum genere fertilissimum deprehendi. Civitatem vero ipsam tanta divitiarum copia, tanto morum elegantia suffertam." *Rosa aurea*, f. VI*v*. I cite the edition: Venice, 1524.

39. "forte me tua inclyta consors rogarit quod offerre debuissem lectionem, scilicet evangelicam qua sese animus qua ocium tueretur, et spiritualibus delitiis refocilatur adversus vicia fortius dunicaret. Tale profecto aliquid me facturum dum inclyta civitas Ferraria turbinibus quateretur, letali valitudine laborans, altissimo tota mente devoueram. Mee igitur sponsioni, illius vero religiose petitioni." *Rosa aurea*, f. VIII*r*–*v*.

40. "Sunt iam anni 30 vel circa, quo tempore Ferraria acriter impugnabatur a Venetis, quod infirmatus apud Mantuam tam graviter, ut mors mea nunciaretur." *Quadragesimale aureum,* f. 15*r.*

41. See R. Creytens, "L'instruction des novices dominicains à la fin du XVe siècle," AFP 22 (1952): 201–25.

42. "ad tollendum multiplicationem fratrum inutilium prohibemus ne aliquis recipiatur ad habitum clericorum nisi fuerit in grammaticalibus sufficienter instructus." Creytens and D'Amato, "Les actes," 254.

43. "Annum agens in mundo quidem sexagesimum. In vita autem regulari sancte congregationis Lombardie quadragesimum quintum. Quadragesimum vero secundum et eo amplius in doctrina angelici divique doctoris Thome Aquinatis." *Conflatum,* f. VI*v.*

44. R.-M. Louis, "Histoire du texte des Constitutions dominicaines," AFP 6 (1936): 334–50.

45. *Acta Capitulorum Generalium O.P., II, ab anno 1304 usque ad annum 1378,* MOPH, vol. 4, ed. B. M. Reichert (Rome, 1899), 12–13.

46. On the evolution and structure of the Dominican curriculum of studies see: C. Douais, *Essai sur l'organisation des études dans l'Ordre des Frères Prêcheurs au XIIIe et au XIVe siècle* (Paris and Toulouse, 1884); I. Taurisano, *L'organizzazione delle scuole domenicane nel secolo XIII* (Lucca, 1928); W. A. Hinnebusch, *The History of the Dominican Order: Intellectual and Cultural Life to 1500* (New York, 1973), 3–98; *Le scuole degli ordini mendicanti (secoli XIII–XIV),* Convegni del Centro di Studi sulla Spiritualità Medievale, XVII (Todi, 1978).

47. See L. E. Boyle, "Notes on the Education of the *Fratres communes* in the Dominican Order in the Thirteenth Century," *Xenia Medii Aevi Historiam Illustrantia Oblata Thomae Kaeppeli O.P.* (Rome, 1978), 1:249–67.

48. "ordinamus . . . nullus exponi vel habilitari possit, nisi per quatuor annos aut saltem per tres . . . in logicalibus et naturalibus studierit." *Acta Capitulorum Generalium O.P., III, ab anno 1380 usque ad annum 1498,* MOPH, vol. 8, ed. B. M. Reichert (Rome, 1900), 260.

49. The chapter of 1459 repeats the ordination of 1456. MOPH, 8:270–71.

50. See, for example, L. Gargan, *Lo studio teologico e la biblioteca dei Domenicani a Padova nel Tre e Quattrocento* (Padua, 1971), 24.

51. An example of the standard formula: "Frater . . . dispensatur ad sacerdotium in 23° anno, dummodo iudicio provincialis, cuius conscientia oneratur, sit sufficiens in grammatica et alias idoneus." MOPH, 17:88.

52. "Hortamur omnes nostri ordinis reverendos provinciales et alios presidentes, ut diligenter invigilent circa fratrum iuniorum erudicionem in moribus et sciencia; et nullus possit ordinari ad sacros ordines, nisi officium congrue dicere sciat et in grammatica sit sufficienter instructus et in via sit ad sciendum." MOPH, 8:425.

53. "Mandatur universis praesidentibus provinciarum et conventuum Italiae, ne quis ad subdiaconatum, nec subdiaconus ad diaconatum, nec diaconus ad sacerdotium, neque sacerdos ad audiendas confessiones exponantur nisi institutus in grammatica; et qui iam longo tempore fuerunt confessores, cassantur, nisi inventi fuerint in lingua vulgari et casibus conscientiae sufficienter instructi. 11 Aug. [1508] Romae." MOPH, 17:10, 76, 108, 196, 205, 233, 256, 289.

54. For example, the chapter of Vicenza 1483 ordained: "Idoneos vero receptos iuxta nostrarum seriem constitutionum studeant educare." Creytens and D'Amato, "Les actes," 254.

55. C. Piana, "Il diaconato di frà Girolamo Savonarola (Bologna, I° Marzo 1477)," *AFP* 34 (1964): 344.

56. On Pietro da Bergamo see: Quétif and Échard, *Scriptores,* 1:863–64; T. Kaeppeli, *Scriptores Ordinis Praedicatorum Medii Aevi,* 3 vols. (Rome, 1970–80), 3:219.

57. I. Colosio, "La *Tabula Aurea* di Pietro da Bergamo (+1482)," *Divus Thomas* (Piacenza), 64 (1961): 119–32.

58. *Rosa aurea,* ff. 476*v,* 498*v.*

59. "epistola illius praeclari Thomiste et viri sanctissimi magistri Petri Bergo." *Rosa aurea,* f. 506*v.*

60. *Rosa aurea,* ff. 472*r,* 502*v.*

61. *Additiones,* ff. 4*r,* 11*v,* 32*r.*

62. "Et dico quod secundum venerabilem Thomistam magistrum Pet. de Bergo. S. Tho. in II Sententiarum intendit quod alchimia, id est alchimistae non faciunt, id est non possunt facere verum aureum." *Summa silvestrina,* 38. I cite the edition Lyon, 1562.

63. "Nullus enim Thomista hactenus vidit istam contradictionem, etiam bone memorie magister Petrus Bergomas, qui in sancto Tho. quando videtur pro singulari generalia magnum acervum coacervasse contradictionum id est 1222." *Conflatum,* f. 157*v.*

64. C. Piana, *Ricerche su le Università di Bologna e di Parma nel secolo XV* (Florence and Quaracchi, 1963), 137.

65. R. Creytens, "Les écrivains dominicains dans la chronique d'Albert de Castello (1516)," *AFP* 30 (1960): 297.

66. "consilium de monte pietatis, cum essem iunior, quod principaliter fuit contra modum et formam servatam, et est Vicentie in archivis." *Conflatum,* f. 299*v.*

67. See the discussion of a letter of Domenico da Gargnano to Gianfrancesco Gonzaga (7 April 1508) in which he pleads for the extermination of the sect of the witches in Zarri. *Le sante vive,* 154, n. 221.

68. On Dominic of Flanders see: Quétif and Échard, *Scriptores,* 1:894; Kaeppeli, *Scriptores,* 1:315–18; C. Prantl, *Geschichte der Logik im Abenlande,* 4 vols. (Leipzig, 1927), 4:272; C. Zucchini, "Le librerie del convento di San Domenico a Bologna," *Memorie Domenicane* 54 (1937): 86–87; U. Schikowski, "Dominicus de Flandria O.P. (+1479). Sein Leben, seine Schriften, seine Bedeutung," *AFP* 10 (1940): 169–221; L. Mahieu, *Dominique de Flandre (XV siècle). Sa métaphysique,* Bibliothèque Thomiste 24 (Paris, 1942); C. H. Lohr, "Medieval Latin Aristotle Commentaries. Authors A-F," *Traditio* 23 (1967): 398–400; A. F. Verde, *Lo Studio Fiorentino 1473–1503. Ricerche e documenti,* 4 vols. (Florence, 1973–) 2:190; A. F. Verde, "Domenico di Flandria: Intransingente Tomista non Gradito nello Studio Fiorentino," *Memorie Domenicane,* n.s. 7 (1976): 304–21.

69. *Summa divinae philosophiae* (= *Quaestiones in XII Metaphysicorum*): Venice, 1499; Cologne, 1621; Bologna, 1622.

70. "Et si dicatur quod secundum hoc subiectum metaphysicae non erit ens com-

mune deo et creature, vel non habebit principium effectivum, dico sustinendo quod sit ens commune deo et creature." *Conflatum,* f. 5*v.*

71. "Secunda [opinio] est Alfonsi [Vargas de Toledo] hic dicentis quod omnis relatio realis in creaturis est res a suo fundamento distincta et cum eo componens. Hanc viam Capreo. et Flandren. et multi Thomistarum sequuntur." *Additiones,* f. 19*r.*

72. "Secunda autem opinio est Alphonsi . . . et hanc viam sequitur Flandren. qui de hac re ad nauseam scripsit." *Conflatum,* f. 206*r.*

73. On Paolo Barbo da Soncino see: Quétif and Échard, *Scriptores,* 1:879–80; Kaeppeli, *Scriptores,* 3:203; Prantl, *Geschichte,* 4:229; MOPH, 8:401; Piana, *Ricerche,* 9, 61, 200–202, 212, 234, 284; C. Piana, "Il suddiaconato di frà Girolamo Savonarola," *Rinascimento,* 2d ser., 6 (1966): 293; Piana and Cenci, *Promozioni,* 172, 174, 176; C. H. Lohr, "Medieval Latin Aristotle Commentaries. Authors N-R.," *Traditio* 28 (1972): 321.

74. *Quaestiones in XII Metaphysicorum:* Venice, 1496, 1498, 1502, 1505, 1576; Lyon, 1579; Venice, 1580; Ursellis, 1622; Cologne, 1622.

75. "Nota quod concertatio est inter philosophelos quosdam, an probare deum esse pertinet ad philosophiam naturalem vel primam, idest metaphysicam, que vana est, quia constat quod in utraque demonstratur, sed in physica sub ratione primi moventis et per medium naturale, in metaphysica autem sub ratione primi entis vel prime partis entis et per medium metaphysicum, quod non incovenit. Metaphysicus tamen necessario utitur quibusdam probatis in physica vel ad eam pertinentibus puta motu, per quem primo cognoscimus aliquid causare aliud, utitur etiam medio physico tanquam extraneo, non autem physica facit econverso, quia ipsa est prior quoad nos et metaphysica posterior." *Conflatum,* ff. 22*v–*23*r.*

76. On Savonarola's student years in Bologna (1475–79 and 1487–88) see: R. Ridolfi, *Studi Savonaroliani* (Florence, 1935), 55–59; Ridolfi, *Vita,* 17, 37–38; Piana, *Ricerche,* 270; Piana, "Il diaconato," 343–48; Piana, "Il suddiaconato," 287–94; Piana and Cenci, *Promozioni,* 177–78.

77. "Nam cum ex studiorum matre Bononia quo me disciplinarum gratia contuleram, Vicentiam remeassem." *Rosa aurea,* f. VI*v.*

78. Forte, "Le Provincie," 452–54.

79. *Rosa aurea,* tractatus 3, casus 59.

80. See n. 66 above.

81. "Sunt iam anni 30 vel circa quo tempore Ferraria acriter impugnabatur a Venetis, quod infirmatus apud Mantuam." *Quadragesimale aureum,* f. 15*r.*

82. Forte, "Le Provincie," 394–98.

83. "Sane commentariola in spheram. Item et in theoricas planetarum, edictionum nostrarum flores et primitias, iam triginta et duobus annis mecum supressa, nunc primo librariis formanda permisi." *In spheram,* f. 2*v.*

84. "Quapropter quia mortem me insequi video, quia insuper nonnulli me adhuc in humanis agente, labores nostros sibi ascribere non verentur, quia demum in his que divina bonitate conscripsi, quedam declaranda sunt, locubrationum nostrarum breve monimentum efficere cogor. Et in primis quidem commentaria in spheram edidi." *Conflatum,* f. 299*v.*

85. "Incipit expositio eruditissimi patris, fratris Silvestri de Prierio, ordinis praedica-

torum sacre theologie professoris, super tractatum de sphera magistri Ioannis de Sacro Busto pro novitiis astronomie." *In spheram,* f. 3*r.*

86. "E secondo che io ho dechiarato in una opereta a lo illustrissimo marchese Mantoano et valoroso cavaliero Francesco Gonzaga, si poe tenire che in terra sia ancora del vero sanguine nutrimentale de Christo, sparso il giorno della passione." *Vita,* f. cV*v.*

87. *Rosa aurea,* tractatus 3, q. 31.

88. "tandem tisi adiudicatus, Saonam missus sum." *Quadragesimale aureum,* f. 15*r.*

89. "Tandem conventui compassus, indigenti predicatoribus villarum, vovi deo, et beatae virgini si possem ea quadragesima predicare, quotidie ieiunare, et confessiones audire, quod uno anno rosarium dicerem, et illud cum gratia recepta, ubique predicarem. Et sic cum febre quidem exivi ad predicandum, sed statim evanuit, et in pauperibus villis 8 vel decem predicavi, per lutum et nives circuiens, et vix leguminibus pastus, domum redii in paschate pinguis, licet vix possem credere me liberatum. Et abinde fui ad labores fortior, et 30 iam ferme annis fui sanus, ita ut pene dicere possim me non decubuisse, quum tamen antea fuerim aegrotativus." *Quadragesimale aureum,* f. 15*r.*

90. "Magnifica contessa e matre in Christo salvatore charissima [Adriana da Thiene], il glorioso Idio per sua infinita pietade et intercessione de la focata Maria Magdalena vi consoli. Come a la magnificentia vostra e chiaro, io za molti giorni composi la rosa aurea, zoe la expositione de li sancti evangeli per la consolatione e laude de la magnificentia del conte vostro consorte e de tuta la fameglia Thienesa, la quale rosa presto se comunicara a li sancti predicatori e tutti li amatori del sacro evangelio." *Vita,* f. aI*r.*

91. "Ego autem qui minimus sum inter scriptores ordinis mei, non modo quia iam annum 60m ago, sed iam per annos fere 30 ex lumine philosophie in hac questione nullum penitus habeo scrupulum, effugatis omnibus tenebris per ea que scripsi in aurea rosa in die s. trinitatis." *Conflatum,* f. 171*r.*

II. Regent Master

1. *Privilegia summorum pontificum, gratiae summorum pontificum, gratiae magistrorum generalium, concesse congregationi Lombardie ordinis predicatorum* (Milan, 1507), f. 44*v.*

2. "Item quod de cetero nullus fiat studens in conventu Bononiensi nisi expositus fuerit a rev.do vicario et deputatis patribus in congregatione. Et ne conventus ipse Bononiensis supra vires suas studentium numerositate gravetur, et nihilominus ad profectum litterarum ydones pateat aditus, ordinamus quod dictus conventus Bononiensis ultra numerum octagenarium non gravetur." Creytens and D'Amato, "Les actes," 257.

3. On the evolution and structure of the curriculum of studies and lecturing duties required of Dominicans proceeding to higher degrees up to the beginning of the sixteenth century, see chap. 1, n. 46.

4. "Habebat tunc congregatio praedicta inter alia bona hoc bonum ne fierent in ea magistri nisi pro necessitate Studii Bononiensis." Bologna, Biblioteca Univer-

sitaria: MS 1999 G. Borselli, *Chronica magistrorum generalium ordinis Praedicatorum*, f. 230r.

5. On Iavelli see my entry in *Dict. d'Hist. et de Géog. Eccl.*, 25:563–66, and the corrections made to it in "Some Renaissance Thomist Divisions of Analogy," *Angelicum* 70 (1993): 114, n. 47.

6. On Francesco Silvestri see G. Sestili, "Francesco Silvestri," *Gli scienziati italiani*, vol. 1 (Rome, 1921), 128–37.

7. On the studium generale in Pavia see: M. P. Andreolli Panzarasa, "Il convento di San Tommaso, la comunità domenicana e l'Università dal Tre al Cinquecento," *Annali di storia Pavese* 18–19 (1989): 29–47; S. Negruzzo, *Theologiam discere et docere. La facoltà teologica di Pavia nel XVI secolo* (Bologna, 1995). The studia of Milan and Turin have not yet received any scholarly attention.

8. On the studium generale in Padua see L. Gargan, *Lo studio teologico.* The studia of Ferrara and Venice have not yet received any scholarly attention.

9. G. Di Napoli, *Giovanni Pico della Mirandola* (Rome, 1965), 237, 255, 513.

10. Cajetan studied as a *studens formalis* for a single year (1491–92), served as master of studies for one year (1492–93), and as bachelor of the *Sentences* for a single year (1493–94). See L. Gargan, *Lo studio teologico*, 156–57.

11. BOP, 2:442.

12. Cajetan explicitly acknowledges his long-standing indebtedness to Carafa in the dedicatory letter in the *Commentaria in Porphyrii Isagogen ad Praedicamenta Aristotelis* (1506), ed. I. M. Marega (Rome, 1934), lxxxii. On Carafa's constant, intrusive exercise of his prerogatives as cardinal protector (1478–1511), especially with regard to academic promotions, see S. L. Forte, *The Cardinal Protector of the Dominican Order* (Rome, 1959), 24–29.

13. On Giovanni Rafanelli, see my "Giovanni Rafanelli da Ferrara O.P. (d.1515): Inquisitor of Ferrara and Master of the Sacred Palace," forthcoming in AFP 67 (1997).

14. E. Menegazzo, "Francesco Colonna baccelliere nello Studio Teologico Padovano di S. Agostino (1473–74)," *Italia Medioevale e Umanistica* 9 (1966): 441–52.

15. M. T. Casella and G. Pozzi, *Francesco Colonna. Biografia e Opere* (Padua, 1959), 1:25–30.

16. "Ordinamus, quod magistri in theologia per bullas aut brevia apostolica sine licencia et favore magistri reverendissimi nostri ordinis vel capitulorum generalium promoti et indocti nullis libertatibus, exempcionibus, graciis, privilegiis eisdem ab ordine concessis gaudere debeant, sed solum pro simplicibus conventualibus habeantur." MOPH, 8:418.

17. On the evolution of the juridical status of the degree of Master of Theology in the Dominican Order see M. Canal, "De gradu Magisterii in S. Theologia apud Fratres Praedicatores. Disquisitio historica," AOP 39 (1931): 101–7, 158–69, 225–33, 405–12.

18. "congregacio Lombardiae, que super omnes alias doctrina et morum viteque sanctimonia ac conventuum multitudine preeminet." *Acta* of the general chapter held in Milan 1505, MOPH, 9:59.

19. For example: "Frater Michael de Ast assignatur baccalaureus ordinarius in conventu Sancti Thomae de Papia ad legendum sententias pro forma et gradu,

dummodo examinatus per magistrum Georgium de Casali vel magistrum Hieronymum de Viglevano iudicio illius in scriptis sit sufficiens. In casu sufficientiae mandatur regenti et aliis illius studii, ut eum recipiant, et ipsi, ut sententias legat diligenter etc. 9 Aug. [1511] Romae." MOPH, 17:268; "Frater Philippus de Ungaria instituitur baccalaureus extrardinarius in conventu S. Dominici de Ferraria, si per examinationem magistri Eustachii de Bononia fuerit repertus sufficiens. 9 Jul. [1509] Romae." MOPH, 17:217.

20. "Ego fr. Silvester de Prierio . . . receptus fuerat in studentem 9 Augusti 1487." Piana, *Ricerche,* 270.

21. Piana, *Ricerche,* 270.

22. See chap. 1, n. 76.

23. Ridolfi, *Vita,* 88–92.

24. "Fr. Thomas de Vio de Caieta assignatur Bononiae. Caietae 8 Apr. 1485." MOPH, 21:47.

25. "Fr. Thomas de Vio de Gaieta assignatur studens artium Bononiae . . . Romae 18 Junii 1488." AGOP IV, 9, MS *Registrum litterarum et actorum fr. Joachini Turriani mag. O.P. pro annis 1487–91,* f. 98*v.*

26. "Fr. Thomas de Vio potest ire ad provinciam et conventum suum Gaietanum, ibique morari et stare quousque plenam recuperaverit sanitatem. Datum Romae 4 Decembris 1488." AGOP IV, 9, MS *Registrum litterarum . . . Turriani,* f. 195*v.*

27. For a reconstruction of the young Cajetan's academic career see my "Valentino da Camerino O.P. (1438–1515): Teacher and Critic of Cajetan," *Traditio* 49 (1994): 287–316.

28. "Ego fr. Silvester de Prierio factus fui magister studentium 1489, regente mag. fr. Angelo de Verona, existente baccalareo fr. Ioanne de Tabia. Coepi autem officium meum Ia die iulii." Piana, *Ricerche,* 270.

29. On the office of master of studies (*magister studii, magister studentium*), see R. Creytens, "Il registro dei maestri degli studenti dello studio domenicano di Bologna (1576–1604)," AFP 46 (1976): 25–114.

30. "Ad fratrem Angelum de Verona sacre pagine professorem celeberrimum . . . Cum studiorum matrem Bononiam sub te mi pater Angele fauste et quam gloriose regente sacrarum litterarum gratia petivissem, forte adolescentibus dialectice rudimenta tradebam." *Compendium dialectice,* f. aIIr.

31. "Dilectis et eruditissimis discipulis suis in studiorum matre Bononia. Frater Silvester de Prierio salutem. Cum diu a vobis desideratus tandem advenissem fratres optimi et in hoc almo gimnasio Bononiensi sacras lectiones adhuc aggredi non liceret quod formatus bachalarius cursorque deesset." *Apologia,* f. aIr.

32. On Giovanni Cagnazzo da Taggia see Quétif and Échard, *Scriptores,* 2:47.

33. "In conventu Bononiensi . . . assignamus . . . ad legendum bibliam pro primo et secundo anno fr. Silvestrum de Prierio." MOPH, 8:401–2. It might be useful to point out that in such academic assignments by general chapters the expressions "pro primo, secundo, tertio, quarto anno" do not mean, as they are erroneously taken to do by many authors, for first, second, third, fourth year students. They mean, rather, for the first, second, third, fourth academic years following the general chapter. In this particular case, since the chapter was held in May 1491, the expressions mean: for the academic years 1491–92, 1492–93, 1493–94, 1494–95.

34. "Eo tempore, quo Cardinalis sancti Petri ad vincula, qui et deinde Julius II, a facie Alexandri Borgiae fugiebat, Saona per Gallos impugnata, sed non expugnata est, Mauro et Venetis suffragantibus, ego Saonam predicationis gratia missus, tempore carnisprivii in Fraschea Terdonam et Serravallem inter peditum ducem quendam Marzochaeum nomine offendi, cum quo ex burgo, quem fornariorum dicunt, Genuam, relictis copiis, adivi, cuius mula cum pedi pedem imposuisset, se adeo vulneravit, ut singulis passibus singulas sanguinis guttas effunderet. Super quo cum plurimum anxiaretur, quod pulchra, et non sua mula esset, rogavit an eam signare noscerem. Respondi, me eam in nomine sanctae Trinitatis signaturum, et confidere quod ei bene esset. Acquievit signo Dei, cum diabolicum habere nequiret. Signata per me mula signo crucis in nomine sanctae Trinitatis, statim sanguis stetit, et sic iuga superantes ad oppidum, qui Punctus Decimus dicitur, devenimus, illudque paululum excessimus. Cumque alius dux peditum nobis obviasset, ut mulam signaret petivit, qui an aliquis signasset, inquisivit, et audito quod ego signassem, suspirans, o diabole, inquit, quasi scilicet ipse vir, ut erat diaboli, nihil posset, ubi Dei servus manum admovisset. Signavit tamen et abinde usque Genuam sanguis, qui steterat, semper refluxit. Ecce coram Deo quia non mentior." *De strigimagarum daemonumque mirandis*, 206. I cite the edition: Rome, 1575.

35. "E che tutte le sopradicte cose siano vere, il confermo per quello che io ho veduto stando nel reame de Napoli del mille quattrocento nonanta quattro e nonanta e cinque viti in alcuni monasterii di lordine di frati predicatori ogni giorno farsi memoria doe volte de la seraphina Magdalena, liquali monasterii credo siano dodice salvo il vero." *Vita*, f. cV r.

36. A. D'Amato, "Sull'introduzione della riforma domenicana nel Napolitano per opera della Congregazione Lombarda (1489–1501)," AFP 26 (1956): 249–75.

37. See n. 35 above.

38. "Cum in Partenope iunior agerem." *Errata et argumenta*, f. CCLVII v.

39. See the bull of Alexander VI (23 January 1494) in BOP, 4:105.

40. "Egregium vel potius divinum opus in Iohannem Capreolum Tholosanum sacri predicatorum ordinis. A fratre Silvestro Prieriano eiusdem ordinis. Sacre theologie baccalario." *Compendium Capreoli*, f. 1r.

41. "Habetis sacre pagine studiosissimi viri compendium ac prope divinum opus velut purissimum simulacrum ab egregio ab nostri seculi viro celeberrimo patre Silvestro Prieriano sacre theologie baccalario eruditissimo." *Compendium Capreoli*, f. bb4r.

42. AGOP IV, 9–13, MS *Registrum litterarum . . . Turriani*.

43. MOPH, 8:416–22.

44. Piana, *Ricerche*, 212.

45. "Excipitur etiam Aureo. ut videtur, cuius tamen scripta habere non potui." *Additiones*, f. 1r.

46. "Anno domini 1498: in festo pentecostes die secunda Iunii celebratum est capitulum generale apud Ferrariam provincie Sancti Dominici sub magistro Ioachino de Venetiis. In quo multa inchoata sunt approbata et confirmata ordinataque. . . . Septimo: Fratris Silvestri de Prierio et fratris Georgii de Casali bachaloriorum Congregationis Lombardie lecture approbate sunt, ad magisteriumque sunt licen-

tiati." AGOP XIV, 52, MS Ambrogio Taegio, *Chronicae Ampliores*, 2, ff. 241*v*–242*r*.

47. E. J. Ashworth, "The Doctrine of Exponibilia in the Fifteenth and Sixteenth Centuries," *Vivarium* 9 (1972): 155, 167, reprinted in *Studies in Post-Medieval Semantics* (London, 1985), and "The Doctrine of Supposition in the Sixteenth and Seventeenth Centuries," *Archiv fur Geschichte der Philosophie* 51 (1969): 262, 271.

48. Prantl, *Geschichte*, 4:292–93.

49. "porta tecum id est epithoma in Iohannem Capreolum pertranseo, quando quidem illud meo nomini inscribendum nolim, nec omnino opus illud proprium verum adulterinum et alienum penitus dixerim. Neque enim illud ego castigavi, ut mihi false ascribitur. Argumentum quoque magna ex parte meum non est, scilicet titulus necnon epistola ipsa insuper et cohortatio ad lectorem exulla. Et non modo mendosum, verum et sententiis depravatum est et usque adeo truncatum, ut plusquam quinque de triginta pagine desint. Quod factum crediderim ut quod aureum et clarissimum, meo originali teste, fuisset difficile, obscurum et truncatum astruatur sed forte librariis formandum integrum inviolatum et in melius commutatum restituam." *Apologia*, f. a1*r*.

50. "deinde aliud epithoma eiusdem cum additionibus opinionum et notabilium, sed per fratrem Nicolaum de Rapallo sciolum fuit depravatum, et per Carolum Darlerii calchographum adeo mendose et truncate elaboratum (cum enim certum precium esset pro quolibet volumine habiturus, notabilia nostra imprimere recusavit, asserens me ea post pacta inita edidisse) ut pro opere quod utilissimum fuisset, erubuerim." *Conflatum*, f. 299*v*.

51. "Deinde brevissimum epithoma Capreoli mei gratia tantum, quod in luce non emersit, sed apud fratrem Marianum de Florentia tenetur." *Conflatum*, f. 299*v*.

52. "Denique illud emendatum et integratum rursus formandum Alexandro Calcedonio amico tradiderim, sed eo interim rebus humanis subtracto, liber est mihi perditus, unde tertio et illud melius refectum reverendo domino Hieronymo episcopo olim Ebudensi tradidi, sed necdum luci restitutum est." *Conflatum*, f. 299*v*.

53. U. Bubenheimer, *Consonantia Theologiae et Jurisprudentiae. Andreas Bodenstein von Karlstadt als Theologe und Jurist zwischen Scholastik und Reformation* (Tübingen, 1977), 64.

54. M. Grabmann, *Mittelalterliches Geistesleben* (Munich, 1956), 3:402–3.

55. J. Eck, *Explanatio Psalmi Vigesimi (1538)* (Münster, 1928), 48 (CC, 13).

56. J. Greving, *Johann Eck als iunger Gelehrter,* Reformationsgeschichtliche Studien und Texte, 1 (Münster, 1906), 23, 45, 115.

57. J. Eck, *Defensio contra amarulentas D. Andreae Bodenstein Carolstatini invectiones (1518)* (Münster, 1919), 66 (CC, 1).

58. *Replica*, 125.

59. G. M. Löhr, *Die Domenikaner an der Leipziger Universität,* Quellen und Forschungen, 30 (Vechta, 1934), 81.

60. "Poi del nonanta e sette, io per divotione mia et per voto andai a visitare le relique e lochi di questa ardente seraphina, a sancto Maximino." *Vita*, f. cV*r*.

61. "Cum anno domini MCCCCXCVII devotionis gratia antrum ubi penituit et sacras eius reliquias apud sanctum Maximianum visitassem." *Rosa aurea,* f. 282*r*.

62. See chap. 1, n. 90.

63. Creytens and D'Amato, "Les actes," 286.

64. A. Chastel, *Luigi D'Aragona. Un cardinale del rinascimento in viaggio per l'Europa* (Bari, 1987), 92–96.

65. "E per la parte mia piacendo a dio e a la sancta religione, ancora unaltra volta intendo visitare quelle sancte relique e sancti lochi." *Vita,* f. dVr.

66. "Non e grave viagio peroche chi vole andare per aqua andando a Pisa overo a Zenova facilmente e securamente po andare, et ilsimile e per terra da Milano andando in Asto overo a Vercelli e passando la montagna a Moncenise overo a Largentera, peroche po cavalcare per tutto sino apresso la speluncha a un tracto di mano et cum assai bona via e bone hostarie e in octo giorni se gli andaria da Milano cavalcando a piacere e in mancho." *Vita,* f. dVr.

67. "Et vogliando io de ogni cosa sapere il vero, pregai il sacristano che mi volesse mostrare il fundamento di queste cose. E lui un libro mi dette dove io lessi una cronica di questa sententia." *Vita,* f. cVv.

68. See B. Montagnes, *Marie-Madeleine et l'Ordre des Prêcheurs* (Marseille, 1984).

69. This MS has been edited by J. Sclafer, "Iohannes Gobi senior OP Liber miraculorum b. Mariae Magdalenae," AFP 63 (1993): 113–206.

70. "E benche una divota persona habbia scripto in vulgaro diffusamente di Marta e Maria e Lazaro non staro pero io di fare questo. Prima e principalmente peroche io voglio scrivere nove historie. E secundario peroche tal persona ha scripto le soe contemplatione piu presto che la vita di questi sancti. Ma io voglio scrivere il certo per certo e niuna cosa incerta per ferma." *Vita,* f. aIr.

71. "in qua multa nova de beata Maria Magdalena conscripsi, et precipue quomodo antrum petiverit, et quid ibi invenit vel egit aut passa est, de quibus quamquam ea a probis accepissem, dubitavi semper." *Conflatum,* f. 299v.

72. See A. Hufstader, "Lefèvre d'Étaples and the Magdalen," *Studies in the Renaissance* 16 (1969): 31–60.

73. G. M. Crescimbeni, *Comentari intorno alla sua Istoria della volgar poesia* (Rome, 1711), 3:214–17.

74. This point has not been noticed by Bandello scholars. See M. Bandello, *Rime,* ed. M. Danzi (Ferrara and Modena, 1989), 180–81.

75. "In studio Bononiensi damus in regentem pro primo anno fr. Iohannem de Tabia magistrum, pro secundo et tercio anno fr. Silvestrum de Prierio." MOPH, 8:431. "assignati sunt conventui Bononiensi pro regente pro primo anno Frater Ioannes de Tabia magister, pro secundo et tertio Frater Silvester." Taeggio, *Chronicae Ampliores,* vol. 2, f. 241v.

76. "Conventui Bononiensi damus in regentem pro primo anno magistrum Silvestrum de Prierio." T. Kaeppeli, "Supplementum ad Acta Capitulorum Generalium editionis B. Reichert," AFP 5 (1935): 291.

77. *Privilegia,* f. 23r.

78. F. Ehrle, *I più antichi statuti della facoltà teologica dell'Università di Bologna* (Bologna, 1932), 126.

79. See Piana, *Ricerche,* 4–22.

80. On San Domenico in Bologna see: A. D'Amato, *I Domenicani a Bologna,* 2 vols. (Bologna, 1988); V. Alce and A. D'Amato, *La Biblioteca di San Domenico in*

Bologna (Florence, 1961); M. H. Laurent, *Fabio Vigili e les Bibliothèques de Bologne au début du XVIᵉ Siècle* (Vatican City, 1943).

81. "Praefuit aliquando Bononiensi Gymnasio tanta cum laude et admiratione, ut ad ipsum audiendum, magnus scholasticorum numerus concurret. Habet enim in docendo cum claritate vocis optimum tradendi litteras modum, cum quadam festivitate, quo fit ut audientes attenti et dociles reddantur. Quod paucis concessum est." Alberti, *De viris,* f. 140*r–v.*

82. "Sub isto reverendo eximioque s. paginae doctore ego fr. Jodocus Pistoris Vomariensis O.P. conventus Wartbergensis fui studens Bononie, quo tempore presenciarum compilator, videlicet mag. Silvester de Prierio, fuit regens in prefato conventu Bononiensi. Et tunc plures postillas huic opera insertas manu mea iussus et rogatus ab eodem conscripsi, praesertim questionem de sanguine Christi, que habetur inserta in questionibus ewangeliorum in festo pasche ut formulare haberet pro. . . . Et fuit idem magister in legendo multum recens et resolutus ac in doctrina S. Thome anno vid. 1500, quo tempore fuit Jubileus sub Alexandro papa VI. Et tandem anno 1510 emi istum librum . . . ob eiusdem patris memoriam ac communem fratrum utilitatem pro libraria conv. Warberg . . . eo quod prefatus magister tempore studii plures michi exhibuit humanitates." Cited by G. M. Löhr, *Die Kapitel der Provinz Saxonia im Zeitalter der Kirchenspaltung 1513–1540* Quellen und Forschungen, 26 (Vechta, 1930), 23.

83. Piana, *Ricerche,* 270–71.

84. Piana, *Ricerche,* 216, 218–20, 222–29.

85. Piana, *Ricerche,* 229–30.

86. ASDB, MS *Liber cons. conv. Bonon.,* vol. 1 (1459–1648): f. 28v (14 July 1499); f. 29r (16 January 1500); f. 29v (17 January 1501); f. 30r. (4 October 1501).

87. "Nam si id dubitatur ex peccato obsessi, aut personae coniunctae, quae in eo puniatur evenisse, remedium primum vera confessio est, deinde exorcismi ecclesiastici, quibus et Deus me praesente nobilem matronam in civitate Bononia liberavit, quae ad instantiam cuiusdam famosae strigimagae annis tredecim arreptitia fuit; quae strigimaga Cimera dicta est, quam tandem inquisitor magister Io. de Tabia, author Tabienae Summae, qui etiam modo vivit, in cineres redegit." *De strigimagarum daemonumque mirandis,* 202.

88. Bologna, Bib. Univ.: MS 430, Floriano degli Ubaldini, *Cronaca,* f. 713v; Bologna, Bib. Com.: MS 99, Fileno della Tuata, *Cronaca della Città di Bologna,* vol. 1, f. 337v; G. Borselli, *Cronica gestorum ac factorum memorabilium civitas Bononie ab urbe condita ad a 1497* (RIS 23, 2), 166.; G. Nadi, *Diario Bolognese* (Bologna, 1866), 238.

89. Specimens of this work are very rare: W. Risse, *Bibliographia Logica* (Hildesheim, 1965), 1:23, lists copies in the library of the University of Leipzig and in the British Library, London. There are six copies in Italian libraries.

90. Silvestro's summary is based on the incunabulum, Paris, per Georgium Mitelhus, 1489.

91. "Tertium [subiective in intellectu nostro] est ipse terminus intellectionis per intellectionem productus, sicut calor ab igne producitur per calefactionem, qui dicitur species non impressa (ut prior) sed expressa sive elicita, dicitur et verbum. Secundum aliquos autem Thomistas differt realiter ab intellectione. Sed mihi videtur

quod non differat ab ea realiter, sicut res a re, sed forte gratia alicuius connotati, quia regulariter secundum scolam sancti Thomae oportet tenere quod motus et terminus productus per motum sunt realiter idem, licet differant modo significandi." *Apologia,* f. Aiir–v.

92. Th. De Vio Caietanus, *Comm. in Ia* (pub. 1507), in Th. Aquinas, *Opera Omnia,* ed. Leonina (Rome, 1886), 4:307; F. Silvestris, *Comm. in I Contra Gentiles* (pub. 1524), in Th. Aquinas, *Opera Omnia,* ed. Leonina (Rome, 1918), 13:153; C. Javellus, *Quaestiones in III De Anima* (pub. 1532) in *Opera Omnia* (Lyon, 1580), 1:695.

93. *Conflatum,* q. 27, a. 1, ff. 198r–199v.

94. Melloni, *Atti,* 3:225–26, points out that this is a summary of a previous work by Ambrogio da Soncino.

95. Rome, Bib. Vallicelliana: S. BORR. S.2.10.

96. "Magister Silvester de Prierio assignatur in regentem in conventum S. Iohannis et Pauli de Venetiis usque ad capitulum generale et praecipitur sibi ut intra decem dies iter arripiat, etc. 17 Maii [1502]." AGOP IV, 15, MS *Registrum litterarum et actorum fr. Vincentii Bandelli mag. O.P. pro annis 1501–05,* f. 44r.

97. "Conventus Sanctorum Iohannis et Pauli eximitur a iurisdictione provincialis, et datur Congregationi Lombardie et incorporatur aliis conventibus dicte congregationis, et datur auctoritas vicario generali eiusdem congregationis absolvendi priorem et alios officiales, aliosque instituendi . . . 18 Maii [1503]." AGOP IV, 15, MS *Registrum litterarum . . . Bandelli,* f. 48v.

98. ASV, Fondo SS. Giovanni e Paolo, Busta 11: MS *Liber consiliorum conv. Ss. Io. et Pauli,* vol. 1 (1450–1524), vol. 2 (1450–1545).

99. "1502 die 26 Semptebris [!] . . . In eodem consilio captum fuit per omnes balotas quod regens conventus quicunque sit ille habeat ducatos duodecim per annum hoc modo ut quolibet mense habeat unum ducatum et sit obligatus legere per totum annum teologiam et loicam, tenere circulos et disputationem publicam in festo sancte Lucie, et facere principium post Dominicam consecrationis ecclesiae nostre, nec possit vacationes inconsuetas facere, hoc est in dampnum studentium nec in quadragesima recedat de conventu sed legat more solito." *Lib. cons.,* 1, f. 32r.

100. "1502 die 3 Octobris. Congregato consilio reverendorum magistrorum et patrum determinatum fuit per maiorem partem consilii quod non fieret electio regentis eo quoniam ut prior dicebat ad r.mum generalem et provincialem spectabat talis electio, et ita captum fuit ut r.do provinciali scriberetur quod provideret vel quod daret nobis licentiam eligendi, et hoc quia magister Silvester dixerat velle ire Bononiam et postea Paduam et quod faceremus provisionem omnino." *Lib. cons.,* 1, f. 32v.

101. "Exacto profitendi in dicto Gymnasio [Bononiensi] tempore, ut Patavii profiteretur a senatu Veneto evocatur." Alberti, *De viris,* f. 140r.

102. "Quod quidem opusculum ea tempestate, qua mihi in Patavino gymnasio metaphisicem disserendam Illustrissimus Venetiarum Princeps Leonardo Lauredanus senatusque contulerat, ex praeclaris auctoribus collegi atque conflavi, ut qui defensivis armis me instructum satis putabam offensivis quoque me instruerem quamquam patribus minime placuerit ut illuc me conferrem." *Malleus,* f. aIIr.

103. G. Contarini, *Notizie storiche circa li pubblici professori nello Studio di Padova scelti dall'Ordine di San Domenico* (Venice, 1769), 152; G. Brotto and G. Zonta, *La*

Facoltà Teologica dell'Università di Padova (Padua, 1922), 202; L. Gargan, *Lo studio,* 150.

104. C. H. Lohr, *Latin Aristotle Commentaries II Renaissance Authors* (Florence, 1988), 368, indicates Silvestro as professor of metaphysics in Padua in 1501 and invokes in support of this Venice, Bib. Marciana: MS Lat. Class. 3.70 (2620). But upon examination, this codex failed to yield any apposite evidence.

105. Contarini, *Notizie,* 152–54; Brotto and Zonta, *La Facoltà,* 202; Gargan, *Lo studio,* 154–55.

106. "sed ista collegi et formavi pene repente cum mihi adeundi Patavium timor incumberet ne in tanto conflictu armis invasivis nudus astarem." *Malleus,* f. sVIIIr.

107. "Die 2 Junii 1494. S. Theologiae Magister F. Valentinus de Perusio in Patavino Gymnasio Metaphysicam agens, Principem adiit, cui se supplicem praebuit, cum electus fuisset Romanae Provinciae Visitator provincialis, petiit ut ad id munus per unum mensem obeundum, sibi concedi, quod cum substitutione alterius Magistri ad lectiones docendas, quousque redierit, obtinuit." Contarini, *Notizie,* 139.

108. Contarini, *Notizie,* 151–52.

109. "Scripsit vero clarissimus ille philosophus Plutharcus Dionisium seniorem siciliarum tyramnum cubiculum filii ingressum cum vidisset poculorum argenteorum et aureorum multitudinem exclamasse. Non es principatui aptus qui tot poculis a me acceptis neminem tibi amicum effeceris." *Malleus,* f. aIIr–v.

110. "Utrum autem duo millia annorum debeat esse tempus messie, non me intromitto, sed sufficit mihi tempus eius esse impletum, quia ipsi principio mundi usque ad presentem annum, scilicet M.cccc quo presens opus fuit castigatum computant [?] ccccc et cc et lx annos." *Rosa aurea,* f. 453v.

111. A. Serra Zanetti, *L'arte della stampa a Bologna nel primo ventennio del cinquecento* (Bologna, 1958), 287.

112. L. F. T. Hain, *Repertorium bibliographicum in quo libri omnes ab arte typographica inventa usque ad annum MD typis expressi . . . recensentur,* 4 vols. (Stuttgart and Paris, 1826–38), vol. 3, 13347; G. W. Panzer, *Annales typographici ab artis inventae origine ad annum MDXXXVI continuati,* 9 vols. (Nuremberg, 1793–1803), 1:453, 440.

113. *Rosa aurea,* f. 471r–v.

114. See: H. A. Oberman, *Forerunners of the Reformation* (New York, 1966), 265–67; J. S. Preuss, *From Shadow to Promise: Old Testament Interpretation from Augustine* (Cambridge, Mass., 1969), 133–37.

III. Prior and Vicar General

1. "praefecturam Coenobii Mediolanensis, Veronensis, Genuensis aegerat." Alberti, *De viris,* f. 140r.

2. "18°—1503–P. Silvestro de Prierio dotissimo maestro in teologia, scrisse alcune opere. Fu Maestro del Sacro Palazzo e Vicario Generale." AGOP XIV, lib. LL: MS G. Gattico, *Descrittione succinta e vera delle cose spettanti alla Chiesa e Convento di Santa Maria delle Grazie,* 89.

3. Forte, "Le Provincie," 399–402.

4. "Fr. Honophrius de Parma absolvitur a prioratu Sancte Marie Gratiarum Mediolani et confirmatur vicarius generalis congregationis Lombardiae . . . Die 22a iunii [1503] Rotomagi." AGOP IV, 15, MS *Registrum litterarum . . . Bandelli*, f. 48*v.*

5. "Fu il Padre F. Silvestro da Prierio Decim'ottavo Priore di questo convento l'anno 1503 desideroso di far anch'egli qualche cosa per sua memoria a beneficio del convento . . . per il che capitando a Milano Monsigr. Illmo Stefano Vescovo di Pariggi suo singolarissimo Padrone l'indusse a far dei suoi denari la Fonte per lavar le mani prima d'entrar in Mensa . . . e di piu a contribuir denari per far gli armari in Sagristia nella parte orientale, per il che avendo il Padre Rmo. Gle di tutto l'ordine Fra Vincenzo Bandello da Castelnuovo . . . mandato a Milano sessanta scudi d'applicarsi a tal impresa, il Sudetto Vescovo diede il denaro per supplire a tutto il rimanente della spesa per compirgli il che fu fatto dal Sudetto Priore l'anno 1504. In oltre rasetto il spazio qual restava fra il Dormitorio grande ed il claustro della Sagristia facendolo purgar da sterpi, pietre ed altre cose e ridusse in piano a guisa di prato." Gattico, *Descrittione,* 36–37.

6. Forte, "Le Province," 450–52.

7. "Sylvester de Prierio magister diffinitor Scocie." MOPH, 4:25.

8. "Anno Domini 1505, die undecima mensis maii, in festo penthecostes celebratum est capitulum generale apud Mediolanum provinciae Lombardiae in conventu Sancti Eustorgii sub magistro Vincentio de Castronovo. In quo quidem capitulo, cum multi deessent diffinitores, ipse magister ordinis, auctoritate apostolica, supplevit loco absentium alios subrogando. Inter eos qui diffinitores constituti sunt, tres fuere congregationis Lombardiae, videlicet frater Marcus de Verona, tunc vicarius generalis, pro provincia Regni Siciliae; frater Honophrius de Parma, tunc prior Bononiensis, pro provincia Anglie; frater Silvester de Prierio, magister in theologia et tunc prior Veronensis, pro provincia Scotie." Taegio, *Chronicae Ampliores,* 2, f. 244*r.*

9. MOPH, 9:25–27.

10. MOPH, 9:27–59.

11. "congregacio Lombardie, que super omnes alias doctrina et morum viteque sanctimonia ac conventuum multitudine preeminet." MOPH, 9:59. "reverendissumus magister ordinis iam multos conventus reformavit et eciam alios conventus intendit reformare quoad substantciam et eciam quoad cerimonalia." MOPH, 9:35.

12. See n. 75 below.

13. "Hoc tempore etiam claret religiosus et doctissimus vir magister Silvester de Prierio qui multa preclara edidit sue doctrine monimenta. Inter que sunt summa de casibus valde utilis et notabilis, et liber super evangelia per totum annum cum multorum casuum declaratione, quem rosam auream nuncupavit. Item impugnationes Scoti in lib. primum sententiarum. Item abbreviationes in Ioannem Capreolum, primo brevi volumine comprehensa, dehinc triplicato volumine clarius enodatas. Item logicam et tractatum de exorcismis et alia plura que adhuc in lucem non venerunt. Perseveratque hic pater et magister optimus continue in dictando, licet etiam prelationis officio laudabiliter deserviat, prestante domino nostro Iesu Christo cui est laus et honor in secula seculorum, Amen." Creytens, "Les écrivains," 298.

14. H. F. Brown, *The Venetian Printing Press* (London, 1891), 61.

15. Forte, "Le Provincie," 381–83.

16. Forte, "Le Provincie," 384–85.

17. "Placuit itidem, et nobile religiosissimumque coenobium, almi ordi. nostri prae-dicatorii, quod S. Maria de Castello inscribitur. Taceo de nonnullis patrum nostrorum, ex nobilissima totius Italie familia flisca, et in primis cum religiosissimi, tum etiam doctissimi, immortalis memoriae patris Reveren. domini protectoris nostri Nicolai a flisco, cuius modestiam vereor laudibus semper afficere, qui ita me primo aspectu traxerit, ut hunc longo tempore occulte coluerim. Quapropter cum declamationes quas memorati coenobii primatum agens, ad nobilitates vestras, quadragesimali tempore habui, postquam ex vestra, immo et mea urbe solvissem, vos plurimum et exoptasse et expetivisse didicerim, nulli rectius eas dedicandas, quam praestantissimis ingeniis vestris putarim." *Quadragesimale aureum,* f. [i] r.

18. "Generosis inclitisque amicis nobilibus, cunctis civibusque Genuatibus, frater Silvester Prierias ex ordine praedicatorum, congregationis Lombardiae, salutem et perpetuam foelicitatem." *Quadragesimale aureum,* f. [i] r. "Mihi vero itidem accidisse minime dubitarim, cui semper, et quidem non vulgariter inclita civitas Genua placuit, non modo caeca natura me agente, verum etiam ratione suadente, quippe quam regionis amenitate, mirandis structuris, immensis opibus, cum publicis tum privati, sanguinis nobilitate, honestate item et civilitate morum, fidei catholicae sinceritate, insignem et nulli civitatum Italiae in cuiusmodi cedentem, ambigat nemo." *Quadragesimale aureum,* f. [i] r.

19. *Quadragesimale aureum,* ff. 24r–25v.

20. "Ego non sum propheta, nec filius prophetae, neque volo prophetare, pono tamen unam conclusionem indubitatam, quod Ianua iam diu flagellata etiam flagellabitur in brevi." *Quadragesimale aureum,* f. 25r.

21. ASMCG, Cassetta 8 Codici: MS *Codice Carbone,* nn. 216, 218–26.

22. "Magistro Sylvestro de Prierio et Magistro Augustino de Gentilibus committitur decisio controversiam inter conventuum Tabiensem et Albiganensem de relictis per magistrum Benedictum de Pervasio. 18 Dec. [1507] Romae." MOPH, 8:250.

23. "Cum autem multis annis admodum R. P. frater Benedictus Siccha de Pornasio diocesis Albiganensis sine licentia superiorum demoratus esset extra congregationem conventuum reformatorum congregationis Lombardiae et magister sacrae theologiae effectus fuisset, et nonnulla bona acquisisset, in se reversus hoc anno 1506 obtenta gratia a R.mo. Magistro Generali ordinis nostri declaratus fuit filius huius conventus Tabiensis in quo receptus fuerat ad habitum et professionem, cui et omnia bona per eum acquisita reliquit, et fuit in eo tamquam in suo originali conventu assignatus. Ortae sunt autem nonnullae controversiae inter hunc conventum et Albiganensem, quae per superiores ordinis facile compositae fuerunt." N. Calvini, ed., *La cronaca dei Calvi* (Taggia, 1982), 222.

24. ASMCG, Cassetta ICI (1425–1528): MS *Doc. 24.*

25. Vigna, *Monumenti,* 1:112–16.

26. Prelormo, *Chronica,* AOP 1 (1893–94): 147; Creytens, "Les vicaires," 252.

27. "[A] patribus in Synodo mantuana anno domini MDVIII acta toti nostrae Congregationi praeficitur." Alberti, *De viris,* f. 140v.

28. "Magister Silvester de Prierio confirmatus declaratur vicarius generalis congregationis Lombardiae cum plenissima auctoritate. 10 Jun. [1508] Romae." MOPH, 17:251.

29. Creytens, "Les vicaires," 253.

30. "Impressum Mediolani per Alexandrum Pelizonum. Anno domini MCCCCCVII, die XII mensis Februarii." *Privilegia,* f. Fviii*v.* Vigna's suggestion is recorded in an annotation in the specimen of the *Privilegia* preserved in ASMCG, Cassetta 8.

31. *Privilegia,* ff. Ci*v*–Cv*v.*

32. BOP, 4:253.

33. "Reverendus magister Silvester de Prierio vicarius generalis impetravit a sanctissimo Domino nostro Iulio papa secundo infrascriptas gratias oraculo vivae vocis supplicante reverendissimo domino Bernardino cardinali Sanctae Crucis qui manu propria se subscripsit in cedula gratiarum impetratarum praesentibus p. fratre Hieronymo de Ianua priore Firmano et fratre Gregorio de Vugonia socio reverendi vicarii praefati, die 3a Feb. 1509. Primo quod si mandatur vicario generali congregationis nostrae per sedem apostolicam quod reformet aliquem conventum ad vitam regularem non expectata secunda iussione nihilominus possit supersedere donec consulat apostolicam sedem an sit de mente suae sanctitatis. Secundo quod prior in nostra congregatione ex causa rationabili in ieiuniis de praecepto possit licentiare fratres ad prandendum per unam horam ante consuetam horam prandii." ASMCG, Cassetta 8: MS addition to *Privilegia.*

34. ASMCG, Cassetta 8: MS *Codice Carbone,* nn. 227–29.

35. "Mediolani quarto calendas martii MDIX." *De sublevatione,* f. 2*r.*

36. "Ex edibus nostris S. Marie gratiarum. Mediolani 14 Kal. Sept. 1509." *De expositione,* f. 1*v.*

37. ASM, Archivio Gonzaga: Busta 1290.

38. ASM, Archivio Gonzaga: Busta 1368.

39. ASM, Archivio Gonzaga: Busta 1462.

40. Creytens, "Les actes," 287.

41. Creytens, "Les actes," 284–86.

42. "Reverendo vicario congregationis Lombardiae pro tempore committitur cura monasteriorum Sancti Dominici et Sancti Pauli de Pisis, cum auctoritate, quam habent provinciales super monasteria sibi subdita, salva in omnibus semper oboedientia Magistri Generalis, cum mandato, ut ipse acceptet et sorores ei obediant. In contrarium facientibus non obstantibus etc. 28 Jan. [1509] Romae." MOPH, 17:81.

43. "Vicario pro tempore congregationis Lombardiae conceditur, ut sorores Mediolanenses sibi subditas de uno monasterio ad aliud eiusdem civitatis possit transmutare et assignare, quando videbitur sibi expediens, usque ad revocationem magistri litteris valituris. 4 Feb. [1509] Romae." MOPH, 17:81.

44. "P. Mattia da Pontecurone: per ordine di P. Silvestro da Prierio Vicario Generale, ammise all'abito, velo e professione le Terziarie del Monastero di S. Lazzaro." C. Santa Maria, "Personaggi celebri di S. Maria delle Grazie," *San Domenico e i Domenicani in Milano* (Milan, 1922), 40.

45. "Magister Sylvester de Prierio instituitur Inquisitor haereticae pravitatis in civitate Brixiae, Crema et aliis locis, quae ad dictam inquisitionem spectant. 17 Jun. [1508] Romae." MOPH, 17:251.

46. The point is stressed by Giovanni Cagnazzo da Taggia in the entry "Inquisitio" in the *Summa Tabiensis* (Bologna, 1516).

47. The convent of San Pietro Martire in Parma was reformed and incorporated into the Congregation of Lombardy by Master General Jean Cleree on 20 July 1507 (MOPH, 21:65). The conventual friar who held the post of inquisitor, master Maffeo da Parma, had been appointed on 20 May 1505 (AGOP IV, 17, MS *Registrum litterarum . . . Bandelli*, f. 43*v*). He was deprived of the office and replaced with a member of the Congregation on 1 August 1507 (MOPH, 21:65). Mortier, *Histoire*, 5:261, affirms that San Domenico in Ferrara was reformed and incorporated into the Congregation of Lombardy during the vicarship of Francesco Silvestri (1518–20) but provides no documentation. Unfortunately the corresponding register of Master General Garcia de Loaysa (1518–24), which would have recorded the event, is lost. Whatever the case, the inquisitor in Ferrara by 1518 was Antonio Beccaria da Ferrara, who belonged to the Congregation.

48. Giorgio Cacatossici da Casale's inquisitorial appointments are recorded in AGOP IV, 15, MS *Registrum litterarum . . . Bandelli*, f. 258*r–v* (Cremona and Piacenza 1502); MOPH, 17:251 (Cremona, Brescia, and Crema 1511): MOPH, 17:96 (Bergamo, Cremona, Brescia, Crema 1512). The bull of Adrian VI of 20 July 1523, addressed to the inquisitors of the Congregation and encouraging the prosecution of witches, refers to him as the late Giorgio and cites an earlier bull addressed to him by Julius II. See B. Spina, *Quaestio de Strigibus* (Rome, 1576), 12–14.

49. B. Spina, *Quaestio de Strigibus*, 37.

50. Alessandria, Bib. Civica: MS 67 *Tabula chronologica inquisitorum Italiae, et insularum adiacentium ex Ordine Praedicatorum compilata et notis historicis illustrata per fr. Dominicum Franciscum Mutium*, f. 76*r–v*.

51. Of the vast literature on witchcraft it will suffice to mention the two works which still remain the principal collections of sources: H. C. Lea, *Materials toward a History of Witchcraft*, 2d ed. (New York, 1957); J. Hansen, *Quellen und Untersuchungen zur Geschichte des Hexenwahns und der Hexenverfolgung im Mittelalter* (Bonn, 1901).

52. See: Hansen, *Quellen*, 47–55; Quétif and Échard, *Scriptores*, 1:576–80; Kaeppeli, *Scriptores*, 1:205–6.

53. Aquinas briefly discusses the *Canon Episcopi* in *De spiritualibus creaturis*, q. unica, a. 2, ob. 14, ad 14. For Aquinas's position on witchcraft, see: G. M. Manser, "Thomas von Aquin und der Hexenwahn," *Divus Thomas* 9 (1922): 17–49, 81–110; C. E. Hopkin, *The Share of Thomas Aquinas in the Growth of the Witchcraft Delusion* (Philadelphia, 1940).

54. See: Hansen, *Quellen*, 66; Quétif and Échard, *Scriptores*, 1:709–17; Kaeppeli, *Scriptores*, 3:156–65.

55. See: Hansen, *Quellen*, 88–99; Lea, *Materials*, 260–65; Quétif and Échard, *Scriptores*, 1:792–74; Kaeppeli, *Scriptores*, 3:500–15.

56. See: Hansen, *Quellen*, 124; Lea, *Materials*, 272–73; Quétif and Échard, *Scriptores*, 1:809–10; Kaeppeli, *Scriptores*, 3:45–46.

57. See: Hansen, *Quellen,* 200–207; Lea, *Materials,* 295–96; Quétif and Échard, *Scriptores,* 2:24–25; Kaeppeli, *Scriptores,* 2:249–50.

58. See: Hansen, *Quellen,* 360–407; Lea, *Materials,* 306–47; Quétif and Échard, *Scriptores,* 1:880–81, 896–97; Kaeppeli, *Scriptores,* 2:341–43.

59. "Unde quidam in agro Comensi mox arsurus, ridens diu, interrogatus de causa dixit se recordari de lenociniis et blanditiis suae Catherinae et daemonis succubi, et cum iam flamora occupabit, idem, inquit, faciam." *De strigimagarum daemonumque mirandis,* 164.

60. Hansen, *Quellen,* 510–11.

61. *Summa silvestrina,* 1:490.

62. *Quadragesimale aureum,* ff. 16*v*–17*v*.

63. See G. A. Dell'Acqua, ed., *La Basilica di Sant'Eustorgio in Milano* (Milan, 1984).

64. L. Airaghi, "Studenti e professori di S. Eustorgio in Milano dalle origini del convento alla metà del XV secolo," AFP 54 (1984): 355–80.

65. T. Kaeppeli, "La bibliothéque de saint Eustorge a Milan a la fin du XV siècle," AFP 25 (1955): 5–74.

66. Mortier, *Histoire,* 5:166–67.

67. *Registrum Litterarum Fr. Thomae de Vio Caietani O.P. Magistri Ordinis 1508–1513,* MOPH, vol. 17, ed. A. De Meyer (Rome, 1935).

68. Gattico, *Descrittione* (see n. 2 above).

69. AGOP XIV, lib. N: MS G. Bugatti, *Istoria del Convento di S. Eustorgio,* 2:771ss.

70. Rome, Ist. Stor. O.P.: MS G. Allegranza, *Additiones et emendationes ad novissimum Bullarium O.P. ex Archivio Monasterii S. Eustorgii Mediol.*

71. "Conventus Sancti Eustorgii, Mediolanensis, eximitur et exemptus declaratur a iurisdictione cuiuslibet inferioris Magistro et fit super illum vicarius Magister Sylvester de Prierio, vicarius congregationis Lombardiae et qui pro tempore fuerit vicarius eiusdem congregationis; cui super illum datur auctoritas eadem in omnibus, quam habent provinciales super conventus suos; et praecipitur omnibus fratribus illius conventus praesentibus et futuris, ut oboediant. In contrarium etc. 14 Mart. [1510] Romae." MOPH, 17:261.

72. "Conventus Sancti Eustorgii praefatus, eximitur et exemptus declaratur a iurisdictione cuiuslibet inferioris Magistro; et unitur ac incorporatur congregationi Lombardiae; et submittitur eius vicario pro tempore cum gratiis, privilegiis etc. congregationis, salva in omnibus semper et per omnia auctoritate Magistri Generalis pro tempore. Imponitur vicario, ut illius curam suscipiat et ei provideat. Prohibetur omnibus fratribus ordinis, sub poena absolutionis ab officiis, si praesidentes sint, et carceris ac gravioris culpae, ne directe vel indirecte haec impedire praesumant. Oppositione et appellatione facta etc. et ceteris in contrarium etc. 15 Mart. [1510] Romae." MOPH, 17:261–62.

73. "Venerandus pater frater Johannes Maria Canisianus, Prior S. Marci de Florentia, fit commissarius ad visitandum et reformandum conventum S. Eustorgii de Mediolano cum auctoritate plenissima etiam ad exigentia mandatum specialissimum, invocato, si opus, brachio saeculari; et possit cogere fratres conventuum per praecepta ad recipiendum fratres, quos ex illo conventu eis assignaverit; et quamdiu in illo negotio est occupatus, habeat locum etiam super praesidentem conventus; praecipitur fratribus illius conventus ut ei oboediant et nullo modo

impediant ab exsecutione huius commissionis. Oppositione vel appellatione facta vel facienda, ceterisque in contrarium etc. 15 Mart. [1510] Romae." MOPH, 17:133.

74. "poiche risolvendosi il Padre R.mo Generale F. Tommaso Cajetano che poi fu Cardinale di S. Chiesa di smembrare dalla Congregazione di Lombardia il Convento di S. Maria delle Gratie [!] di Viterbo, procurando li padri di detta Congregazione di risarcirsi di detta smembrazione di farsi unire mediante la riforma al Convento di S. Eustorgio di Milano." Gattico, *Descrittione*, 68.

75. "questo Generale [Vincenzo Bandello] fece poi ogni diligenza col Governatore di Milano per far dare il Convento di S. Eustorgio alla Congregazione . . . nientedimeno non consenti per all'hora il detto Governatore . . . per non inimicarsi i primi della città difensori di S. Eustorgio . . . Tal disegno però essendo tuttavia nella memoria impresio di questi Frati della Lombardia (come sempre è restato et ancora resta) morto che fu l'anno seguente detto Generale procuravano col suo successore Fr. Giovanni Normanno Francese che fu eletto in Pavia, il medesimo negotio ch'egli eseguiva certo col favore de Ministri Galli; ma in Pavia in breve anco mori l'anno 1508." Bugatti, *Istoria,* 803.

76. MOPH, 17:256.

77. Mortier, *Histoire,* 5:12, 18, 91.

78. *De expositione missae,* f. Aiv.

79. "in S. Eustorgio vivevano 60 Frati avanti che i P.P. della Congregazione di Lombardia avendo per il Capo il P. Maestro F. Eustachio da Bologna Vicario loro Generale ne li discaciassero col favore de' Francesi l'anno 1510 16 Luglio." Allegranza, *Additiones,* 247.

80. "il Padre Maestro Frat'Isidoro Isolano da Milano uomo di grandi meriti e lettere e di gran negoziatura . . . se n'ando a Brescia da Monsieur d'Ambasia chiamato Carlo Padrone di Chiaramonte e plenipotenzario Vice Re per Ludovico Re di Francia all'ora Padrone dello stato di Milano, con pregarlo interponesse sua mano a rarettar tal negozio qual cortesemente scrisse lettere a due Cardinali Francesi che si ritrovavano in Milano, accio operassere che il Vicario Generale Archiepiscopale rarettando, i rumori facesse che li Padri di S. Eustorgio si contentassero di lasciarsi ridure a miglior osservanza delle loro leggi e percio unirsi all'osservante Cong. di Lombardia. Ma accorgendosi che il Vicario Generale sudetto trascurava tal Fonzione, si risolse di scrivere una lettera con grand' efficacia al Re in Francia e raccomandarla di ricapito per accompagnarla con calde preghiere nel presentarla al Confessore dello stesso Re con il quale aveva stretissima amicizia qual lo servi da amico poiche ottenne dal Re lettere efficacissime con le quali commetteva al suo Senato di Milano che con ogni potente mezzo facesse che li frati di S. Eustorgio s'unissero alla Sudetta Congregazione . . . finalmente dopo aver di novo ricevuto dupplicato e tripplicato lettere dal Re con minaccie se non l'inseguivano . . . si risolse Goffredo Presidente del Senato e Senatori d'andar a S. Eustorgio con corte armata il che fu li 16 Agosto del 1510 ed indussero quei Padri ad obbedire." Gattico, *Descrittione, 68.*

81. *De Regum Principumque omnium Institutis Liber Fratris Isidori Isolani Mediolanensis ordinis predicatorum ac congregationis Lombardiae* (Milan: Pietro Martire Mantegazzo, n.d.), f. Av.

82. See: F. Lauchert, *Die italienischen literarischen Gegner Luthers* (Freiburg, 1912), 200–215; N. Defendi, "La *Revocatio M. Lutherii ad Sanctam Sedem* nella polemica antiluterana in Italia," *Archivio Storico Lombardo*, 8. 4 (1953): 67–132.

83. "Magnifico Domino Jaffredo Carolo Senatus Mediolanensis presidi frater Thomas Radinus Todischus Placentinus Ordinis Praedicatorum congregationis Lombardiae humiliter se commendat . . . Hoc multa fatentur preclara per vos gesta facinora, inter que quod nuper de divi Eustorgii reformato coenobio actum est eminentius protestatur. Almi siquidem Dominici veris filiis et heredibus iustissima vestri providentia domus propria restituta est . . . Ex divi Eustorgii coenobio quarto nonas Septembris a deiparae Virginis partu trecentesima secunda olympiade." *Syderalis abyssus*, f. 1*r*–*v*.

84. "Conventus Sancti Eustorgii de Mediolano eximitur a quocumque inferiori Magistro; unitur congregationi Lombardiae et eius vicario submittitur, cum gratiis etc., salva oboedientia Magistri in omnibus. Assignantur illic pro hac vice, quos vicarius nominaverit. Absolvuntur omnes praesidentes. Mandatur vicario et patribus congregationis et conventus pro tempore, ut studium generale inibi conservent sicut Bononiae; cuius provisio prima committitur vicario. Gaudeat studium et officiales ac studentes intranei et extranei omnibus privilegiis Bononiensibus. Submittuntur vicario pro tempore omnia monasteria et collegia tertii habitus, et earum personae in civitate et districtu Mediolanensi, quae per fratres Sancti Eustorgii aut provincialem huius provinciae regi solebant. Praecipitur omnibus ne haec impediant etc., oppositione vel appellatione etc. Haec omnia tamen salva in omnibus oboedientia, subiectione, iurisdictione et auctoritate Magistro debita. 4 Aug. [1510] Reate." MOPH, 17:263–64.

85. Julius II's bull of 13 August 1510 is reproduced in Dell'Acqua, *La basilica*, 234.

86. See chap. I, n. 32.

87. "Vicario congregationis Lombardiae, praesidenti et patribus conventus Sancti Eustorgii mandatur, ut fratres omnes filios nativos conventus reformationem acceptantes et manere volentes recipiant et retineant non obstante, quod se opposuerunt aut recesserunt; illi fratres habent annum integrum ab eorum ingressu ad experiendum vitam regularem, intra quem libere cum bonis suis, quae eis interim salva sint, poterunt exire; et provideatur eis de bonis conventus interim de omnibus opportunis. Si completo anno stabiliant se, ubicumque fuerint, in conventu aliquo, semper sic esse intelligatur, quod Magister Ordinis pro tempore libere de eis et bonis eorum possit disponere . . . 14 Aug. [1510] Reate." MOPH, 17:263–64.

88. "Magistris Johanni Antonio de Cremona et Georgio de Casali committitur, ut iudicent, qui fratres Sancti Eustorgii de Mediolano debeant ab observancialibus fratribus recipi iuxta priores litteras in priori facie signatas, et qui non, ne recipiantur fratres destruere volentes reformationem, etc. Non recipiendis autem et recipi nolentibus assignent provisionem vel unicam vel annuam, ad tempus vel ad vitam, dummodo tamen tam recipiendi quam illi, quibus assignanda est provisio, acceptent reformationem et renuntient omnibus in contrarium facientibus et eam nullo modo molestent; alias ipso facto careant provisione. Item quamdiu steterint in ordine praecipitur illis, ut commisionem exsequantur. Praecipitur praesidenti et patribus conventus Sancti Eustorgii, ut oboediant ordinationi eorum. Reser-

vatur tamen auctoritas plenaria Magistri Generali pro tempore mutandi, addendi, diminuendi, etc. In contrarium. 2 Sept. [1510] Reate." MOPH, 17:264–65.

89. "Vicario generali congregationis Lombardiae pro tempore imponitur et datur plena auctoritas recuperandi quaecumque bona ablata et alienata, quae pertinent ad conventum Sancti Eustorgii et omnes ei quoad haec obediant etc. 18 Sept. [1510] Romae." MOPH, 17:265.

90. "Eidem vicario datur plena auctoritas capiendi, puniendi, expellendi a Mediolano fratres illic vagantes, scandala perpetrantes et reformationi nocere machinantes. Prohibetur fratribus, ne quis contra eius voluntatem in burgo portae Ticinensis morari possit praetextu cuiuscumque licentiae praesentis vel futurae, quorum nulla ei ad hoc suffragetur. In contrarium etc. 18 Sept. [1510] Romae." MOPH, 17:265.

91. "Vicario congregationis Lombardiae et patribus conventus Sancti Eustorgii insinuatur, quod nullum tenentur ex emissis fratribus in conventu illo recipere, nisi quos et illo modo, quo iudicaverint commissarii deputati per litteras datas Reate 2 Septembris. Et contra illam commissionem nullae aliae emanarunt. Et si quis contrarias exhibeant, tamquam falsarii puniantur. Item imponitur vicario, ut litteras Romae 18 Sept. datas exsequatur contra fratres vagantes Mediolani; sic tamen, quod singillatim possint venire ad iudices. Quod si ex accessu illo tumultus periculum sit, mandatur iudicibus, ut extra Mediolanum in alia civitate vicina iudicium faciant, insinuantes fratribus locum sui iudicii. In contrarium etc. 29 Oct. [1510] Romae." MOPH, 17:266–67.

92. "si ribellarono e con il favore di un Potentato Grande mandarono in Francia del Re ove anche ando il Sudetto P. Isidoro et il Padre Frate Matteo Bandello nipote del Generale Bandelli e vedendo il Re l'ostinata durezza d'ambo le parti, dubitando di qualche grande scandalo oprò che si pacificassero e che ciaschedun convento restasse alla sua primiera congregazione e nel suo primiero stato." Gattico, *Descrittione,* 69.

93. Reverendo magistro Silvestro de Prierio, committitur cognitio et exsecutio causae insulti facti a conventualibus in conventum et fratres sancti Eustorgii de Mediolano, cum plena provincialium auctoritate inquirendi, incarcerandi et puniendi, et specialiter et simpliciter, super conventum Sancti Thomae de Papia; et ut inquirat de percussione fratris Alberti, absolvat, mutet et puniat, etc. Conceditur quoque eidem, ut possit assumere sibi collegam vicarium provinciae Sancti Petri Martyris; qui si videatur non recte incedere, soli suae paternitati committitur; cum praecepto omnibus et singulis et sub poena absolutionis ab officiis et privationis omnium bonorum etc. 13 Feb. [1512] Romae." MOPH, 17:270–71.

94. "i nostri uniti con la maggior parte de Scuolari dello Studio di Pavia (condotti da Maestro Gioacchino Beccaria nobile Pavese, e più nobile Predicatore, e da Maestro Vincenzo d'Odo Reggente qui dello studio della Provincia armati) fecero empito per poter entrarvi; nella quali azzione riuscendo più stremito e più tumulto . . . (perchè i Francesi sospettosi toccavano all'armi) l'impresa per l'hora fu vana." Bugatti, *Istoria,* 804–5.

95. "Citatur Magister Vincentius Dodius, ut compareat coram Reverendissimo Magistro ad dicendum, quare non debeat puniri et privari voce activa et passiva et

gravius ex conclusione provinciae proposita contra observantiam etc. 28 Maii, [1512] Romae." MOPH, 17:274.

96. "Committitur et mandatur reverendis magistro Damiano et magistro Hieronymo de Viglievano, ut cognoscant causam insulti facti in conventum Sancti Eustorgi, cum potestate citandi etc. puniendi etc. absolvendi et liberandi et propter irregularitates suspendendi etc. et omnia alia ad hoc necessaria faciendi etc. 29 Maii [1512] Romae." MOPH, 17:274.

97. "magister Hieronymus de Viglevano assignatur in regentem in conventu S. Eustorgii; frater Franciscus de Ferraria in baccalaureum et frater Ysidorus [de Mediolano] in magistrum studentium pro presenti anno etc. 5 Aug. [1511] Romae." MOPH, 17:91.

98. "In conventu S. Eustorgii de Mediolano, in regentem assignatur frater Vincentius de Vincentia, dummodo sit magister; cui conceditur, ut servatis servandis magisterium accipere possit; in baccalaureum praesentis anni frater Franciscus de Ferraria; pro secundo anno frater Chrysostomus de Casali; in magistrum studentium frater Bartholomaeus de Pisis. 19 Jun. [1512] Romae." MOPH, 17:296.

99. See R. Potter, *Zwingli* (Cambridge, 1976), 33.

100. "ma poi rientrando nella città Massimiliano Sforza Primogenito di Ludovico Maria Moro già morto col Corpo della Lega (degli Svizzeri del Papa, Venetiani et altri) accompagnato dal Cardinal Seduntasi, Condottiere, Capo e Parte degli Svizzeri, da questo Cardinale i nostri Frati hebbero ogni favore; onde cacciarono i detti Frati Lombardi con altro anch'ora che con parole; e vi rientrarono gli antichi Eustorgiani nel nome d'Iddio." Bugatti, *Istoria,* 805.

101. "Praecipitur et singulis fratribus vitae communis cuiuscumque gradus et dignitatis existant, sub poena gravioris culpae et sub poena excommunicationis latae sententiae, quam ipso facto contrafaciendo incurrant, ut infra spatium sex horarum, quarum duae pro primo, duae pro secundo, et aliae duae pro tertio et peremptorio termino assignatur, a receptione praesentium, exeant de conventu Sancti Eustorgii de Mediolano et liberum fratribus congregationis Lombardiae dimittant etc. 4 Jul. [1512] Romae." MOPH, 17:276–75.

102. "Julius Papa II. dilecte fili noster salutem et Apostolicam benedictionem. Exposuit nobis dilectus Filius noster Nicolaus de Flisco Ord. Praed. [Protector] quod licet bonae memoriae Cardinalis Neapolitanus una cum moderno Generali dicti Ordinis reformassent Conventum Sancti Eustorgii dicti Ordinis Mediolani, et in eo Fratres Congregationis Lombardiae dicti Ordinis de Observantia nuncupatos introduxissent Conventum huiusmodi Congregationi eidem addendo, in quo Conventu sive Domo Fratres ipsi pacifice usque in hanc rerum et temporum varietatem, immo felicitatem permanserunt. Nihilominus nuper Fratres Conventuales, qui, priusquam reformaretur, Conventu erant egressi, Conventum illorum absque licentia Magistri Generalis occupaverunt, et occupant. Quare idem Cardinalis Protector, et Generalis, et Fratres Observantiae praedicti nobis supplicaverunt, ut eorum indempnitati ac quieti paterne consulere dignaremur. Nos igitur, qui cultum divinum augeri, non minui, nostris praesertim temporibus, summis desideramus affectibus, huiusmodi ut pote justis supplicationibus inclinati praemissa paterne considerantes circumspectioni tuae per praesentes com-

mittimus, ut constito tibi prius de praemissis summario et extrajudicialiter eosdem Fratres de Observantia in pristinam Conventus seu domus S. Eustorgii possessionem, in qua erant, visis praesentibus, amotis exinde dictis Fratribus Conventualibus, reintegres atque restituas, restituosque nomine et auctoritate nostra adversus quoscunque manu teneas, atque defendas, dictos Conventuales Fratres ac contradictores omnes per censuras Ecclesiasticas, et alia opportuna remedia compescendo, invocato ad hoc, si opus fuerit, auxilio brachii secularis. In contrarium facient. non obstant. quibuscumque. Datum Romae apud Sanctum Petrum sub annulo Piscatoris di VI Julii MDXII. Pontificatus nostri anno IX. Balthasar Iuverdus." Allegranza, *Additiones*, 247–48.

103. "In nomine Domini Amen. Pridem Sanctissimus in Christo Pater et Dominus noster Dominus Julius divina providentia Papa II nobis Mattheo miseratione divina tituli Sanctae Potentianae sacrosancte Romane Ecclesiae Presbitero Cardinali Sedunensi totius Germaniae et Lombardiae eiusdem Domini nostri Papae et Sedis Apostolicae Legato Breve Apostolicum praesentari fecit quod nos cum ea qua decuit reverentia recepimus . . . Cujus quidem Brevis vigore non volentes in causa rite procedere ac Partibus breve justitiae complementum ministrare, Fratres Conventuales S. Dominici Praedicatorum, ad Fratrum de Observantia noncupatorum in praeinserto Brevi principaliter nominatorum instantiam legitime ad comparendum coram nobis in certo cum eis prefixo termino citari et vocari jussimus ac mandavimus. Termino itaque adveniente ac Partibus hinc inde coram nobis comparentibus, et ad hoc consentientibus gravioribus implicite causam et causas praedictas juxta tenorem dicti Brevis dilecto nobis in Christo Joanni Angelo Arcimboldo Sedis Apostolicae Protonotario audienda ac probanda et deducenda in eadem ab utraque parte recipienda, nobisque acta et deducta fideliter referenda, reservata in nobis eandem causam toties quotiens nobis placeret reassumendi, et in eadem sententiandi et pronunciandi facultati subdelegarimus." Allegranza, *Additiones*, 247–49.

104. "Reverendissime et Illustrissime SS. D. N. Pape et Sedis Apostolicae Legate. Non levi molestia affecti fuerunt Cives Mediolanenses et praesertim Vicecomites, et caeteri quorum Maiores sepulcra erexerunt in Ecclesia et Monasterio S. Eustorgii Mediolani quod Fratres nuncupati de Observantia Ord. S. Dominici conati fuerint veteres ipsius Monasterii Religiosos expellere, et Monasterium ipsum cum redittibus occupare. Nec sine causa haec eorum molestia procedit. Nam ipsi Fratres de Observantia amplum et magnum habent Monasterium extra Portam Vercellinam Mediolani, et propterea pessimum exemplum praebent secularibus dum non alienum Monasterium, sed alieni Monasterii opes et redditus affectaverunt. Quamdiu enim in ipso Monasterio fuerunt ne dum redditus ipsius Monasterii consumpserunt denegaveruntque alimenta pauperibus expulsis, sed etiam multas alienationes immobilium fecerunt et demum vasa argentea et statuas argenteas magni ponderis, inter quas etiam aderant statuae quorundam Vicecomitum satis antique aliaque ipsius Monasterii ornamenta et Ecclesiae paramenta seu vendiderunt, seu rapuerunt. Et forte hujusmodi sacram pecuniam in detestabili et pudendo litigio consumunt. Praeterea avidissimi erant in exigendis legatis, et tamen leges legatorum observare recusabant. Nam si quispiam Civis aliquam Capellam erexisset, eamque certo Legato ditasset cum lege et conditione

ut in ea Missas cantarent certis diebus, hoc facere recusaverunt impudenter dicentes, hoc non esse professionis eorum, et tamen, non erubescabant satis contumaciter efflagitare legata. Aliaque multa servabant ex quibus Cives ipsi non immerito praeponunt ipsos Conventuales praedictis nuncupatis de Observantia. Praesertim cum et isti Conventuales deposita hypocrisi forte non minus religiose vivant. Et profecto Religiosis saltem suae res, et quidem non modicae satis esse debent, nec decet eos aliis exemplum praebere ut aliena appetant. Reverendissima igitur Dominatio vestra parte ipsorum Civium humiliter supplicatur, ut dignetur illa providere quod ipsi Fratres de Observantia amplius non vexent ipsos veteres Fratres et Religiosos S. Eustorgii, et huic rei perpetuum silentium imponere et providere quod ipsi de Observantia restituant ea quibus Ecclesiam ipsam et Monasterium spoliaverunt." Allegranza, *Additiones,* 250–51.

105.   "Quin immo Breve ipsum surreptionis, et obreptionis vitio subiacere retulit. Nos igitur cognitis causae hujusmodi meritis, ac consideratis considerandis necnon Fratrum de Observantia nuncupatorum nihil penitus pro verificatione praefato SS. D. N. expositorum et narratorum in Brevi deducere et probare curantium contumacia Partibus coram nobis ac toto Mediolanensis Civitatis Senatu ad audiendam deliberationem nostram personaliter constitutis, praefatos Fratres Conventuales apud nos de Religionis zelo, vitae ac morum honestate, fide dignorum testimonio multipliciter prout ex infrascripta apparet supplicatione nobis porrecta commentatos, de juris peritorum et totius senatus praefati consilio et assensu ab impetitione Fratrum de Observantia, nec non vexatione molestatione et impedimentis super Conventu S. Eustorgi per eosdem de Observantia ipsis Conventualibus quomodolibet praestitis, illatis, et factis absolvimus et absolutos fore et esse decernimus et declaramus. Ad restitutionem omnium et singulorum bonorum tam mobilium quam immobilium, jocalium, et aliorum quorumcumque per eosdem Fratres de Observantia quomodolibet ablatorum et alienatorum, si quae sint eosdem condemnando, ipsumque Monasterium, ac Fratres Conventuales oboedientiae et jurisdictioni Provincialis Provinciae S. Petri Martyris Lombardiae cui ab antiquo subesse dignoscitur, subiiciendo et submittendo eidemque Provinciae pro ut prius fuit incorporando et reuniendo . . . In quorum fidem praesentes nostras patentes literas fieri, et per Secretarium nostrum subscribi ac sigilli nostri jussimus appensione communiri. Actum et datum Mediolani anno a nativitate eiusdem millesimo quingentesimo duodecimo, indictione quintadecima, die vero Jovis nono Mensis Septembris, Pontificatus praefati D. N. Julii Papae Secundi anno nono, praesentibus ibidem nobilibus et egregiis Viris D.D. Johanne Francisco de Marliano J. U. Doctore, Nicolao Arcimboldo, Johanne Francisco de Brippio, ac multis aliis fide dignis testibus ad praemissa vocatis specialiterque rogatis. Idem Mattheus Card. praedictus Legatus a Latere. M. Sandeii de Man.to." Allegranza, *Additiones,* 250–52.

106.   "Matheus miseratione divina tit. Sanctae Potentianae Sacrosanctae Romane Ecclesie Presbyter Cardinalis Sedunensis totius Germaniae et Lombardiae, et ad quaecunque loca nos declinare contingerit, SS. D. N. Papae et Apostolice Sedis Legatus dilectis nobis in Christo Praeposito S. Michaelis Papien. Mediolani commoranti, et Vicario Mediolanen. in spiritualibus generali salutem in domino sempiternam. Conquesti sunt nobis dilecti nobis in Christo modernus Prior et

Conventus Monasterii S. Eustorgii Mediolan. Ord. S. Dominici quod quidam Frater Silvester de Prierio ac nonnulli alii fratres dicti Ordinis de Observantia nuncupati quaedam bona tam mobilia quam immobilia, ac varia et diversa clenodia jocalia aliasque res et bona ad praefatum Monasterium legitime spectantia et pertinentia asportaverunt alienarunt et vendiderunt, ac quaedam indebite occupata detinent non curantes illa Priori et Conventui restituere in grave animarum suarum periculum et Monasterii damnum et praejuditium non modicum aliasque diversimode supra dictis et aliis bonis et rebus ad Monasterium praefatum pertinent. injuriantur eisdem, ideoque discretioni vestrae auctoritate Ap.a qua per literas Ap.cae Sedis sufficienti facultate muniti fungimur in hac parte, per praesentes mandamus quatenus vocatis qui fuerint evocandi et auditis hinc inde Praepositis, quod justum fuerit decernatis, facientes quod decreveritis per censuram ecclesiasticam firmiter observari. Testes autem qui fuerint nominati si se gratia odio vel amore subtraxerint censura simili compellatis testimonium veritati perhibere. Non obstante si Ordini praefato a Sed. Ap.la indultum existat quod ipsius Ordinis personae ad iudicium trahi suspendi vel excomunicari, seu eiusdem Ordinis loca interdici non possint per literas Ap.las non facientes plenam et expressam ac de verbo ad verbum de indulto huiusmodi mentionem et qualibet alia dictae Sedis indulgentia generali vel speciali cuiuscunque tenoris existat, per quam praesentibus non expressam vel totaliter non insertam vestrae iurisdictionis explicatio valeat in hac parte quomodolibet impediri, quae quod ad hoc ipsis nolumus aliquatenus suffragari. Quod si non ambo hiis exequendis interesse potueritis, alter vestrum ea nihilominus exequatur. Datum Laudae Anno Incarnationis Dominicae Millesimo Quingentesimo duodecimo nonis Octobris Pontificatus SS. D. N. Domini Julii Papae II Anno nono. Sep. M. Sanderi. C. Meyr. M. Sanderi." Allegranza, *Additiones,* 252–54.

107. "Durando poi per il tempo, che dissi, questi venerandi Padri osservanti in S. Eustorgio si portavano con quei segni di clemenza, di Religiosità e carità (e sia perdonato il detto per il uevo che pur perdono non richiede) come al grido di una terra data a manifesto sacco essendo che diffalcavano dell'Ordinario annuale del Convento più di quaranta mila libre Imperiali di Milano, oltre gli argenti forse venduti, come consta per loro libri d'oncie 721 e oltre i paramenti e libri con altri mobili portati via. Colpa se detto Convento non habbia da indi in qua (cioè dall'anno 1512 che furono cacciati di Giugno) mai potuto nodrire il solito numero de Frati." Bugatti, *Istoria,* 804.

108. "Praesidenti, patribus et officialibus studii Bononiensis intimatur, quod magister Silvester de Prierio succedat in officio regentiae magistro Eustachio, si a patribus congregationis ad hoc fuerat deputatus, non obstante assignatione magistri Georgii de Casali in actis, si fuit per errorem facta, etc. In contrarium etc. 2 Jan. [1509] Romae." MOPH, 17:80. The reference is to the *Acta* of the general chapter of Rome, 1508. See MOPH, 9:90.

109. ASDB, MSS: *Moderatores stud. Bonon.,* f. 8r; Prelormo, *Chronaca,* f. 135r.

110. "Magister Georgius de Casali assignatur Bononiae in regentem . . . 5 Aug. [1511] Romae." MOPH, 17:91.

111. ASDB, MS *Liber cons. conv Bon.,* vol. 1 (1459–1648), f. 31v.

112. Piana, *Ricerche,* 257.

113. "Committitur reverendis magistro Silvestro de Prierio et magistro Hieronymo de Viglevano, revocando alios iudices quoad hoc, examen praedicatorum generalium provinciae [S. Petri Martyris], ut in eis servetur ordo constitutionum, cum potestate citandi et absolvendi seu destituendi; et si numerus sufficientium sit maior, primus in ordine sit potius in iure etc. 27 Maii [1511] Romae." MOPH, 17:274.

114. "Qua peracta Coenobii nostri Bononiensis cura fratrum suffragiis illi demandata est." Alberti, *De viris,* f. 140*v.*

115. "Millesimo quingentesimo undecimo Die decimo Julii. R.dus pater frater Silvester de Prierio ordinis Predicatorum, Sacre Theologie professor et conventus Sancti Dominici de Bononia Prior preposuit infrascriptis patribus de consilio dicti conventus congregatis qualiter domina Joanna condam Magnifici D. Joannis de Ludovisis et uxor condam Magnifici equitis aurati atque Doctoris utriusque iuris eximii Domini Ludovici de Bologninis, habens capellam in ecclesia nostra iuxta caput divi Dominici et desiderans ad eius altare cotidie imperpetuum pro anima sua unam missam celebrari et in dicta ecclesia singulis annis tria anniversaria per fratres dicti conventus imperpetuum debere persolvi. Unum videlicet pro anima sua, secundum pro anima patris sui, tertium pro anima matris sue Petit Rogat et instat pro dictis missis celebrandis et officiis persolvendis ut supra promittens se daturam Mille Libras bolennorum conventui pro elemosina. Unde maturo habito consilio super hoc conclusum fuit quod et missa ad altare et anniversalia in Ecclesia ut supra persolverentur iuxta devotionem dicte D. Johanne. Et quod dicta elemosina aut in totum aut in parte investirentur in aliqua re stabili quatenus perpetuus afficus etiam posteris imperpetuum correspondeat Missis et anniversariis supradictis. In quorum fidem propria manu se subscripserunt infra scripti patres. Ego frater Silvester de Prierio or. praed. prior. bonon. affirmo ut supra . . . Ego frater Eustachius de Bononia ordinis predicatorum vicarius generalis congregationis Lombardie superveniens suprascriptis omnia supra deffinita confirmo et retifico." ASDB, MS *Liber consiliorum,* vol. 1 (1459–1648), f. 31*r.*

116. Milesimo quingentesimo undecimo die sexta novembris. Frater Silvester de Prierio ordinis predicatorum, Sacre theologie professor et Conventus Sancti Dominici pro meritis Prior, congregatis Patribus dicti conventus exposuit eis qualiter quidam domini Bononienses, dicti domini de la guerra, pecierant mutuo et cum promissione infra biennium vel triennium restituendi quingentos ducatos ex quibus in absencia sua iam receperant centum, quos conventus maxima difficultate mutuo acceperant illos brevi restituiturus. Et post paucos dies cum ipse rediisset ad conventum vocatus sive citatus a dictis Dominis pecierant ab eo iterum sibi dare alios centum, sine ulla omnino spe evadendi ne illos tradere cogerent. Ex qua re consuluit patres convocatos et infrascriptos de modo dandi dictos centum aureos et plures si foret opportunum. Exponens pro datione talium pecuniarum unum de tribus fore necessarium. Aut videlicet fratres emittere et frumentum et alia pro victu et vestitu eorum vendere et satisfacere, aut calices, cruces et aliqua alia argentea ad ornatum ecclesie et Arche Patriarchis nostri Dominici pertinentia conflare et agere ut ex eis dicta pecuniarum quantitas fieret et illis satisfacere. Aut certe aliquid de immobilibus pro dicta satisfactione distrahere. Et maturo facto super hoc conscilio per patres convocatos et infrascriptos

unanimiter conclusum fuit, ne fratres ullomodo emitterentur et id multis quidem rationibus pertinentibus ad bonum studentium et aliorum iuniorum emittendorum tam spirituale quam corporale et temporale. Unde concluserunt et decreverunt dicti patres una cum dicto patre Priore nemine discrepante aut discentiente potius conflare calices etc. aut aliquid de immobilibus distrahere et solvere quam fratres cum tanto eorum periculo et discrimine animarum et corporum vagos emittere. Praesertim in tanto armorum strepitu, tanta locorum et victus penuria, tanta omnium aliorum nostrorum conventuum gravedine et breviter tanta istorum temporum malicia. Hac deliberatione peracta commisit R.us Pater Prior duobus patribus videlicet P. fratri Dominico de Morano et P. fratri Ioanni de Bononia ut viderent Calices cruces et alia argentea tam ad ornatum et necessitatem Sacristie quam Arche etc. pertinentia et illa que minus incommodarent conventum traderent ad conflandum pro dicta necessitate; quorum dicti patres conflari fecerunt unam capanulam et duo candelabra de argento probatissimo ponderis librarum quinque et unciarum quinque optime deaurata tradita per quondam serenissimam olim reginam yspaniarum ob devotionem quam habebat ad S. Dominicum, item calices quattuor et crucem unam de argento basso. Que omnia conflata ascenderunt usque ad libras duodecim uncias duas et tres quartas unius ontie. Et sic conflata fuerunt valoris circiter centum quattuor ducatorum. Hoc consilium voluit idem R.us P. Prior anotari in hoc libro Consiliorum Patrum Conventus Bononiensis sicut de more talia Conscilia solent in isto libro anotari cum subscriptione patrum consulentium. Ego frater Silvester de Prierio prior." *Liber consiliorum,* vol. 1 (1459–1648), f. 31*v.*

117. "1512 die 16 Januarii. Fra Innocenzio da Bologna de Paselli fu ricevuto all'habito dal P. Maestro Silvestro da Prierio alhora Priore di questo convento e finito l'anno fece la sua professione. lascio cento lire di questa moneta di Bologna al Convento." *Liber consiliorum,* MS 12, f. 3*r.*

118. "Milesimo quingentesimo duodecimo die vigesimasecunda Apprilis. Fr. Silvester de Prierio ordinis predicatorum. Sacre Theologie Professor et Conventus Sancti Dominici de Bononia pro meritis Prior de unanimi Conscilio Patrum dicti Conventus: ex legiptimis et honestis imo neccessariis et urgentibus causis: ordinavit quod Fr. Petronius de Bononia Conversus de cetero habeat Socium qui continue commoretur secum in Possessione Caude Longe ad faciendum opportuna ibidem, que hactenus facta sunt per aliquem secularem sicut facere coquinam et gubernare galinas, habere curam domus ac cetera talia peragere. Item quod tempore triture et vindemie deputentur eidem fratri Petronio socii pro diversis possesionibus, ad levandum frumenta et alia blada et uvas, annotando seu anotari faciendo quidquid et quantum de area levaverint et ad conventum miserint. Que etiam scribantur per deputatum in conventu immediate delata.

"Ordinavit insuper dictus Pater Prior eadem die et in eodem Consilio ac unanimi Conscensu omnium patrum dicti conventus infrascriptorum quod in loco Ronciani stet aliquis frater qui habeat curam loci et usque ad quinquennium possit retinere redditus dicti loci et illos expendere in utilitate et reparatione et bonificatione dicti loci maxime in augmentatione et plantatione vitum olivarum ac aliorum fructuum et arborum ac secundum quod videbitur de conscilio patris prioris qui fuerit pro tempore et patrum conventus melius expedire ita tamen quod casu quo P. Prior et dicti patres vellent pro conventu vinum aut aliquid aliud tale pertinens ad redditus dicti loci teneantur ad equivalens pro subsidio loci ut dictum est. Et de omnibus teneatur optima ratio. Has duas ordinationes voluit pro earum memoria dictus R.us. Pater Prior anotari in hoc libro consciliorum Patrum Conventus Sancti Dominici de Bononia iuxta consuetudinem cum subscriptione patrum conscentientium et considentium. Ego frater Silvester de Prierio Prior." *Liber consiliorum,* vol. 1 (1459–1648), f. 32r.

119. "Cum vero bononiae prioratum agerem presente Iulio pontifice max." *Errata et argumenta,* f. 248v.

120. "Magister Sylvester de Prierio fit inquisitor in civitatibus Mediolanensi et Laudensi et locis, ad quae huiusmodi inquisitio hactenus se extendit, quibus additur civitas Placentina et eius diocesis, destituto omni alio, si quis forte in aliquo locorum hactenus fuisse inquisitor. 5 Aug. [1511] Romae." MOPH, 17:268.

121. *Tabula Chronologica,* f. 137v.

122. Hieronymus Lucensis, *In pomponacium de anime immortalitate* (Milan, 1518), f. 2r.

123. L. Fumi, "L'inquisizione Romana e lo Stato di Milano," *Archivio Storico Lombardo,* 1910, 37:11.

124. V. M. Fontana, *Monumenta Dominicana* (Rome, 1675), 413.

125. Fontana, *Monumenta,* 414.

126. T. J. Rocaberti, *Bibliotheca Maxima Pontificis* (Rome, 1695–9), 19:227–367.

127. J. A. Mirus, "On the Deposition of the Pope for Heresy," AHP 13 (1975): 233.

128. U. Horst, *Zwischen Konziliarismus und Reformation. Studien zur Ekklesiologie im Dominikanerorden* (Rome, 1985), 23.

129. Erasmus, *Opus Epistolarum,* ed. P. S. and H. M. Allen (Oxford, 1906–58), vol. 4, Ep. 1006, p. 46.

130. P. M. Domaneschi, *De rebus coenobii Cremonensis Ordinis Praedicatorum* (Cremona, 1768), 15–31.

131. "1512. Pater Frater Sylvester Mazzolini Prieras seu De Prierio Pedemontanus. Fuit Magister S. Palatii et insignus Scriptor." AGOP XIV, lib. O, I: MS E. Tedeschini, *Monumenta Coenobii S. Dominici Cremonae,* 6. Domaneschi, *De rebus,* 428.

132. "Datis Cremonis pridie Kal. Iul. 1513." *Commentaria in spheram ac theoricas planetarum* (preface: Bainbridge), f. 2v.

133. See chap. 4, n. 33.

134. "Date Cremone pridie Kalendis Julii. 1514." *Commentaria in spheram ac theoricas planetarum* (preface: Fieschi), f. 2v.

135. BOP, 4:271.

136. ASM, Archivio Gonzaga: Busta 2487.

137. Domaneschi, *De rebus,* 37–42.

138. Forte, "Le Provincie," 449–50.

139. "Reverendi Patris Fratris Silvestri de Prierio or. Pre. de observantia, Sacre Theo. doctoris eximii: et conventus Venetensis divi dominici Prioris Meritiss." *Quadragesimale aureum,* f. 1r.

140. "[I]n conventu Venetensi divi Dominici functus est Prioris officio." Ambrosius de Altamura, *Bibliothecae Dominicanae* (Rome, 1677), 245.

141. G. D. Armani, *Monumenta selecta conventus Sancti Dominici Venetensis* (Venice,

1729), 145–46; F. Cornelio, *Ecclesiae Venetae Antiquis Monumentis* (Venice, 1749), 7:325.

142. Armani, *Monumenta*, 143–44; Cornelio, *Ecclesiae*, 325.

143. "Anno MDXIV. More Veneto [= 1515] die I. Januarii. Ego Fr. Silvester de Prierio Prior proposui Ven. PP. an vellent habere in filium sui Conventus P. F. Bartholomaeum de Pisis, et responderunt ut infra. In primis Ego idem Prior sum valde contentus etc." *Liber consiliorum* cited by Cornelio, *Ecclesiae*, 7:325.

144. Cornelio, *Ecclesiae*, 7:325.

145. Serra Zanetti, *L'arte della stampa*, 288.

146. BAV, MS Vat. Lat. 9451, f. 109*v.*

147. Vigna, *I Domenicani illustri*, 384.

148. See: P. Michaud-Quantin, *Sommes de casuistique et manuels de confession au moyen âge* (Louvain, Lille, and Montreal, 1962), 101–3; T. N. Tentler, *Sin and Confession on the Eve of the Reformation* (Princeton, 1977), 32, 34–37.

149. See: J. Kirschner, "Discounting Genoese Paghe 1450–1550," AFP 17 (1977): 141–49; R. Savelli, "Between Law and Morals: Interest in the Dispute on Exchanges during the 16th Century," *The Courts and the Development of Commercial Law* (Berlin, 1987), 39–102.

150. J. Heumann, *Documenta literaria varii argumenti* (Altdorf, 1758), 23, 30.

151. "ex praeclaris auctoribus collegi atque conflavi." *Malleus*, f. 2*r.*

152. Thomas Anglicus, *Liber propugnatorius super primum sententiarum contra Johannem Scotum* (Venice, 1499).

IV. Master of the Sacred Palace

1. "Tandem anno MDXV per eundem Leonem pont. max. . . . vita functo Ioanne Ferrariensi . . . sacri pallatii magister Romae consistens dictus est." Alberti, *De viris,* f. 140*v.* On Rafanelli see chap. 2, n. 13 above.

2. See R. Creytens, "Le *Studium Romanae Curiae* et le Maître du Sacré Palais," AFP 12 (1942): 5–83.

3. See: V. M. Fontana, *Syllabus magistrorum sacri palatii apostolici* (Rome, 1663); J. Catalano, *De magistro sacri palatii apostolici* (Rome, 1751); I. Taurisano, *Hierarchia Ordinis Praedicatorum* (Rome, 1916); I. Taurisano, "L'insegnamento domenicano a Roma. I maestri del sacro palazzo," *Memorie Domenicane* 43 (1926): 527–36; A. Zucchi, *Roma Domenicana*, vol. 3 (Florence, 1941), 66–86; R. Loenertz, "Saint Dominique écrivain, maître en théologie, professeur à Rome et Maître du Sacré Palais d'après quelques auteurs du XIVᵉ et XVᵉ siècle," AFP 12 (1942): 84–97.

4. "Ego enim, quanquam urbis et orbis domini nostri spontaneo munere inquisitor ac perinde sive ordinarie sive delegato iure inspectantibus ad fidem iudex." *Replica,* 117.

5. See A. F. Verde and E. Giacconi, *Epistolario di Frà Vincenzo Mainardi da San Gimignano Domenicano 1481–1527*, vol. 1 (*Memorie Domenicane*, no. 23 [1992]), 64.

6. Città del Vaticano, Arch. Vat., Armadio 29, vol. 65, f. 83. It has been published by P. Kalkoff, *Forschungen zu Luthers römischen Prozess* (Rome, 1905), 173–74.

7. Fontana, *Monumenta*, 414; Quétif and Échard, *Scriptores*, 2:55.

8. "Tandem anno MDXV per eundem Leonem pont. max. Bononiae existentem; qui ad colloquium cum Francisco primo Gallorum rege venerat, vita functo Ioanne Ferrariensi, Thoma Caietano Generali Magistro ordinis nostri procurante, (licet antea ad id faciendum Pontifex dispositus fuerit) sacri pallatii magister Romae consistens dictus est." Alberti, *De viris*, f. 140*v*.

9. See: J. Schweizer, *Ambrosius Catharinus Politus (1484–1553) ein Theologe des Reformationszeitalters* (Münster, 1910); Lauchert, *Gegner*, 30–133.

10. *Speculum vite pro rerum et temporis necessitate confessoribus principum et aliorum prepotentum* . . . (Cologne, 1518). See N. Paulus, *Die deutschen Dominikaner im Kampfe gegen Luther (1518–1563)* (Freiburg, 1903), 118, n. 4.

11. "Hoc etiam tempore claret reverendus vir magister Silvester de Prierio, sacri palatii dignissimus magister, qui multa dictavit et continue dictat. Inter que est conflatum sancti Thome, in quo omnia dicta sancti Thome in diversis locis dicta in unum decentissime congregat et per commentum declarat. Item summam de casibus que Silvestrina dicitur, et Summam Summarum, opus sane perutile et necessarium. Item aliam summam quam Rosam auream appellavit, in qua exponit evangelia occurrentia egregie pro predicatoribus, superaddens decisiones quorumdam casuum magistrales et curiosas. Item abbreviavit totum scriptum Capreoli super sententias; dehinc iterum eundem Capreolum in maiori volumine comprehendit. Item scripsit impugnationes in primum librum Scoti in uno tractatu quem Maleum Scoti appellavit. Item logicam. Item tractatum de exorcismis. Item librum de sublevatione morientium, et quosdam tractatus in astrologia et de sphera. Item sermones quadragesimales. Hic vir insignis ob sui eminentem scientiam a domino Leone papa decimo ad legendam sacram theologiam evocatus publice id munus gratiose agit in urbe. Et nihilominus continue dictat et componit nova et singularia opuscula." Creytens, "Les écrivains," 300.

12. Borzino, *Memorie,* f. 108*r*.

13. BOP, 3:611.

14. BOP, 4:124.

15. At the behest of Cardinal Oliviero Carafa, Alexander VI united the four convents of Savonarola's Congregation of San Marco with five convents of the Congregation of Lombardy and seven unreformed convents of the Roman province. See: R. De Maio, *Savonarola e la Curia Romana* (Rome, 1969), 98 ff.; R. Creytens, "Les actes capitulaires de la congrégation Toscano-romaine O.P. (1496–1530)," AFP 40 (1970): 131.

16. AGOP IV, 13, MS *Registrum litterarum et actorum fr. Joachini Turriani mag. O.P. pro prima parte anni 1500*, f. 145*r*.

17. E. Rodocanachi, *Una Cronaca di Santa Sabina sull'Aventino* (Turin, 1898).

18. "cathedra primum, mox vero ex suo proprio motu (ita munus accipio, tametsi apud eam pro me non ex me oratores non defuerint) officio hoc sacri apostolicique palatii donavit, quod gratissimum non tam honoris quam quietis gratia non inficior, eo vel maxime quod eque ut ipse ultimus, ita beatus Dominicus primus hoc munere functus est, et uterque Sancte Sabine claustra incoluit." *Conflatum*, f. +2*v*.

19. Fontana, *Monumenta*, 431.

20. "Priori conventus Perusini per clausas conceditur cum assensu consilioque Magistri Sacri Palatii quod recipere possit quemdam apostatam et cum eo agendi etc. quia magis in foro conscientiae etc. 15 eiusdem [May 1521]." MOPH, 21:101.

21. "Hora (non è molto) ragionandosi di questa materia ne l'horto de le Gratie, ove essendo da Roma venuto a Milano Frate Silvestro Prierio, Maestro del Sacro Palazzo, vi si ritrovò anco M. Francesco Montegazzo, patritio Milanese." M. Bandello, *La terza parte delle novelle* (Lucca, 1554), f. 52*v*.

22. Fontana, *Monumenta*, 433.

23. "Ioannes Capreoli Tholosanus, super quem requievisse spiritus intelligentiae doctrinae videtur Angelicae. Cuius volumina magno ingenio primum Paulus Soncinas sub divino deduxit epithomate. Deinde Silvester Prierias, nostra tempestate, Sacri palatii Magister." I. Isolani, *De Laudibus Aureae Mensae Solis Oratio* in *Ex Humana Divinaque Sapientia Tractatus de Futura Nova Mundi Mutatione* (Bologna, 1523), f. 25*r*.

24. "Data fuit licentia die 9 Septembris 1523 fr. Ioanni de Albingana, converso, posse esse in societate R. Magistri S. Palatii cum potestate redeundi ad propriam provinciam." MOPH, 11:156.

25. "Incipit practica brevissima quonam modo sacerdotes audire, et penitentes confiteri oporteat, ad Clementem VII Pont. Max. magistri sacri Palatii fratris Silvestri de Prierio." *Brevissima practica, qua et sacerdotes audire et peccatores confiteri docentur, gratia reformationis, latine et vulgariter per magistrum sacri palatii edita* (no place, no date), f. aII*r*. A specimen of this work is in Rome, Biblioteca Angelica.

26. "1524. Fra Silvestro Prierio maestro del Sacro Palazzo tiene un horticello del convento e paga dui scudi l'anno, et era quello avanti la chiesa, hoggi dietro alla capella." Rodocanachi, *Cronaca*, 16.

27. See my "An Unedited *Oratio* by Tommaso Radini Tedeschi O.P. (1488–1527)," AHP 32 (1994): 43–63.

28. See my "Gaspare di Baldassare da Perugia O.P. (1465–1531): A Little-Known Adversary of Cajetan," *The Thomist* 60 (1996): 595–615.

29. See: J. W. O'Malley, *Praise and Blame in Renaissance Rome: Rhetoric, Doctrine, and Reform in the Sacred Orators of the Papal Court, c. 1450–1521* (Durham, N.C., 1979); M. G. Blasio, *Cum gratia et privilegio. Programi editoriali e politica pontificia, Roma 1487–1527* (Rome, 1988).

30. See O'Malley, *Praise*, 17–21, on the role of the Master of the Sacred Palace, and 19, 26, 31 for his account of Silvestro.

31. Quétif and Échard, *Scriptores*, 2:58.

32. *Cum gratia*, 57, n. 111.

33. "Desiderium ingens Romam adeundi sese ingerit mea praecordia ac vexans, quo Reverendissimo D. V. frui in Domino queam." *In spheram* (preface Bainbridge), f. 2*v*.

34. "Siquidem agente maxime Dominico Grimano tum Portuensi episcopo a Julio II audita viri praestantia, Romam accitus est anno MDXII, ut sacras ibidem literas publice profiteretur." Quétif and Échard, *Scriptores*, 2:55.

35. Michalski, *De Sylvestri Prieriatis . . . Vita et Scriptis*, 14.

36. See chap. 3, nn. 37, 38, 39.

37. See chap. 3, nn. 115, 116, 118.

38. "Verum anno MDXIIII Leo X pont. max. audita viri praestantissima doctrina, procurantibus litteratissimis viris Cardinalibus videlicet sanctae Crucis et Grimano, Romam ut sacras litteras publice profiteretur statuto stipendio, accivit." Alberti, *De viris,* f. 140r.

39. Bubenheimer, *Consonantia,* 60, n. 218.

40. F. M. Renazzi, *Storia dell'università degli studi di Roma* (Rome, 1803–06), 2:236; E. Conte, *I maestri della Sapienza di Roma dal 1514 al 1787: I rotuli e altre fonti* (Rome, 1991), 1:2.

41. "Nam gravissimo prelationis iugo cervicibus meis excusso (quod tamen longo tempore sine murmure traxi, dicente domino, si diliges me pasce oves meas) cathedra primum, mox vero suo proprio motu (ita munus accipio, tametsi apud eam pro me non ex me oratores non defuerint) officio hoc sacri apostolique palatii donavit." *Conflatum,* f. +2v.

42. See note 11 above.

43. See note 41 above.

44. "verum etiam hic Romae per fratrem Io. Bapt. de Viqueria priorem Brixianum, necnon fratrem Hiero. de Berthenorio socium protolectoris in Gymnasio magistri Thomae Placentini vicarii nostri." *De strigimagarum daemonumque mirandis,* 137.

45. T. Radini Tedeschi, *Orazione contro Filippo Melantone,* critical edition with Italian transl. by F. Ghizzoni (Brescia, 1973), 79.

46. Bubenheimer, *Consonantia,* 59–66.

47. Bubenheimer, *Consonantia,* 63, n. 230.

48. Leandro Alberti, *Descrittione di Tutta Italia* (Bologna, 1550), f. 335v.

49. "Inter quos . . . et Silvester Prierias, sacri palatii Magister, vir omnium modestissimus et facetus, olim in divinis literis praeceptor meus in urbe Roma." J. Fabri, *Malleus in haeresim Lutheranam,* vol. 1, Corpus Catholicorum 23 (Münster, 1941), 3.

50. The standard account of the case is still that by L. Geiger, *Johannes Reuchlin* (Leipzig, 1871), 205–404. But see also J. H. Overfield, *Humanism and Scholasticism in Late Medieval Germany* (Princeton, 1984), 247–97.

51. See chap. 3, n. 129.

52. Heumann, *Documenta,* 146.

53. "Adiicis, ut nil odiosum dimittas, et de Reuchelino, quasi ordo praedicatorum illum insequatur, et non universitas Parisina et Coloniensis et caeterae. Quis autem eum tueatur, veritas an Hebrei an Chrisostomus an utrique, nescio: unum tamen scio, quod officia mea, que sunt viri iusti et misericordis, ignoras." *Replica,* 128.

54. See Cajetan, *De cambiis* in *Opuscula Omnia* (Venice, 1588), 2:164.

55. See, for example, chap. 2, n. 92 above.

56. *Conflatum,* f. +6v.

57. "Conflatum vero ipsum ex divo Thoma propter sui vastitatem, necdum plene expletum est, sed quantum ad textum quidem, totum perfeci uniformiter, excepto eo quod secundum secundi ne magnitudo eius excresceret in immensum, edidi quasi per modum epithomatis, sic tamen quod nullum verbum s. Thomae mutatum est, et nullum verbum doctrinalem omissum, et forte hec pars ceteris gratior erit. Commentaria autem nostra in Conflatum, expleta sunt quo ad pri-

mum volumen plene, quo ad secundum idest primum secundi expleta sunt ex parte magna, sed non plene." *Conflatum,* f. 299*v.*

58. *Brevissima practica,* f. Ciiir.

59. Creytens, "Les écrivains," 298, 300; Alberti, *De viris,* f. 140*v*; *Francisci Silvestri Ferrariensis . . . Quaestiones luculentissimae in tres libros De Anima. Cum additionibus ad easdem . . . R. P. F. Matthiae Aquarii . . .* (Venice, 1601), 109, 138; *Commentaria et controversiae in Primam Partem Summa D. Thomae Aquinatis* (Bologna, 1620), 2:12.

60. Borzino, *Memorie,* f. 109*v.*

61. "Cupio enim quantum possum exhibere legendum non me, qui nihil sum, sed divum Tho. cui ut lectores acquirerem, tantum laborem arripui." *Conflatum,* f. 1*v.*

62. "Testor etiam quod peracto hoc primo volumine, illud totum per duos viros doctissimos et fidelissimos feci examinari ad originalia divi Tho. uno audiente et legente altero, et omnia sunt inventa ad unguem conformia . . . Porro ipsa originalia s. Tho. inveni multipliciter mendosa, et magno labore emendavi, et ubi verum textum inveni, illum recitavi, ubi autem remansi dubius, in glosa explicabo." *Conflatum,* f. 1*r.*

63. "Nota quod hinc dantur due responsiones, et quidam volunt quod s. Tho. aliud intendat in prima aliud in secunda . . . Ego autem dico quod secunda responsio non est s. Tho. sed fuit glossa alicuius Thomiste, per errorem inferta textui, ut patet consulenti originalia s. Tho." *Conflatum,* f. 187*r.*

64. The Leonine editors include the passage in question on the ground that it appears in all codices consulted by them. See Thomas Aquinas, *Opera Omnia* (Rome, 1888), 1:291. The edition of Lyons 1686 mentions, though, that the passage does not appear in some MSS.

65. "Pro materia huius argumenti nota quod bacchalarii iurant deferre magistris, quod tamen intelligitur citra veritatem maxime fidei. In materia ergo magistrali theologica bacchalarius non habet fundare opinionem novam ubi opiniones magistrorum sunt sustentabiles. Quod etiam s. Tho. tanquam humilissimus observavit. In primo ergo Sen. scribens bacchalarius, usus est opinione sustentabili que suo tempore currebat . . . In Summa autem scribens ut magister, dictam opinionem recitavit, nec reprobavit sed ostendit eam non fuisse suam, dicens, quidam dicunt, et deinde prefert suam." *Conflatum,* f. 259*r–v.*

66. "Plerique autem hucusque ad doctrinam sancti Thome aspirantes, ob voluminum multitudinem in quibus eedem difficultates pertractantur, multiplicibusque sententiis resolvuntur, quarum alie sine aliis limpide intelligi minime possunt, ab huius sacrate scole Thomistice voto quasi impossibili sese retraxere. Plerique vero eamdem audacius quam hucusque licuerit aggredientes, nec terminos ipsius ob longa requisita in variis voluminibus studia attingentes, solis quibusdam sententiis magis in promptu se offerentibus inspectis, oblique multa in eadem doctrina interpretati fuere, profitentes se Thomistas, cum potius a sancti Thome doctrina deviaverint, quasi recti naturam et complementum distorta diminutaque regula examinantes." *Conflatum,* f. +3*v.*

67. "Prima [opinio] fuit Hervei, qui cognomen sibi subtilissimi nec immerito vendicavit, ut sua opera testantur, et quem ubique inveni meo iudicio profundissime

s. Thome mentem penetrasse, quamquam aliquando ab eius sententia declinet, dubitative tamen et cum magna reverentia, sicut de distinctione essentie et esse ... Post hunc nobilissimum Thomistam venit Io. Capreo. qui tametsi Herveo par ingenio non fuerit, fuit tamen prestantissimus doctor et accerrimus defensor s. Tho. post cuius doctrinam propalatam in Italia, iam nullus ex discipulis s. Tho. vel mediocriter doctus, aut Scotistas aut alios adversarios s. Tho. facit alicuius momenti." *Conflatum*, f.110r.

68. "hec dico pro veritate et honore Capreoli, qui fuit pater omnium theologorum nostri temporis, et a quo omnes Thomiste presentes habent quicquid boni habent, unde non est facile, et sine testimonio alicuius solemnis doctoris, ab eius dictis recedendum, vel sine evidenti ratione." *Conflatum*, f. 286 v.

69. "quidam dicunt idest Caieta. quod [s. Tho.] ademit sibi omnem viam concordie cum doctrina Arist. iuxta suam expositionem, quia tenet Arist. putasse animas intellectivas immortales, et numeratas secundum numerum corporum, et constat Arist. tenuisse generationem eternam, ex quibus manifeste sequitur animas humanas esse actu infinitas, quod hic decernitur impossibile, hec ille, qui ex his vult habere quod oportet s. Tho. aut negare Aristotelem, aut dicere animas rationales de mente eius esse mortales, de quo infra erit sermo. Sed ego dico primo Aristotelem errasse in eternitate generationis, et consequenter eum negare non solum non incovenit, sed est necesse, non solum secundum fidem, sed philosophice loquendo." *Conflatum*, f. 48 v.

70. *Conflatum*, ff. 86 v–87 r. For a brief discussion and further references see my "Some Renaissance Thomist Divisions of Analogy," *Angelicum* 70 (1993): 93–122.

71. *Conflatum*, ff. 110r–112r. Silvestro's critique of Cajetan on this issue has been briefly discussed by F. Stegmüller, *Francisco de Vitoria y la Doctrina de la Gracia en la Escuela Salmantina* (Barcelona, 1934), 19–23, who argues that Silvestro exercised some influence on Francisco de Vitoria. Silvestro's opinion is still mentioned by Luis Molina, *Concordia Liberi Arbitrii* (1595), disp. 48 and 51. I shall consider elsewhere Francisco de Vitoria's personal connections with Silvestro as well as his dependence on him in speculative matters.

72. *Conflatum*, ff. 206r–207 v. The history of the debate on this issue in the Thomistic School has been traced by A. Krempel, *La doctrine de la relation chez Saint Thomas* (Paris, 1952), but Krempel was not familiar with Silvestro's lengthy and bitter attack on Cajetan.

73. Cajetan, *Comm. in Ia*, q. 28, a. 2, n. 8 (Thomas Aq. *Opera Omnia*, 4:323).

74. "Varia, proinde, erat de futuro Magistro sententia. Adderant quippe viri re et nomine clari, et qui ad tantum gradum provehi merito possent non pauci. Hi precipue fuere: Silvester de Prierio, lector Curiae ac in Urbe magni factus." Olmeda, *Chronica*, 196.

75. Borzino, *Memorie*, f. 108r.

76. See particularly: F. Fiorentino, *Pietro Pomponazzi. Studi storici sulla scuola bolognese e padovana del secolo XVI* (Florence, 1868), 156–241; E. Verga, "L'immortalità dell'anima nel pensiero del Card. Gaetano," *Rivista di Filosofia Neo-Scolastica* 27 (1935) Supplemento: 21–46; M.-H. Laurent, "Introductio. Le Commentaire de Cajétan sur le *De Anima*," in Thomas de Vio Cardinalis Caietanis, *Scripta philo-*

sophica, ed. P. I. Coquelle (Rome, 1938), 1:7–53; C. Giacon, *La seconda scolastica*, 3 vols. (Milan, 1944–51), 1:53–90; E. Gilson, "Autour de Pomponazzi. Problématique de l'immortalité de l'Ame en Italie au début du XVIᵉ siècle," *Archives d'Histoire Doctrinale et Littéraire du Moyen Age* 36 (1961): 163–279, and "L'affaire de l'immortalité de l'âme à Venise au début du XVIᵉ siècle," *Umanesimo europeo e umanesimo veneziano*, ed. V. Branca (Florence, 1963), 31–61; G. Di Napoli, *L'immortalità dell'anima nel rinascimento* (Turin, 1963), 179–338; M. L. Pine, *Pietro Pomponazzi: Radical Philosopher of the Renaissance* (Padua, 1986), 124–234.

77. For example, the most recent account has only two passing references to Silvestro, which seem to make of "the Master of the Sacred Apostolic Palace, Silvestro Mazzolini" and "Silvestris de Prieras, a theologian in the court of Leo X" two different persons. See Pine, *Pietro Pomponazzi*, 126.

78. I first argued this in my "Silvestro da Prierio and the Pomponazzi Affair," *Renaissance and Reformation* 19 (1995): 47–61.

79. Spina's three tracts were completed in late 1518 and published in Venice on 10 September 1519 as part of a collection entitled *Opulscula [!] edita per fratrem Bartholomeum de spina pisanum ordinis predicatorum*. . . .

80. Gilson, "Autour de Pomponazzi," 196; idem, "L'affaire," 43.

81. "1519, die 24 Octobris.—Ego fr. Hieronymus de Laude, prior Bononiensis, de communi consilio patrum discretorum dicti conventus, misi ad librorum venditorem qui habebat quosdam libros impressos Venetiis contra Rev.mum D. Card. S. Sixti: De immortalitate animae humanae, et feci omnes quotquot habere potui, deferri in conventum sub deposito, et scripsi manu propria fratri Bartholomeo Pisano, auctori predicti libri, praecipiens ei in virtute sanctae obedientiae, ne aliquem librum qui in sua esset potestate cum illo titulo contra Thomam Caietanum et Peretum, vendere vel publicare auderet, nisi expressam in scriptis ostenderet se habere licentiam a rev.do vicario generali etc. Ipse rescripsit manu propria inter cetera, quod libellum contra Thomam Caietanum imprimi fecerat sine licentia et scitu rev.di vicarii congregationis Lombardiae, et de industria id fecerat, ne Rev.mus Cardinalis praedictus causam haberet indignationis contra congregationem, sed tantum contra ipsum fratrem Bartholomeum, qui dixit se zelo Dei et pro salute studentium tale opus edere voluisse. Postquam rev.dus vicarius, scilicet magister Franciscus de Ferrara id scivit, acriter reprehendit ipsum fratrem Bartholomeum, tunc lectorem Mutinensem. Ego idem fr. Hieronymus scripsi Rev.mo Cardinali S. Sixti quod Pater vicarius congregationis non concessit licentiam fratri Bartholomeo Pisano publicandi librum praedictum." *Lib. cons. conv. Bon.*, f. 36Av, cited by Creytens, "Les vicaires," 256–57.

82. Franciscus Ferrariensis, *In Summam contra Gentiles*, vol. 2, chap. 79, n. 8.

83. "Diu etiam et per litteras et per amicos curavi, habere quendam tractatum viri eminentissimi Magistri Silvestri de Prierio sacri palatii apostolici magistri, quem quidam ex eiusdem ordinis fratribus, adversus nos composuisse rettulerunt. Verum cum proximi his diebus, Magister Ioannes de Augusta frater eiusdem ordinis ex urbe rediens, ad nos se contulisset retulit, Magistrum Silvestrum nihil adversus nos scripsisse, quamquam forsan scripsisset adversus quendam confratrem, asserentem Arist. sentire animos esse mortales." Pomponazzi, *Apologia* (Bologna, 1518), f. 23r.

84. "Audes et intermiscere mendacia sicut supra de magistro Vincentio Vincentino, sic in presenti loco de Magistro sacri pallatii viro doctissimo, integerrimo ac fidei zelantissimo preceptore meo singularissimo. Licet enim librum ut hereticum non damnaverit propter hoc quod contineat demonstrative non posse probari animam esse immortalem vel philosophum hoc non tenere et huiusmodi, que a multis opinata sunt. Non tamen librum commendavit, in hoc quod astruis demonstrative probari oppositum per rationes naturales quas induxisti, et hoc esse simpliciter et absolute verum, illud vero esse deliramentum et principiis philo. repugnans, et qui illud praedicarunt legumlatores fuisse deceptores. Hec et alia plura extrema damnatione digna, quibus liber ille tuus refertus est non commendavit Magister sacri pallatii, immo abhorruit. Quod certe experireris, si sua principaliter interesset." Spina, *Flagellum,* f. kIV *v.*

85. Gilson, "L'affaire," 38, has misread Spina's "preceptore meo singularissimo" as referring to Vincenzo Colzado.

86. See chap. 3, n. 143.

87. "Deinde textum dialectice, qui quoniam prima fronte quaedam subtiliora per se fert, lectores deterret, cum tamen dilectus et eruditissimus discipulus meus Bartholomeus Pisanus commentaria in illum moliretur mutationem eorum ei signans, quo loco inserenda essent ostendi." *Conflatum,* f. 299 *v.*

88. For example, G. Di Napoli, *L'immortalità,* 298, remarks: "Nell'Apologia II (42) il Pomponazzi ricorda tra i contradittori i domenicani Vincenzo Colzade da Vicenza e Silvestro Prierias . . . dell'uno e dell'altro noi non possediamo scritti riguardo al problema dell'immortalità."

89. "Et si mei non est instituti, quid de immortalitate nostri animi senserit philosophorum sapientissimus Aristoteles afferre, quippe qui non humana authoritate probare cupio quod sentio, incidenter tamen de sententia et opinione Arist. in re hac cogor rationem habere, quo me ipsum ab iis quae mihi falso et leviter (idest me non audito) verbo aut scripto Petrus Pomponatius in Apologetico suo imposuit, expurgem, quod scilicet viso suo libro quem de immortalitate (imo de mortalitate) animae cudit, subriserim et probarim. Haec enim falso et leviter dicuntur, quin potius eo viso, ingemui ac dolui, quod ita catholica fides in parvulorum mentibus per christianos elidatur, et enervetur, et erroribus innumeris sit occasio data, quo iam experientia docet, et si meum fuisset, in librum per ignes, Venetorum exemplo, animadvertissem. Illustrissimos autem dominos Venetos potius laudavi, et miratus sum, quod nulla habita ratione amicitie ad Perretum Venetiis id effecerunt, quod ubique faciendum erat, tantum scilicet scelus flammis ultricibus expiasse. Quamquam vero copiosissime luculenter et eruditissime, dilectus et filius, et discipulus Bartho. Pissanus ordi. Praedi. eiusmodi opinionem confutarit, adducam tamen et ego quae quondam in Commentaris primi voluminis nostri conflati contra eiusmodi opinionem; antequam scriberet Perretus, compendiose edideram, etsi nec in hanc diem propalata sint." *De strigimagarum daemonumque mirandis,* 19.

90. "Ad Perretum respondi minime, quia de his ante eum scripseram, nunc vero respondere non oportet, quia per Fratrem Hieronymum Fornarium Bachalarium et per Fratrem Bartholomaeum Pisanum fundamenta eius eversa sunt." *De strigimagarum,* 42.

91. "Castiga igitur propositum, et hunc qui libello huic tuo proprius est prepone titulum, petri pomponatii mantuani tractatus de mortalitate anime intellective." Spina, *Tutela veritatis*, f. dIIIr.

92. "Non potui ultra resistere spiritui sancto aut zelo animarum et veritati frenum imponere, qui solus (deus testis est) me impulsit ad scribendum." See the letter *Ad lectorem* at the end of Spina's *Flagellum*.

93. *Conflatum*, q. 39, ff. 266r–272v.

94. See, for example, Paolo Nazari da Cremona, *Commentaria et controversiae*, 2:307.

95. See K. Mueller, "Luthers römischer Prozess," ZKG 24 (1903): 46–85; P. Kalkoff, "Zu Luthers römischen Prozess," ZKG 31 (1910): 48–65, 368–414; 32 (1911): 1–67, 199–258, 408–56, 572–95; 33 (1912): 1–72; *Forschungen zu Luthers römischen Prozess* (Rome, 1905); *Zu Luthers römischen Prozess. Der Prozess des Jahres 1518* (Gotha, 1912); Lauchert, *Gegner*, 7–30; J. N. Scionti, *Sylvester Prierias and His Opposition to Martin Luther* (Ph.D. diss., Brown University, 1967); J. Wicks, *Cajetan und die Anfänge der Reformation* (Münster, 1983) and "Roman Reactions to Luther: The First Year (1518)," *Catholic Historical Review* 69 (1983): 521–62; P. Fabisch, "Silvester Prierias (1456–1523)," *Katholische Theologen der Reformationszeit*, vol. 1, Katholisches Leben und Kirchenreform 44 (Münster, 1984), 26–36; P. Fabisch and E. Iserloh, *Dokumente*, 33–201; D. R. Janz, *Luther on Thomas Aquinas: The Angelic Doctor in the Thought of the Reformer* (Stuttgart, 1989); D. N. Bagchi, *Luther's Earliest Opponents: Catholic Controversialists, 1518–25* (Minneapolis, 1989).

96. Wicks, "Roman Reactions," 523.

97. See *Dialogus*, 52. I cite the edition in P. Fabisch and E. Iserloh, *Dokumente*, 1:52–107.

98. Kalkoff, *Forschungen*, 175–76.

99. *Luther's Works*, ed. J. Pelikan and H. T. Lehmann, 55 vols. (St. Louis and Philadelphia, 1955–86): 27:156, 157, 158, 397, 398; 31:316, 334; 34:311; 36:11, 13, 14; 39:55–56, 173; 41:286; 47:72, 81, 110, 167; 54:83, 263, 265.

100. *Conflatum*, f. 299v.

101. *Replica*, 126.

102. "Commentaria autem nostra in Conflatum, expleta sunt quo ad primum volumen plene, quo ad secundum vero, id est primum secundi expleta sunt ex parte magna, sed non plene, quia inde me invitum Martinus avulsit, cito vero ea deo favente explebo, sed quantum ad secundum secundi et tertium sive ultimum volumen puto commentanda relinquam alicui discipulorum eorum, nisi beatissimus dominus noster Leo sua bonitate qua me semper est prosequutus reddat religioni, ubi iam a prelaturis immunis et quietus omnia brevi tempore explerem." *Conflatum*, f. 299v.

103. See Bagchi, *Luther's Earliest Opponents*, 4–8.

104. Wicks, "Roman Reactions," 561.

105. Lauchert, *Gegner*, 7–30.

106. Quétif and Échard, *Scriptores*, 2:57–58.

107. W. Klaiber, *Katholische Kontroverstheologen und Reformer des 16. Jahrhunderts. Ein Werkverzeichnis*, Reformationsgeschichtliche studien und Texte, vol. 116 (Münster, 1978), 238, n. 2598, and 240, nn. 2616, 2621.

108. H. A. Obermann, "Wittenbergs Zweifrontenkrieg gegen Prierias und Eck," *ZKG* 80 (1969): 331–58.

109. C. Lindberg, "Prierias and His Significance for Luther's Development," *Sixteenth Century Journal* 3 (1972): 45–64.

110. R. Bäumer, "Silvester Prierias und seine Ansichten über das ökumenische Konzil," *Konzil und Papst* (Padeborn, 1975): 277–301.

111. Fabisch, "Silvester Prierias," 35–36.

112. Horst, *Zwischen Konziliarismus und Reform,* 126.

113. *Luther's Works,* 18:314–15.

114. Wicks, "Roman Reactions," 530.

115. *Table Talk,* 6 April, 1533 (*Luther's Works,* 54:83).

116. "Dixit se Pontifici declarasse de tiniente grossulo, indignabundum exclamasse: O ribaldo! O porcaccio! coripuisse etiam Silvestrem Prieratem, quod tam pueriliter scripserit opus non tribus diebus, sed mensibus pensandum, ha dato uno bono rabuffo, ut suis verbis utatur, et hominem haberi ludibrio." Christoph Scheurl, letter to Luther, 20 December 1518, in E. L. Enders, *Dr. Martin Luthers Briefwechsel* (Leipzig, 1884), 1:327; "Pontifex non parum dicitur indignatus Prieratis rusticitati, cui magis trimestre quam triduum opus erat." Christoph Scheurl, letter to Eck, 22 December 1518, in Enders, *Briefwechsel,* 1:331.

117. "Horum intemperiis Lutherus opposuit sua Problemata. Indignabantur quorum res agebatur. Missa sunt ad Leonem X. Respondit Sylvester Prieras, tam feliciter ut ipse Pontifex indixerit illi silentium." Erasmus, letter to Francisco de Vitoria, 29 November 1527, *Opus,* 7, Ep. 1909, 257–58.

118. See: N. Paulus, *Johann Tetzel der Ablassprediger* (Mainz, 1899), 164; Lauchert, *Gegner,* 15.

119. "Etenim praeceptor etiam meus Theologus profundissimus Magister Sylvester Prierias, receptus fuit ad osculum oris a Leone Decimo." Spina, *Quaestio de strigibus,* 112.

120. See A. Charles Fiorato, *Bandello entre l'Histoire et l'Ecriture* (Florence, 1979), 579–618.

121. "Se Papa Lione X. Pont. Mass. nel principio che Martino Lutero cominciò à sparger il pestifero veleno de le sue heresie, havesse prestato benigne orecchie al Maestro del Sacro Palazzo, era cosa assai facile ad ammorzar quelle nascenti fiamme, che hora tanto sono accresciute, che se Dio non ci mette la mano, elle sono più tosto per pigliar accrescimento che per iscemarsi." Bandello, *La terza parte delle novelle,* novella 10, f. 43r.

"Nel principio, che la Setta Luterana cominciò a germogliare, essendo di brigata molti Gentilhuomini, ne l'hora del merigge, in casa del nostro vertuoso Signor L. Scipione Attellano, e di varie cose ragionandosi, furono alcuni, che non poco biasimarono Leone X. Pontefice, che ne i principii non ci metesse rimedio, a l'hora che Frate Silvestro Prierio, Maestro del Sacro Palazzo, gli mostrò alcuni punti d'heresia, che Fra Martino Lutero haveva sparso per l'opera, la quale de le Indulgentie haveva intitolata, perciò che imprudentemente rispose, che Fra Martino haveva un bellissimo ingegno, e che coteste erano invidie Fratesche. Che se à l'hora ci havesse proveduto, era facil cosa la nascente fiamma smorzare, che dapoi ha fatto, con danno irreparabile di tutta la Christianità, cosi grande incendio." Bandello, *La terza parte delle novelle*, novella 25, f. 96r.

122. "Cum dilectus filius Silvester de prierio or. pre. et theologie professor ac sacri palatii magister, aliqua contra scripta Martini luter ordinis fratrum heremi. s. augu. professoris, que ac ipsum martinum in eventum in quem scripta sua huiusmodi infra tempus expressum non revocaverit, de fratrum nostrorum consilio partim ut heretica partim ut scandalosa, partim vero tanquam pias aures offendentia, damnavimus, canonice scripserit." Letter of Leo X, 21 July 1520, *Errata et argumenta,* f. 4.

123. See R. E. McNally, "Pope Adrian VI (1522–23) and Church Reform," AHP 7 (1969): 253–85.

124. *Concilium Tridentinum* (Freiburg/B., 1930), 12:32–39.

125. See, for example, J. Wicks, *Cajetan Responds: A Reader in Reformation Controversy* (Washington, 1978), 32.

126. J. Paquier, *Jérôme Aléandre* (Paris, 1900), xxxiii.

127. P. Kalkoff, "Kleine Beiträge zur Geschichte Hadrians VI," *Historisches Jahrbuch* 39 (1919): 71–72.

128. *Concilium Tridentinum,* 12:32.

129. *Vita,* f. cVv.

130. BOP, 4:253.

131. McNally, "Pope Adrian VI," 277.

132. "Tota haec Lutherana tempestas ex leuioribus initiis huc vsque incruduit. Dominicani commendabant impudentius indulgentias pontificias; Lutherus opposuit articulos. Siluester inepte respondit: Lutherus acriter resistit." Ep. 1875 to John Vergara, 2 September 1527, *Opus,* 7:167. "Lutheranum incendium quam friuolis initiis huc vsque progressum est! Primus iocus erat et ludus. Rescripsit Prieras: mox monachorum clamores ad populum, articuli, bullae, aedicta." Ep. 1891 to John Gacy, ca. 17 October 1527, *Opus,* 7:211. "Primum, ubi prodierunt Luteri placita de indulgentiis, silentium erat optimum. Respondit Prieras satis gloriose, et primus cicadam, vt Graeci dicunt, ala corripuit." Ep. 2445 to Mathias Kretz, 11 March 1531, *Opus,* 9:170. "Occasio data est per Dominicanos quosdam, qui Pontificias indulgentias praedicabant tam impudenter, ne dicam impie, ut populus ferre non posset. His Lutherus opposuit suas conclusiones, ad quas primus respondit Prieras, sed sic, ut tantum irritarit crabrones. Mox praeproperis ac stultis quorundam apud populum vociferationibus, deinde maledicis libellis utrinque provolantibus, ex parva scintilla late sparsum est incendium." *Apologia adversus debacchationes Sutoris, Opera Omnia,* ed. J. Clericus (Leiden, 1703–06), 9:789E. "Dominicani quidam haec nimis adulanter et impudenter, ac prope dixerim blaspheme jactantes apud populum, excitarunt Lutherum, ut proponeret aliquot propositiones disputandas. Quibus sic respondit Prieras, ut exarserit incendium." *Apologia brevis ad viginta quatuor libros Alberti Pii, Opera,* 9:1141E.

133. "Vidi Sylvestri insulsissimam responsionem." Ep. 872 to John Lang, 17 October 1518, *Opus,* 3:409.

134. "Sylvestri libellus e mantica sublatus est; itaque rogo ut exemplar mittas." Ep. 877 to Wolfgang Fabricius Capito, 19 October 1518, *Opus,* 3:416.

135. "Prieratem et Cajetanum dico parum feliciter scripsisse, non quod indocte, sed

quod nihil profecerint. Nam Prieras irrisus est ab omnibus. Cajetanus ne lectus quidem, qui tamen acutissime tractavit hoc negotium. De eventu loquor, non de eruditione." *Apologia brevis ad viginta quatuor libros Alberti Pii, Opera,* 9:1136A.

136. "Verum ante te scripsit Prieras. Fateor. Sed it ut causam Indulgentiarum fecerit deteriorem. Scripsit Cardinalis Cajetanus. Subtilius quidem ille, sed quod ad causae successum attinet, nihilo felicius." *Ad exhortationem . . . Alberti Pii . . . Responsio, Opera,* 9:1119D.

137. "Ausus est moderatius loqui de potestate Romani Pontificis, sed de qua isti nimis immoderate prius scripserant: quorum praecipui sunt tres Praedicatores, Aluarus, Sylvester, et Cardinalis S. Sixti." Ep. 1033 to Albert of Brandenburg, 19 October 1519, *Opus,* 4:103.

138. "Quod tamen citra fraudem Lutherii dictum velim. Ego illius nec accusator sum nec patronus nec iudex. Viderint ii quibus hanc prouinciam nominatim delegauit Rhomanus Pontifex." Ep. 1041, ca. November 1519, *Opus,* 4:121. "Pontificis primatum satis iam asseruerunt Caietanus, Sylvester et Eccius, ut mea opera nihil sit opus." Ep. 1275 to John Glapion, ca. 21 April 1522, *Opus,* 5:50.

139. "Interea quum eruditorum hominum literis Romam inuitaret, et complurium et eorum quibus fidere tuto poteram—sed praesertim R. Card. Sedunensis . . . et eodem prouocaret literis humanissime scriptis Syluester ille Prieras, coepi et de Roma adeunda cogitare." Ep. 1342, *Opus,* 5:210.

140. "Sylvestrum Prieratem neque probasti apud amicos unquam, neque cum nunc vis, probandi causas habes; laudas tamen, et ut bonum virum praedicas, qui humaniter erga te affectus sit, in Lutheri, ut manifeste cognosci datur, invidiam, quo magis videaris adversari huic si inimicis ipsius secunda facias." Ulrich von Hutten, *Hutteni cum Erasmo Expostulatio* (1523), in *Ulrich von Hutten Schriften,* ed. E. Böcking (reprint Aalen, 1963), 2:212.

141. "Male habet et illud Huttenum, quod in quadam Epistola per occasionem infero, Sylvestrum Prieratem humaniter et amanter ad me scripsisse, cum tamen illum ne titulo quidem honorifico digner. Tantum ajo, Sylvester ille Prieras. Illius ad me litteras dico humanissime scriptas. O miram adulationem! Sed ista scribis, inquit, in invidiam Lutheri. Imo in hoc scripsi, ut ostenderem esse causam, cur de Roma adeunda cogitarem." *Spongia adversus adspergines Hutteni, Opera,* 10:1647F.

142. Ep. 1412 to Silvester Mazolini, ca. 19 January 1524, *Opus,* 5:386–87.

143. See *The Correspondence of Erasmus,* vol. 9, trans. R. A. B. Mynors, annot. J. M. Estes (Toronto, 1989), 280–81.

144. See H. de Jonge, "Introduction," *Apologia respondens ad ea quae Iacobus Lopis Stunica texaverunt in prima Novi Testamenti aeditione, Opera Omnia Desiderii Erasmi Roterodami* (Amsterdam and Oxford, 1969–), 9:22–27.

145. *The Correspondence of Erasmus,* vol. 8, trans. R. A. B. Mynors, annot. by P. G. Bietenholz (Toronto, 1988), 341.

146. "Scripsi Prierati, indicaret quibus locis offenderetur; obmutuit. Et hic est animus quem tu putas praefractum et intractabilem." Ep. 1581 to Natalis Beda, 15 June 1525, *Opus,* 6:94.

147. For a further reference to Silvestro's efforts to enlist Erasmus's support against Luther see *Opus,* 3:409, note to line 16.

148. See: C. Ginzburg, "Stregoneria e pietà popolare. Note a proposito di un processo

modenese del 1519," *Annali della Scuola Normale Superiore di Pisa. Lettere, Storia e Filosofia*, 2d ser., 30 (1961): 269–87; A. Biondi, "Streghe ed eretici nei domini estensi dell'epoca dell'Ariosto," *Il Rinascimento nelle corti padane* (Bari, 1977), 165–99; M. Bertolotti, "Le ossa e la pelle dei buoi. Un mito popolare tra agiografia e stregoneria," *Quaderni Storici* 14 (1979): 470–99; A. Biondi, "G. F. Pico e la repressione della stregoneria," *Mirandola e le terre del basso corso del Secchia* (Modena, 1984), 1:331–49: A. Biondi, "Introduzione," in G. F. Pico, *Libro detto Strega* (Venice, 1989), 9–41.

149. I shall consider elsewhere the complex issue of the possible connections between the contemporaneous, fifteenth-century spread of the Dominican reform, revival of Thomism, and intensification of the persecution of witches.

150. "Immo nunc in Apennino tantum excreuerunt, ut dicant se brevi plures fidelibus futuras, et se propalandas in publicum, et erit sicut Valdensibus in Valle Lucerna." *De strigimagarum daemonumque mirandis*, 161.

151. "Et hoc totum ideo eis accidat oportet, quia capitulum istud non intellectum, sed creditum quod sit intellectum, obturat sensus eorum, adeo ut Romae viri peritissimi, propter capitulum istud contra quendam strigimagum procedere recusarent, qui ab inquisitore peritissimo et expertissimo Fratre Aug. Papiensi ordinis Praedicatorum citatus fugerat, cum nihilominus esset propter fugam inchoato processu iudicatus: et insuper laboraret infamia huiusmodi apostasiae, probata per testes 14 essetque per testes viginti et duos accusatus, quorum nonnulli essent incinerati, et nonnulli paenitentes. Et in causa erat capitulum Episcopi solum: cuius rei gratia cum essem ego coniudex, coactus hoc opusculum coepi." *De strigimagarum daemonumque mirandis*, 133.

152. "Contingit et secundum interiorem sensum apparitiones daemonem causare . . . Sive per unctionem corpoream: ut accidit his qui ire se credunt vespere quintae feriae ad ludos Dianae, vel similia diabolica . . . Ego quoque ab una muliere amante quendam scio quod diabolus unxit eam nudam, suadens illi quod sic duceret eam ad domum sui dilecti: et postmodum, postquam fuit extra se multo tempore, et crederet se cum suo dilecto fuisse, etc., invenit se in suo loco ita lassatam quod refocillatione indiguit etc.; et nisi ego declarassem ei quod imaginatio fuit, et ex tali nuditate ita laesa esset, nesciret forte usque hodie quod illud non fuerit in veritate. Per haec tamen non negamus quin diabolus, Deo permittente, quandoque personam aliquam voluntariam etiam corporaliter ducat de loco ad locum. Sed hoc rarissime videtur accidere." Th. De Vio Caietanus, *Comm. in IIa–IIae* in Th. Aquinas, *Opera Omnia*, vol. 9, ed. Leonina (Rome, 1897), 316–17.

153. "Ad haec, ne et ludi ipsi diabolici atque spectacula somnia putentur, aliud quoque referam. Crebro pueri puellaeque duodecim, aut decem, vel octo annorum, doctrina et cohortatu inquisitorum resipiscunt, qui et in tantae rei miraculum instar illius ludi saltare iubentur: idque ita faciunt, ut nullus sapiens negare possit, quin altiori quadam arte, et quae humanam transcendat, sint edocti. Nam cum illae choreae per omnia humanis dissimiles sint: quod in illis femina post dorsum masculi teneatur, et non antecedendo, sed retrocedendo saltetur: et in fine cum reverentia praesidenti diabolo solvenda est, ei terga dantes inclinent caput, non in ante, sed retro: et pedem non flectant retro, sed in ante elevantes in altum. Id

totum vero tanta gratia et venustate perficiunt, ut id statim et in pueritia sit impossibile didicisse. Siquis vero haec aut negat, aut dubitat, certus effici potest non modo in agro Comensi, ac Brixiano . . . Id vero summopere cupio, ut reverendissimus aliquis ex dominis nostris Cardinalibus id muneris assumat, ut decem ex his puerilis et puellis Romam traduci curet (quod facillimum est) quo et urbi Romae spectaculum grande praebeat, et incredulis velamen grandius auferat cecitatis." *De strigimagarum daemonumque mirandis,* 136–37.

154. P. Grillandus, *Tractatus de Haereticis, et Sortilegiis, omnifariam Coitu, eorumque poenis: Item de Quaestionibus et Tortura ac de Relaxatione Carceratorum* (Lyon: Bened. Bonini, 1536).

155. See n. 148 above.

156. All the standard collections of sources on witchcraft include excerpts from the *De strigimagarum daemonumque mirandis* and the *Summa silvestrina:* Lea, *Materials,* 354–65; Hansen, *Quellen,* 317–23; G. Bonomo, *Caccia alle streghe. La credenza nelle streghe dal sec. XIII al XIX con particolare riferimento all'Italia* (Palermo, 1971), 336–39; S. Abbiati et al., *La stregoneria. Diavoli, streghe, inquisitori dal Trecento al Settecento* (Milan, 1984), 218–29.

157. See P. Zambelli, *L'ambigua natura della magia* (Milan, 1991), 220–28.

158. *De rerum praenotione* in *Opera* (1573; Turin, 1972), 2:468–70.

159. *De strigimagarum daemonumque mirandis,* 242.

160. See G. Romeo, *Inquisitori, esorcisti e streghe nell'Italia della Controriforma* (Florence, 1990), 27.

161. "Frater Augustinus Costantini de Florentia assignatur Florentiae in S. Maria Novella in studentem theologiae cum hac conditione ut maneat cum magistro Thoma de Placentia magistro sacri palatii, dans omnimodam auctoritatem praefato magistro super ipsum, prout habent priores super subditos suos." AGOP IV, 20, MS *Registrum litterarum et actorum fr. Francisci Silvestri mag. O.P. pro annis 1524–28,* f. 49*v.*

162. Borzino, *Memorie,* f. 108*r.*

163. "mortem me insequi video . . . iam lentissimus mortem obibo." *Conflatum,* f. 299*v.*

164. See chap. 1, n. 33 above.

165. "1522 . . . At cum grassantem nimis in Urbe eo tempore luem videret, multosque sine Sacramentorum receptione deficere cognosceret, petita Pont. licentia, se in Aulicorum spirituale solamen exposuit . . . 1523 . . . Rapitur a mortalibus doctissimus vir Sacri Palatii Mag. P. Silvester de Prierio dira peste percussus, dum in ministrandis Sacramentis aegrotantibus Aulicis pontificiae Curiae esset intentus." Fontana, *Monumenta,* 433–35.

166. Quétif and Échard, *Scriptores,* vol. 2, 53.

167. J.-J. Berthier, *Le Couvent de Sainte-Sabine à Rome* (Rome, 1912), 448, 721.

168. "At Silvester de Prierio, Pedemontanus, ibidem alter pro Scotia, quantus verbo et scripto fuerit, opera quae fecit testimonium perhibent de illo. Refertissimam Summam, de Casibus Conscientiae dictam, novissime post alios plures de Ordine compilavit; quam ex suo nomine, aut certe ex fructifera silva, Silvestrinam intitulatam, Leone X Pontifici Maximo dicavit. A quo Romam accersitus ut sanctam Theologiam inibi edoceret; id munus multo tempore gratiose egit in Urbe: magis-

ter etiam sacri Palatii prae multis designatus, demum dira peste (quasi non esset untus oleo scientiae et virtutis prae aliis) sublatus, in Minerva humi conditus est." Olmeda, *Chronica*, 191.

169. Borzino, *Memorie*, f. 108*r.*

170. Taurisano, *Hierarchia*, 50.

171. P.-T. Masetti, *Monumenta et Antiquitates* (Rome, 1864), 2:37–39.

172. Taurisano, *Hierarchia*, 51. Taurisano confesses his inability to fill the gap in the series of Masters of the Sacred Palace between the death of Nicola Columbi (1 October 1527) and the appointment of Tommaso Badìa (17 February 1529). It is likely, though, that the intervening incumbent was Stefano di Cassano. See Teodoro Valle da Piperno, *Breve Compendio* (Naples, 1651), 219.

173. "Pro reverendis provincialibus huius provinciae defunctis et fratre Silvestro de Prierio, quondam magistro et lectore Sacri Palatii, caeterisque fratribus ac sororibus citra ultimum capitulum defunctis quilibet sacerdos unam missam." *Acta Capitulorum Provinciae Germaniae Inferioris Ordinis Fratrum Praedicatorum ab Anno MDXV usque ad Annum MDLIX,* ed. S. P. Wolfs (The Hague, 1964), 95.

174. Silvestro is so described in a marginal annotation in the *Codice Carbone* (ASMCG, Cassetta 8), n. 376.

175. Alberti, *Descrittione,* f. 335*v.*

176. The chronicle of Santa Sabina mentions the Sack rather laconically and solely in terms of the financial consequences for the convent: "1527. In questo anno fu il sacco di Roma e per le molte ruine che furono ordinò il vicario del papa che le risposte de' canoni fossero solo per quarta." Rodocanachi, *Cronaca,* 16. On the complete destruction during the Sack of the convent's reputedly very rich library, see A. Martinelli, *Roma ex Ethnica Sacra* (Rome, 1653), 296.

177. See A. Cossio, *Il Cardinale Gaetano e la Riforma* (Cividale, 1902), 431–37.

178. *Conflatum,* f. 299*v.* The "fore demonstravi" is a reference to the *Errata et argumenta.*

INDEX OF MANUSCRIPTS

Index of Names

Cagnazzo, Giovanni da Taggia, OP, 25, 34–35, 37, 56, 73, 122, 124
Cajetan. *See* De Vio, Tommaso da Gaeta
Calò, Pietro, OP, 33
Calvi, Niccolò, 50
Canigiano, Giovanni Maria, OP, 61
Capreolus, John, OP, 28, 30–31, 38, 45, 95
Carafa, Oliviero, cardinal, 21, 51, 63, 92, 113, 118
Cardano, Girolamo, 125
Carli, Goffredo, 63
Carvajal, Bernardino, cardinal, 52, 85, 89, 90
Charles II of Anjou, 33
Charles V, emperor, 90, 115
Cimitri, Gentile, 37
Clement VII, pope, 3, 75, 81, 84, 106, 115–16, 120, 124, 127, 129
Cleree, Jean, OP, 51
Cochlaeus, Johann, 73
Colonna, Francesco da Venezia, OP, 22
Columbi, Nicola da Perugia, OP, 129
Colzado, Vincenzo da Vicenza, OP, 64, 67, 98
Comazzio, Bartolomeo da Bologna, OP, 23
Comestor, Petrus, 11, 45
Contarini, Gaspare, 98
Contarini, G., 43
Cornelio, F., 72
Corrado d'Asti, OP, 19
Crasso, Damiano da Rivoli, OP, 64
Crescimbeni, G. M., 34

D'Amato, A., 27
Darlieri, Carlo dei, 30
D'Auria, Oberto, 50
Da Vinci, Leonardo, 47–48
Della Porta, Giambattista, 124
De Vio, Tommaso da Gaeta, OP, cardinal, 5–7, 11, 13, 21–24, 38–39, 43, 50–52, 55, 60–69, 71, 78, 80–81, 90–104, 106, 113, 115, 117–19, 121–24, 131
Dodo, Vincenzo da Pavia, OP, 64
Domaneschi, P. M., 70–71
Domenico da Catalonia, OP, 46

Dominic, Saint, 36, 48, 75, 79
Dominic of Flanders, OP, 13–14, 31
Dominici, John, OP, 3, 71
Duglioli Dall'Olio, Elena, 2

Échard, J. *See* Quétif, J. and Échard, J.
Eck, Johann, 31, 106
Erasmus, Desiderius, 69, 81, 90, 108, 110, 114, 119–22, 127
Este, Ercole I d', duke of Ferrara, 21
Este-Gonzaga, Isabella d', 32, 53, 71, 85
Eugene IV, pope, 49, 82
Eymerich, Nicholas, OP, 57, 124

Faber, Johann von Augsburg, OP, 101
Fabisch, P., 109, 138 n13
Fabri, Johann, 88
Faella, Angelo da Verona, OP, 24–25, 29, 35
Fantoni, Girolamo da Vigevano, OP, 64
Federico d'Aragona, king of Naples, 26–27
Ferdinando I d'Aragona, king of Naples, 26
Fiandino, Ambrogio, 98
Ficino, Marsilio, 125
Fieschi, Niccolò, cardinal, 42, 65, 66, 70, 73, 84, 93
Fontana, V. M., 56, 68–69, 78, 80, 128–29
Fornari, Girolamo da Pavia, OP, 67, 102
Francis I, king of France, 78, 90

Gabriele da Barcellona, OP, 46
Gaspare di Baldassare da Perugia, OP, 81, 92, 93, 95
Gattico, G., 60–64
Gemmingen, Uriel von, 89
Geynges, Gregorius de, 83
Ghinucci, Girolamo, 80, 105
Ghislardo, Bartolomeo, 39, 53
Giacomo da Brescia, OP, 46
Giacomo da Pavia, OP, 35
Gibboni, Mattia da Aquario, OP, 94
Gilson, E., 99
Giorgio, Marino, doge, 71

Nazari, Giovanni Paolo da Cremona, OP, 94

Neri, Philip, Saint, 39

Nicholas V, pope, 48

Nider, Johann, OP, 58, 124

Nifo, Agostino, 98, 104, 125

Obermann, H. A., 108–109

Olmeda, Sebastian, OP, 128–30

O'Malley, J. W., 82–83

Onofrio da Parma, OP, 47

Otto da Pavia, 29

Panzer, G. W., 45

Paquier, J., 115

Pastor, L., 115

Patrizi, Agostino, 82

Paul III, pope, 100, 115

Paul IV, pope, 78

Paulus, N., 114

Pelati Gerolamo, 70

Peñafiel, Jeronimo, OP, 7, 80, 128

Peter of Verona, saint, 60

Petit, Guillaume, OP, 62

Petrarch, 34

Peuerbach, Georg, 70

Pezzotelli, Andrea da Brescia, OP, 26

Pfefferkorn, Johann, 88–89

Piazzesi, Eustachio da Bologna, OP, 51, 54, 62–63, 66

Pico della Mirandola, Giovanfrancesco, 14, 127

Pico della Mirandola, Giovanni, 21, 125

Pirckheimer, Willibald, 73, 91

Pirris, Domenico da Gargnano, OP, 13, 122, 124

Pistoris, Judocus, OP, 37

Pius II, pope, 3, 15, 34, 46, 48, 71

Pius V, pope, 2

Politti, Lancelotto de'. See Ambrogio Caterino

Pomponazzi, Pietro, 43, 67, 81, 91, 97–104, 124–26

Ponchier, Etienne, 47, 106

Ponte, Gotardo da, 53, 70

Porcellaga, Andrea da Brescia, OP, 50

Prantl, C., 30

Quétif, J. and Échard, J., 5–6, 56, 78, 83–84, 108, 128

Rab, Hermann, OP, 105

Radini Tedeschi, Tommaso da Piacenza, OP, 63, 81, 86, 88, 128, 130

Rafanelli, Giovanni da Ferrara, OP, 21, 75, 77, 84, 86

Raffaele da Pornassio, OP, 4

Raymond of Capua, OP, 3–4

Razzi, S., 39

Renazzi, F. M., 86

Reuchlin, Johann, 81, 88–91, 104

Rocaberti, T. J., 69

Rovetta, A., 6

Ruggeri, Ugo, 38

Savonarola, Girolamo da Ferrara, OP, 5, 14–15, 23, 30, 49, 61, 79, 113, 131

Schönberg, Nikolaus von, OP, 77, 84

Securo, Francesco da Nardò, OP, 43

Sforza, Ludovico Maria, duke of Milan, 47

Sforza d'Aragona, Camilla, 39

Shinner, Mattias, cardinal, 60, 65–66, 120

Silvestri, Francesco da Ferrara, OP, 13, 20, 38, 64, 92, 99, 100–102, 124, 128

Silvestro da Mantova, OP, 23

Sixtus IV, pope, 79

Soardi, Lazzaro dei, 74

Sommi, Cacciaconti, 69

Spina, Bartolomeo da Pisa, OP, 2, 13, 64, 67, 72, 92, 97, 99–104, 114, 124, 127

Spinola, Theodorina, 39–40

Sprenger, Jacob, OP, 58, 124

Suso, Henry, OP, 39, 41

Taegio, Ambrogio, 48

Taurisano, I., 129–30

Tedeschini, E., 70

Tetzel, Johann, OP, 105

Michael Tavuzzi is Professor of Philosophy at the University of St. Thomas, Rome, and a member of the Dominican Historical Institute. His principal research interest is scholasticism, especially Thomism, on the eve of the Reformation.

Library of Congress Cataloging-in-Publication Data
Tavuzzi, Michael M.
    Prierias : the life and works of Silvestro Mazzolini da Prierio,
    1456–1527 / Michael Tavuzzi.
        p. cm. — (Duke monographs in medieval and Renaissance
    studies ; 16)
        Includes index.
        ISBN 0-8223-1976-4 (cloth : alk. paper).
        1. Mazzolini, Silvestro, da Prierio, 1456–1527? 2. Theologians—Italy—Biography.
3. Dominicans—Italy—Biography. I. Title. II. Series: Duke monographs in medieval
and Renaissance studies ; no. 16.
BX4705.M474T38 1997
230′.2′092—dc21
[B]   96-54041
                                                                    CIP